FASHION HISTORY

DRESS, BODY, CULTURE

Series Editor: Joanne B. Eicher, *Regents' Professor,*
University of Minnesota

Advisory Board:
Djurdja Bartlett, *London College of Fashion, University of the Arts*
Pamela Church-Gibson, *London College of Fashion, University of the Arts*
James Hall, *University of Illinois at Chicago*
Vicki Karaminas, *University of Technology, Sydney*
Gwen O'Neal, *University of North Carolina at Greensboro*
Ted Polhemus, *Curator, "Street Style" Exhibition, Victoria*
and Albert Museum
Valerie Steele, *The Museum at the Fashion Institute of Technology*
Lou Taylor, *University of Brighton*
Karen Tranberg Hansen, *Northwestern University*
Ruth Barnes, *Yale Art Gallery, Yale University*

Books in this provocative series seek to articulate the connections between
culture and dress, which is defined here in its broadest possible sense as
any modification or supplement to the body. Interdisciplinary in approach,
the series highlights the dialogue between identity and dress, cosmetics,
coiffure, and body alternations as manifested in practices as varied as plas-
tic surgery, tattooing, and ritual scarification. The series aims, in particular,
to analyze the meaning of dress in relation to popular culture and gender
issues and will include works grounded in anthropology, sociology, history,
art history, literature, and folklore.

ISSN: 1360-466X

Previously published in the Series
Helen Bradley Foster, *"New Raiments of Self":*
African American Clothing in the Antebellum South
Claudine Griggs, *S/he: Changing Sex and Changing Clothes*
Michaele Thurgood Haynes, *Dressing Up Debutantes:*
Pageantry and Glitz in Texas
Anne Brydon and Sandra Niessen, *Consuming Fashion:*
Adorning the Transnational Body
Dani Cavallaro and Alexandra Warwick, *Fashioning the Frame:*

Fashion History

A Global View

LINDA WELTERS AND ABBY LILLETHUN

BLOOMSBURY VISUAL ARTS
LONDON • NEW YORK • OXFORD • NEW DELHI • SYDNEY

BLOOMSBURY VISUAL ARTS
Bloomsbury Publishing Plc
50 Bedford Square, London, WC1B 3DP, UK
1385 Broadway, New York, NY 10018, USA
29 Earlsfort Terrace, Dublin 2, Ireland

BLOOMSBURY, BLOOMSBURY VISUAL ARTS and the Diana logo are trademarks
of Bloomsbury Publishing Plc

First published in Great Britain by Bloomsbury Academic 2018
This edition published by Bloomsbury Visual Arts 2018
Reprinted 2019 (twice), 2020 (twice), 2021 (twice)

For legal purposes the Acknowledgements on p. xv constitute an extension of this
copyright page.

Cover design: clareturner.co.uk
Cover Image: Cartography by Henricus Hondius, Amsterdam, 1630.
Illustrated copperplate. (© DEA PICTURE LIBRARY/De Agostini/Getty Images)

A catalogue record for this book is available from the British Library.

A catalog record for this book is available from the Library of Congress.

ISBN: HB: 978-1-4742-5363-5
PB: 978-1-3501-0569-0
ePDF: 978-1-4742-5364-2
eBook: 978-1-4742-5365-9

Series: Dress, Body, Culture, 1360-466X

Typeset by Deanta Global Publishing Services, Chennai, India
Printed and bound in India

To find out more about our authors and books visit www.bloomsbury.com
and sign up for our newsletters.

CONTENTS

LIST OF ILLUSTRATIONS

ACKNOWLEDGMENTS

This book is the result of a series of conversations at conferences and symposia. We acknowledge all those who listened to our ideas and encouraged us in our efforts to expand fashion history beyond the West. We are especially indebted to Joanne Eicher, our "dress mother," for advice and encouragement throughout the entire project.

The ideas in this book were first presented at the Costume Society of America in 2011, and subsequently published (at the invitation of editor Sally Helvenston) as a Forum in *Dress*, the Society's scholarly journal (Lillethun, Welters, and Eicher 2012). The discussion continued at the annual conferences of the International Textile and Apparel Association in 2011, 2012, and 2013. Our thanks go to colleagues who participated in the panel discussions: Linda Arthur Bradley (Washington State University), Seunghye Cho (Framingham State University), Joanne Eicher (University of Minnesota), Dilia Lopez-Gydosh (University of Delaware), and the late Charlotte Jirousek (Cornell University).

Further paper presentations and informal talks took place at the second biannual "Non-Western Fashion Conference" in London, England, in 2013 and the "Dressing Global Bodies" Conference in Edmonton, Canada, in 2016. Presenters and participants at the Textile Museum's 2015 Symposium in Washington D.C., "Picturing China: Qing-Dynasty Photography and Fashion," also unraveled new threads. These academic gatherings succeeded in doing what conferences and symposia are intended to do: share research and information and alert attendees to what other scholars are thinking. Thanks to all presenters and attendees for their insights.

The editorial staff at Bloomsbury has been extraordinarily helpful and patient. We thank Kathryn Earle and Anna Wright, who initially shepherded the idea for a book through to a proposal. Once the proposal was accepted, Hannah Crump, Frances Arnold, and Pari Thomson took over the reins. We appreciate their guidance and good humor.

Many institutions provided gratis images to illustrate our ideas. These include Special Collections at the University of Rhode Island Library, the Historic Textile and Costume Collection at the University of Rhode Island, the Rhode Island School of Design Museum of Art, Yale University's Bienecke Library and The Lewis Walpole Library, the Laskaridis Foundation in Athens, National Gallery (UK), the Victoria and Albert Museum, the Wellcome Library (London), and the Artifact Museum in Haenam City (Korea). For assistance at these and other repositories, we extend our thanks. Individuals who facilitated image acquisition include Tina

Bates, Joanne Eicher, Axel Langer, Kyung-Eun Lee, Yoonsup Chung, Hyungsik Yun, Sengkheang Penh, and anonymous donors.

We are extremely grateful to the University of Rhode Island Center for the Humanities for awarding a subvention grant to partially fund acquisition of rights and permissions for photographs.

Individuals who aided us in other ways include our respective university's interlibrary loan specialists (Emily Green at URI and Kevin Prendergast at Montclair State University), Susan Jerome of URI's Historic Textile and Costume Collection, Fafar Bayat for illustrative material, and James Middleton for consultation. For other assistance, great and small, we thank Mae Chae, Kristen Chaney, Allison Ellston, Ji-Hye Kang, Anna Rose Keefe, Rebecca Kelly, Sheng Lu, Lauren Mione, Lindsay Michael, Joseph Shemtov, and Cara Tremain.

Finally, the authors thank friends and family for tolerating reduced levels of socialization while this book was being written.

FOREWORD

Joanne B. Eicher

What an exciting book to read on fashion history! Linda Welters and Abby Lillethun's volume is based on the premise that all human beings are open to change, a basic idea of fashion. Not only are *Homo sapiens* open to change, we are creative. The usual histories, however, of what we call costume, dress, or fashion, ethnocentrically declare that fashion is a Western phenomenon not acknowledging the possibility of fashion in non-Western cultures. Welters and Lillethun refreshingly smash this ethnocentrism, call it a fallacy, and provide documentation of fashion changes across the globe, historically and contemporaneously. Chapter 1 is a landmark presentation that outlines the case for why a comprehensive history of fashion *must* be global, buttressed by a broad array of scholarly views. Arguments first developed by Eric Wolf, the anthropologist who wrote *Europe and the People Without History* in 1982, feature prominently.

Chapters 2, 3, and 4, in Part 1, follow with review of the lexicon used in writing about how we dress our bodies and assessment of key fashion theories and fashion historiography. I consider Part 2 their tour de force, however, which rests on case studies of fashions beyond the West, examples from India and China, cultures existing centuries before the rise of the West. In addition, it reports fashion change in precolonial and colonial societies in the Americas, Africa, and Southeast Asia. These case studies include examples from their own research on New England natives and in Greece, Latvia, Indonesia, and the Bronze Age. From these, they move on to fashion in indigenous cultures, using Jennifer Craik's (2009) notion of the "fashion impulse" that reinforces the idea of creativity existing in *Homo sapiens* from prehistory to the present. They report on archaeological findings and early trade networks regarding resources for jewelry, silk textiles, and tailored garments. Grave finds and rock art are some of the early forms of archaeological evidence of dress and fashion change along with tools used. Embellishment of the body with beads and tattoos certainly demonstrates the creative urge of human beings through time.

To intrigue readers more, a few of my favorites follow. Although Native Americans' wearing of untailored furs, skins, and pelts did not appeal to Europeans who interacted with them, the Native Americans demonstrated change in moccasins, leggings, various body coverings acting as garments, and hairstyling. A first-century CE example came from a ship captain based in Egypt who wrote about purple cloths and "clothing in the Arabian style with sleeves; plain, ordinary, embroidered, or interwoven with gold." Welters and Lillethun found extensive Chinese examples: a colorful one comes from Chinese fashions of imperial court ornaments of imported kingfisher feathers of iridescent blues from lapis to turquoise used over the years from BCE into CE. Byzantine hairstyles and various garments are another case of changing styles over time, sometimes the choice of a style distinguishing them from the dominant Romans. Braudel and Lipovetsky, often cited about fashion, claim that the Chinese seldom altered what they wore. This included, for Braudel, not only China but also Japan, India, Turkey, and Algeria. Welters and Lillethun successfully contradict that claim arguing that Braudel and Lipovetsky often fell into the trap of being blinded by seeing only tailored clothing as possibly having fashion, not understanding that simply cut or wrapped and draped garments also change over time. Shapes, however, can change in ways of draping and wrapping. Also types of textiles, colors, patterns, motifs, and trims change, which indicates fashion.

I particularly enjoy the example of Chinese makeup of dark lips, painted eyebrows, and no facial powder described by a poet of the ninth century that contrasts with reports of white powdered faces in sixteenth-century China. Readers will treasure these and other examples, too, when they are read and savored beyond my small number of selections reported here. The extensive documentation from China, reinforced with Korean, Japanese, Indian, and Javanese examples in Chapter 7 illustrates that in this range of Asian settings, fashion has been a vibrant part of life. Moving from Eastern examples, in Chapter 8 Welters and Lillethun turn to unexpected Western illustrations citing earlier dates than the fourteenth century, often used to pinpoint fashion's birth by fashion historians. They mention Sara-Grace Heller using French romance literature as documentation prior to the fourteenth century for fashion change. Welters and Lillethun also quote Greek and Roman sources with BCE dates, pointing out the challenges related to archaeological finds.

Chapter 9 investigates what they call "global fashion," reviewing the impact of the West on the rest of the world, but also the rest of the world on the West. They begin with citing several authors who point to the impact of the West in colonization. They also discuss native-made bark cloth change in Hawai'i and the dress called holokū, although a result of Western introduction becomes a fashion that had Hawaiian stylistic input. African examples include comments by a merchant from the Dutch West India Company in 1705. He observed that the African females were committed to elaborate dressing to allure Westerners. Another compelling example of fashion comes from the research of Karen Tranberg Hansen, who documented clearly that fashion arose when Zambians purchased secondhand clothing shipped from Western countries, then choosing to refashion their purchases to suit their own tastes.

In Chapter 10, Welters and Lillethun conclude: "The increase in published research relevant to the globalization of fashion history is heartening." They have done yeoman service by bringing together many examples of such research to date from across the globe, paving the way for a much bigger enterprise than their first step toward accomplishing that goal. Such an enterprise would be writing a chronological account of global fashion from prehistory to present, a gigantic task. These two authors, however, have made a strong, compelling argument and provided an excellent foundation for such an accomplishment.

1

INTRODUCTION: EUROPE AND THE PEOPLE WITHOUT FASHION

We have been taught, inside the classroom and outside of it, that there exists an entity called the West, and that one can think of this West as a society and civilization independent of and in opposition to other societies and civilizations. Many of us even grew up believing that this West has a genealogy, according to which ancient Greece begat Rome, Rome begat Christian Europe, Christian Europe begat the Renaissance, the Renaissance the Enlightenment, the Enlightenment political democracy and the industrial revolution.

ERIC R. WOLF

Eric Wolf penned the above quotation about the discipline of history in his landmark book *Europe and the People Without History* (1982: 5). An anthropologist by training, Wolf's objective was to marry anthropology, sociology, and political economy with history to develop an account of global interconnectedness. He objected to the then dominant privileging of the West in chronicles of human history. Wolf claimed in the new preface to the 1997 reprint that "human societies and cultures would not be properly understood until we learned to visualize them in their mutual interrelationships and interdependences in space and time" (Wolf [1982] 1997: x). Wolf's book could just as easily have been written about fashion history. Indeed, the genealogy of fashion in locations around the globe shows "mutual interrelationships and interdependences in space and time" just as in the discipline of history.

The argument for a global history of fashion

It is the central contention of this book that the history of fashion should be understood as a global cultural phenomenon. Two problems have prevented such an understanding to date: first, the oft-repeated claim that fashion did not exist before the late medieval period, and second, the assumption that it did not exist outside the West. An adjunct issue is the focus on elite dress, to the exclusion of folk dress and the everyday dress of common people in Europe and elsewhere from fashion history.

Returning to *Europe and the People Without History,* we point out that Wolf recognized the problem of linking the advance of civilization to the rise of capitalism; the emergence of market economies in medieval Europe serves as a common explanation for European dominance. Wolf framed his critique on a time line that began in 1400, a century after Marco Polo; his father, Niccolo; and his uncle Maffeo returned from their travels across Asia, when China had the largest naval fleet in the world and when Europe embraced a market economy that gave rise to wealthy merchants who rivaled kings and queens in sartorial display. Wolf briefly traced the development of the social science disciplines, citing history's propensity to focus on the achievements of dominant political entities and anthropology's concentration on the study of present-day cultures while ignoring the history of those cultures. Wolf was intent on starting in 1400 because that is when Europe began expanding outside of its geographical boundaries, and because through expansion Europeans began encountering societies that had complex cultures and long histories. He argued that these histories should not be ignored. That is why he chose the title *Europe and the People Without History.*

Many scholars in the academy heard Wolf's cry. As globalization advanced in the 1990s, attention shifted beyond the borders of Euro-America, mostly to the East, with the rise of China and India as powerful economic forces. Another anthropologist, Jack Goody, also critiqued the Western-centric framing of history. In 2006, twenty-four years after Wolf's book appeared, he titled his own book *The Theft of History* (2006), echoing Wolf's assessment of the history discipline. Goody countered accepted interpretations of fashion and declared that he suspected that "we could trace it [fashion] earlier and probably everywhere" (265).

In the last decades of the twentieth century, scholars began to question the hegemony of Western Europe in the history of dress. Cynthia Jasper and Mary Ellen Roach-Higgins focused on teaching; they suggested more accurate naming of costume history courses (e.g., "Heritage of Western Dress") and including assignments that introduced influences from other cultures (Jasper and

Roach-Higgins 1987). Suzanne Baizerman et al. argued for a more holistic approach to the study of dress after observing the discourse surrounding Eurocentrism in the disciplines of anthropology, art history, and folklore (Baizerman, Eicher, and Cerny 1993). Brydon and Niessen's *Consuming Fashion: Adorning the Transnational Body* (1998) challenged the class, race, and economic dichotomies embedded within fashion theory. The edited book introduced new views into fashion systems. In the new millennium, anthropologists Jane Schneider (2006a) and Karen Hansen (2004) criticized the dominance of Western fashion in dress studies. Schneider argued that the history of the dress of courtly societies in non-Western countries demonstrated the same fundamental elements of fashion—changing styles and elitism—as did the court fashions of Europe, an argument we took to heart in developing the case studies for this book. In the twenty-first century, globalization has created what Hansen terms a "new world in dress" (Hansen 2004: 372). Australian Jennifer Craik raised the globalization issue in her two books on fashion (Craik 1994, 2009). Craik argued that the term "fashion" needs revision, that fashion systems operate globally, and that non-Western dress has its own fashion system. Robert Ross (2008) and Margaret Maynard (2004) examined colonialism's effects on the dress of the colonized. Historian Beverly Lemire, who has published extensively on textiles and early modern dress, edited a collection of essays that explore fashion as a powerful force in politics and society (2010). Finally, Giorgio Riello and Peter McNeil addressed fashion *and* history in their introductory essay and selection of extracts for *The Fashion History Reader: Global Perspectives* (2010). As Riello and McNeil note in their introductory essay, "If we wish to understand fashion beyond Europe, we must refrain from thinking that this has suddenly emerged in the last few decades as the result of globalization and the growth of new middle classes" (2010: 4), thus directing the fashion history field to critically assess embedded assumptions. These scholars helped to form the basic assumptions for this book.

Sandra Niessen was one of the first to reimagine fashion history as global. In *Re-Orienting Fashion* (2003: 243), she expounded upon the problems inherent in separating the dress of the West from other dress systems and also the assignment of fashion only to Europe and its diaspora. Niessen discussed the boundaries built into the study of dress and fashion, one of which is Eurocentrism. Eurocentrism refers to a conception of the world that focuses on European cultures while giving little attention to other geographical areas, such as Asia, Africa, and Latin America. It is a subset of ethnocentrism, which can be described as viewing other cultures through the lens of one's own culture; often with the "other" assessed as lacking the attributes that the viewer, attached to their own culture, perceives as superior. In reference to dress history, Eurocentrism means that the dress practices of Europe and the ancient Mediterranean cultures that contributed to European civilization are the only dress histories that matter.

The ten-volume Berg *Encyclopedia of World Dress and Fashion* (2010) went a long way to rectify that neglect as did Giorgio Riello and Peter McNeil's *The Fashion History Reader*. General editor Joanne Eicher and her team of volume editors selected contributing authors for their research expertise, some of whom are world-renowned experts on their topics (Eicher 2016).

This book is an extension of that perspective. We advance the argument to consider the *history* of fashion—not just contemporary fashion—as a phenomenon that happened in many locales around the world. Fashion, as applied to dress, is commonly described as changing forms of dress that are adopted by a group of people at a certain time and place (Welters and Lillethun 2011). This definition is not time or place specific, yet fashion has long been conceptualized as the product and domain of Western capitalism. The widely accepted premise is that fashion did not exist before the fourteenth century and that it developed in European courts with the rise of market economies. In this conception, fashion spread to the rest of the world through the expansion of Euro-American power. This is a major fallacy in dress and fashion studies. While some scholars of contemporary fashion have embraced a more pluralistic view, dress *historians* have been slow to envision or accord importance to fashion outside the West.

We contend that fashion existed in Europe before the mid-fourteenth century and in cultures outside the West prior to modern times. Adjunct to this view we argue that European folk dress also developed in the fashion sphere and should be included in the history of fashion. While selected examples and case studies (of varying detail) are provided to illustrate our points, this book is not intended to be comprehensive of *all* cultures across time and space. We have chosen examples from both the Northern and Southern Hemispheres as well as from prehistory to the twenty-first century. In doing so, we highlight several great ancient civilizations that are ignored in costume history textbooks (e.g., China, India, Meso- and South America). It is hoped that this work will inspire new, inclusive fashion histories that incorporate cultures beyond the West and before the rise of capitalism in Europe. While some recent authors extend the discussion of dress history beyond Europe and America, such as Daniel Hill (2011) and Robert Ross (2008), they do not contextualize changing dress practices as "fashion." This book proposes that changing dress practices should be interpreted as fashion.

The conceptualization of fashion's birth in fourteenth-century Europe gained credence in the cultural studies field when Fernand Braudel, a non-dress specialist, published his three-volume tome *Civilization and Capitalism, 15th–18th Century*. Braudel, a French historian, was responding to the growing interest in social history. Published in French, then translated to English in 1981, his work reached a wide academic audience interested in the emerging field of cultural studies.

He devoted twenty-three pages to "costume and fashion," a subject that had previously been ignored by historians in academia. He distinguished between "costume" and "fashion" based on the pace of change in dress. In Braudel's eyes, costume refers to the clothing of Europe's peasants, Peruvian Indians, and sub-Saharan Africans, whereas fashion applies only to Europe's elite. He described costume as a manifestation of stable societies, whereas dress remained the same for generations, even centuries. Yet, in apparent contradiction, he stated that costume the world over was "subject to incessant change" (Braudel 1981: 311).

He made the clear claim that fashion began in Europe as a way for the elite to distinguish themselves from those lower than them on the social scale. He stated that this change occurred around 1350 when men's tunics suddenly became shorter. He went on: "One could say that fashion began here. For after this, ways of dressing became subject to change in Europe" (Braudel 1981: 317). He supported his claim by emphasizing the rapidity of changing forms of dress, which he contrasted with the "changelessness" in the courtly costumes of India, Japan, China, and the Islamic countries as well as the poor in Europe. He deliberately excluded the changing tastes in fabrics that characterize court dress in Eastern countries. His argument centered on tailoring, or "fashioning," clothes to the body, which ignored body modifications and hairstyling, as well as changing tastes in textiles. These elements are hallmarks of fashion change in Eastern cultures, such as India, Japan, and China. In fact, every culture manipulates these features of dress and appearance. His Eurocentric narrative possesses the two problems outlined earlier and that bear repeating: first, the claim that fashion did not exist before 1350, and second, that fashion did not exist outside the Euro-American zone. Dress historians subsequently fixed on the mid-fourteenth century as the "birth of fashion," and it appears in many texts since the 1980s. A few scholars and historians have countered Braudel on these views, including Antonia Finnane (2008: 6), a well-known sinologist, historian Beverly Lemire (2010: 11), and Jack Goody (2006: 263–4).

The long-standing structure of "costume" history classes perpetuated this Eurocentric approach to the study of fashion history. In the early twentieth century, the typical narrative began with the dress of ancient Egypt, Greece, and Rome and progressed through European historical periods to the French Republic (Fales 1911). This structure has not changed fundamentally since then. British, French, and German authors wrote the early costume history books following the art history model. Gradually, textbooks were published for use in colleges and universities. All of these books traced the history of dress as it reflects Western civilizations. Although some recent publications and museum exhibitions explore the influence of other cultures, such as China, on Western dress, the notion of a fashion system—that is, a process of innovation in dress and appearance practices, and diffusion to others—operating independently of Western influence is almost nonexistent in the museum world.

Some authors have looked to the history of fashion in Asian cultures. Toby Slade, writing about Japan, hoped to "demonstrate that there are other modernities, and different fashion histories beyond the canon of European and American dress narratives, which dominate nearly all interpretations of the practices, styles, institutions and hermeneutic structures of clothing in the modern age" (Slade 2009: 1). Antonia Finnane, in her book *Changing Clothes in China*, claims that "the fact remains that little is known in the English-speaking world about changes in material culture in non-Western societies" (Finnane 2008: 8). The volume of essays edited by Niessen, Leshkowich, and Jones—*Re-Orienting Fashion*—critically reframed the perceptions of Asian fashion systems in tribal, urban, diasporic, and local contexts.

Excluding the rest of the world from fashion

Eric Wolf, as discussed at the beginning of this chapter, understood the consequences of studying only the West. His work acknowledged both the "people who claim history as their own and the people to whom history has been denied," allowing them to "emerge as participants in the same historical trajectory" (Wolf 1982: 23). We apply this approach to fashion history. To deny peoples outside the West the possibility of being agents in a fashion system is reductive and Eurocentric. Baizerman, Eicher, and Cerny made this observation in 1993, expressing the need for a new model to study dress in the modern, globally connected world. As mentioned above, it was Sandra Niessen who first brought the notion of the West/Rest to fashion in her essay "Afterward: Reorienting Fashion Theory" (2003). In fact, she used the phrase "Europe and the People without Fashion" as one of her subheadings. The construction of a divide among people based on having or not having fashion may appear ridiculous at face value, but setting the "having" or "not having" of fashion as a cultural marker has allowed for the construction of otherness with a very wide scope (Niessen 2003). If the others are seen as outside the fashion system, then they are viewed as people without change/progress, taste/style, preferences/dislikes, and so on. Those said not to have fashion are denied the basic human impulse to decorate the body. The ability to purposefully decorate the body distinguishes *Homo sapiens* and *Neanderthals* from apes according to Gillian Morriss-Kay (2010), a professor of anatomy who also specializes in developmental psychology and cultural anthropology. She traced the cognitive shift in human prehistory leading to art creation, positing that body painting was "likely to have been an important precursor to the creation of art separate from the body" and that making a strand of shell beads indicates "recognition of a symbolic importance in the wearing" (2010: 161).

Craik claimed that "fashion is *not* exclusively the domain of modern culture and its pre-occupation with individualism, class, civilization, and consumerism" (Craik 2009: 19). As she explained,

> Fashionable impulses (constantly changing clothing codes and stylistic registers) occur in non-Western and non-modern societies too. Yet the perception (and the myth) has been that non-Western cultures have stable and unchanging clothing codes (called costume or customary dress), a perception perhaps driven by the "snapshot" (or synchronic) approach to ethnographic case studies as well as the desire to emphasize the difference between "us" (civilized individuals) and "them" (pre-civilized groups). (Craik 2009: 19–20)

Craik coined the phrase "the fashion impulse" (2009), a term we find to be an apt one that we use when describing the attire, and change to it, of non-Western and preindustrial cultures worldwide. We apply the phrase "the fashion impulse" to societies in which a fashion system is in place.

We argue that it is time to reconceptualize the history of fashion. Western fashion is only one dress system to consider. Courtly fashion in China, Korea, Japan, Thailand, Indonesia, India, the Middle East, and Mesoamerica are just as important to understand in today's global world as European courtly fashion because it is part of human history; ditto goes for preindustrial and tribal dress across the world. Dress has never been static in any culture; the desire to use the human body to express a host of changing meanings, what Craik terms the "fashion impulse," has been present in societies since time immemorial. Our call for reconceptualizing fashion history extends to the way we teach the subject at colleges and universities as well as the way dress is exhibited in museums.

To summarize, we emphasize three points that will be expanded upon in the following chapters. First, it is our belief that fashion history as currently conceptualized is Eurocentric. Second, the paradigm around fashion scholarship is shifting. We argue, as do some others, that it is a fallacy to define fashion as exclusive to post-1350 Europe and its diaspora. Third, the problem of exclusion can be resolved by reconceptualizing fashion history as a global phenomenon.

***

The remainder of the book is divided into two parts. Part 1, Understanding Fashion and its History, consists of chapters 2–4, which address the terminology, theory, and historiography of fashion. Readers who are already familiar with fashion scholarship on these subjects may wish to start with Part 2, which consists of case studies presented in chapters 5–9.

We note that dress histories of many areas of the world are not available in English, and for these we relied on entries in the aforementioned Berg *Encyclopedia of World Dress and Fashion*. Additionally, international experts authored many entries based on decades spent researching dress and fashion in specific locales, and their entries represented their most recent analysis of dress. We incorporated information from a few selected entries into our case studies.

Chapter 2 elucidates the terminology surrounding the study of fashion. Definitions and contexts from a variety of vantage points in usage by fashion/dress historians and cultural historians are dissected. We illuminate terms often conflated with fashion such as "costume" and "dress." We explain why we prefer the term "fashion" during a time of change in the terminology; we note that the terms themselves seem to be subject to fashion.

In Chapter 3, fashion systems are explained through theories generated by Western scholars. We explicate key theoretical developments in dress and fashion scholarship in chronological order to help readers comprehend how historical context shapes fashion scholarship.

Chapter 4 illuminates the historiography of published scholarship on dress history, primarily in English. It reviews salient literature from the earliest costume books illustrated with engraved images to the present day's abundance of fashion titles. It traces the rise of Eurocentrism in the study of dress history and the recognition in the 1980s of Eurocentrism as a problem in the study of dress. We look at how the old costume history became the new fashion history. The development of the field of cultural studies as it affects the study of fashion undergoes examination. We recognize the scholarship of authors who have been influential for the new fashion history and discuss the state of fashion history discourse at a threshold moment.

Part 2 presents case studies of fashion beyond the temporal and spatial boundaries of those normally included in standard histories of fashion. We selected locations to feature examples from around the globe, and from the earliest time periods evidencing self-decoration to our current period of globalized fashion. We stress that this book is not a global history of fashion and that it is not universal in its coverage. Instead, we feature examples from our own research; for example, Linda Welters conducted ethnographic research in Greece and Latvia, and has analyzed archaeological textiles of New England native peoples; Abby Lillethun's dissertation on batik includes Indonesia and West Africa, and she researches Bronze Age dress. We read widely on world dress, focusing on studies that incorporated the notion of fashion into their analyses, and our reading influenced our case selections. Some cases are brief in comparison to others. We illustrate the potential for further study of what has formerly been called "traditional dress" as part of a fashion system.

In Chapter 5, we give detail to the argument to include indigenous cultures in the fashion sphere. We reinforce the position that the impulse to decorate the body is a universal human behavior, and as such it extends to small-scale, nonindustrial cultures where fashion can occur (Cannon 1998). In light of the universal human behavior to decorate the self, we incorporate Jennifer Craik's notion of the "fashion impulse" in considering the dress practices of indigenous cultures, including prehistory (2009). Because sources of information on the dress of indigenous cultures are extremely limited until contact with Europeans, the chapter discusses what can be deciphered through archaeology. The cultures discussed include a group from Paleolithic France, the Narragansett tribe of southern New England and other cultures across the Canadian fur-trade region, and from Meso- and South America. We include the effects of colonization, an outside influence rather than an internal dynamic.

Chapter 6 considers early trade networks in terms of their contributions to changing styles of dress in the Eastern Hemisphere. We believe that responses to innovations by ancient world consumers should be interpreted as fashionable behavior. A lively trade network between Mediterranean cultures began as early as the Bronze Age, which allowed for exchange of both materials and styles for dress. Trade expanded north, east, south, and west in ancient Eurasia. Examples of the trade in fashionable items and the trade's effects from the Bronze Age to the eighteenth century include precious and semiprecious materials for jewelry, silk patterned textiles, evolving taste in textiles, and cross-cultural exchange of styles such as tailored garments. The Byzantine, Persian, and Ottoman Empires are highlighted. An example is made of the kebaya of Indonesia, which developed in the context of international trade.

Chapter 7 examines fashion systems in East, South, and Southeast Asia. The changing fashions of the courts of selected Asian cultures enlighten understanding of fashion outside the West prior to the current century. The examples are drawn from the dress histories of China, Korea, Japan, India, and Indonesia. While dress forms remained stable for long periods of time in many Asian societies, the textiles that comprised the outfits went in and out of fashion as did trims, embellishments, and hairstyles. Acknowledging that dress embraces all aspects of appearance, changing tastes in cosmetics are included.

Chapter 8 explores alternative fashion histories in Europe and America, that is to say, prior to the so-called birth of fashion in mid-fourteenth-century Europe, and beyond the court system. We contend that the date of the origin of fashion is not fixed to one time and region. We question the exclusion of folk dress from standard costume and fashion histories.

Chapter 9 extends discussions initiated earlier in the book about the spread of Western fashion from the Age of Exploration to the present, and of so-called non-Western influences on Western fashion. One type of fashion change occurred when the colonizers' styles gradually displaced indigenous dress, although locales responded individually to the introduction of European fashions in fabrics and garment styles. The Pacific region, most notably Hawai'i, serves as an example. Other examples are drawn from sub-Saharan Africa. In the later twentieth century, few areas of the globe had not been introduced to Western fashion, and in the desire to be modern, youth everywhere created their own fashion microsystems. We propose that there is no "West" in terms of fashion anymore, either in contemporary fashion change or in the overarching history of fashion. At the same time, we recognize the influence of the local on fashion systems.

In Chapter 10, we offer concluding remarks. We summarize the major points and call on others to write new, inclusive fashion histories.

Each chapter begins with a quotation that emphasizes the chapter's main points. Some of these are drawn from primary sources, while others come from research or secondary sources key to our argument.

Books in the *Dress, Body, Culture* series are generally illustrated in black and white. Further, the number of illustrations is limited to fifty. While all publications on such a visual subject as dress and fashion would be served by plentiful color images, the cost becomes an issue for a series that aims to advance the discourse on dress and culture through publication of many innovative viewpoints. This book incorporates just enough images to support its points.

Likewise, we did not conduct exhaustive reviews of literature for all of the geographic areas we discuss in this book. We concentrated, where possible, on those scholars who address fashion in history. We crossed disciplinary boundaries, but with the recent expansion of disciplines interested in fashion and its history, we may have missed some important new works. We apologize to any scholars we neglected to include in this book, which is intended as an argument to consider dress systems throughout the world as emblematic of the fashion process. Critical to the development of our ideas were scholarly conferences as well as museum exhibitions and catalogs. We look forward to continued discussion in the future.

PART ONE

UNDERSTANDING FASHION AND ITS HISTORY

2
THE LEXICON OF FASHION

There is a rage of fashion which prevails here with dispotick Sway, the colour and kind of silk must be attended to; and the day for putting it on and off, no fancy to be exercised, but it is the fashion, and that is argument sufficient to put one in, or out of countenance.

ABIGAIL ADAMS ON FASHIONABLE
DRESS IN LONDON

When Abigail Adams, the future First Lady of the United States, joined her husband, John, in London, she made the above observations in a letter dated July 26, 1784, to her sister Mary Cranch back home in Massachusetts (Ryerson 1993: 379). Her comments elucidate key features of the nature of fashion in the West in the late eighteenth century. She saw fashion as a powerful force in society, almost a dictatorial one. She implied that a time element was involved and that styles were occasion specific. In other letters, she compared French styles to those of England and America, revealing that fashion in the West varied from place to place (Winner 2001). Surely prevailing dress practices outside the West shared these same qualities: changing styles of dress accepted by a group of people, at a specific time, and in a specific place.

Fashion means different things to different people. While this book considers fashion related to dress and appearance, the word also encompasses other cultural expressions such as furniture, interior design, the food we eat, even the novels we read. Regardless, the one feature that everyone agrees on is that fashion involves currency, implying change over time.

To consider the argument that fashion historically existed beyond the West and in premodern times, we must elucidate the terminology. This chapter explores fashion's various meanings. We consider the range of its meanings as well as its synonyms and antonyms. Not all scholars interpret the terms in the same way; these varied interpretations are presented in the following sections.

Etymology of fashion terms

In this section, we dissect common fashion terms, going back to their first appearance in the English language and their changing meaning over time. This investigation of fashion terms in English is appropriate, although limiting, considering our discussion of terms in other languages below. We note that English is the most widely spoken language in the world after Hindi and the various languages spoken by the ethnic groups living in the People's Republic of China. For this dissection of terms, we rely on the *Oxford English Dictionary* (OED), which differs from a typical dictionary in that its objective is to trace changes in a word's usage over time in addition to providing detailed definitions. Dictionaries such as *Webster's Dictionary* or the *Oxford Dictionary of English* simply define commonly used words with short notes about origins. In the days before the internet, dictionaries generally consisted of a single volume. By comparison, the most recent printed version of the OED, which was published in 1989, numbers twenty volumes. The OED is available online (OED Online) and is free to patrons of any library with a subscription, including many public libraries.

Words equated with the term "fashion," or used as descriptors for fashion, include "mode," "dress," "clothing," "costume," "toilette," "apparel," and "habit." Additional words related to fashion, a term with broad meanings, include the more specific descriptors "taste," "style," "fad," "classic," and "trend." Each of these terms is discussed below, along with some others. We include current debates on usage, noting that the terms themselves are subject to change over time.

Fashion and related terms

Fashion

Fashion is both a verb, as in "to fashion something," and a noun, as in "to wear the latest fashion." In the OED, fashion carries no fewer than fourteen different meanings. Relevant for the current discussion are the following: "manner, mode, way" and "a prevailing custom, a current usage, especially one characteristic of a particular place or period of time," and "conventional usage in dress, mode of life, etc., *esp.* as observed in the upper circles of society; conformity to this usage." And finally, "the mode of dress, etiquette, furniture, style of speech, etc., adopted in society for the time being . . . to be in the fashion: to adopt the accepted style" (OED 1989 s.v. "fashion").

The word "fashion" derives from the Latin words *factio*, the act of making, and the verb *facere*, to make. This meaning correlates to one of the earliest definitions of fashion, to make something, to "fashion" something. By the late

Middle Ages, fashion came to mean a "style, fashion, manner (of make, dress, embellishment)" as well as a "way or mode (of behavior)" (Kurath 1952: 358). The word in Middle English had various spellings (*fassioun*, *faschyoun*, *faccioun*, etc.). An early example of its use as a noun is dated 1475, when the peascod belly, the padded front of a doublet, appeared in Western fashion for men: someone was being advised to stuff his doublet with wool if he desired the "newe *faccion*" (Kurath 1952: 358).

These definitions show that fashion involves styles and ways of dressing confined to a moment in time and space. Fashion is both temporal and geographical. Fashion is often associated with modernity, as we shall see in later discussions. It is a sign that a people, a place is current, of the moment, up with the times, and thus it is a social expression. The OED illustrates the temporal nature of fashion with a 1739 example: "Taste and fashion with us have always had wings."

One of the OED's definitions associates fashion with "the upper circles of society," which sheds light on interpretations of fashion among some academics. Several scholars view fashion as an expression of social hierarchy in the industrial era, a sartorial signal that separates the cognoscenti from the masses (Benjamin 1999; Lipovetsky 1994; Simmel [1904] 1954). It is true that most fashion histories focus on the dress of the elite, especially prior to 1800, simply because ample evidence of dress practices does not survive for those of lower social status. Sociologist George Sproles provides a more relevant explanation of fashion diffusion for contemporary society in that he views fashion as no longer simply emulation of the elite. New styles can be introduced at all levels of society, rendering fashion leadership more inclusive (Sproles 1974).

Note that none of the meanings of fashion in the OED exclude dress outside the West. The geographical designation of applying the term "fashion" in history only to the West possibly originates in the word's Latin roots. However, this is not the only possible reason. Additional reasons for the widespread acceptance that fashion began in the West are discussed elsewhere and include its ties to the rise of capitalism, market economies, and socially mobile societies.

The temporal component—the underlying concept that fashion developed in modern times—evolved presumably because the word "fashion" did not exist before the late Middle Ages, precisely when current scholarship has determined that "fashion" as a social phenomenon began. One problem with this interpretation is that the word's usage is examined only in English. Other languages not derived from Latin, both ancient and modern, have words that imply changing forms in dress adopted at a given time and place. Take, for example, the Chinese words *shiyang* and *shishizhuang*, which appeared before 1100; the words meant "the prevalent style fit for the time" (Tsui 2016: 52–53). Even in Latin, there is a word implying something "of the moment." That Latin word is *modo*, meaning "right now, present." It evolved into the French and

German *mode,* and the Italian, Spanish, and Portuguese *moda* (Paulicelli 2014: 5). In English, "mode" is a synonym for fashion.

Phyllis Tortora delves into the issue of temporality in her essay "History and Development of Fashion" (Tortora 2010). She explains fashion as acceptance of something by a large number of people, which implies a relatively short duration. The key element, she explains, is change. She does not specify the precise length of time meant by "short duration." In other work, Tortora has suggested that fashion prevailed when styles "lasted less than a century" (Tortora and Marcketti 2015: 104).

For the purposes of this book, we employ the definition of fashion advanced in our previous work: "Changing styles of dress and appearance that are adopted by a group of people at any given time and place" (Welters and Lillethun 2011: xxvii). As applied to dress, fashion is then the dominant adoption pattern by a group of people in a particular geographic location. To be called fashion, a mode of dress need not be adopted by all of a society or even its majority; depending on its size a society may include subgroups that develop distinct fashions. Further, we do not put a specific time limit on the duration of a particular style; thus, change is not restricted to clothing or other styles that pass out of fashion in less than 100 years. If that were the case, the common business suit could not be considered fashion because it has been in use since the mid-nineteenth century.

Dress

Dress, like fashion, is both a verb and a noun. The OED presents a much narrower definition of the noun dress, a meaning that most people outside the academy would understand. Dress is defined as "a suit of garments or a single external garment appropriate to some occasion when adornment is required—a lady's robe or gown made not entirely to clothe, but also to adorn." The "Walking Dresses" seen in Figure 2.1 exemplify this definition; the fashion plate illustrates two women's gowns inspired by neoclassicism, a major influence on the arts in the 1790s and early 1800s.

The OED also gives "dress" a more general meaning of "personal attire or apparel." The period example of this definition, seemingly a critique on excessive interest in fashion, comes from 1638: "Your dresses blab your vanities." Inclusion of "personal" in the definition suggests individual choice in creating an identity.

The word "dress" has been proffered as a more inclusive term than fashion in scholarly circles, a word that is distinct from fashion. Mary Ellen Roach-Higgins and Joanne Eicher suggested that the word "was broadly interchangeable with several other terms used by social scientists" such as clothing, adornment, and costume (Roach-Higgins and Eicher 1992: 1). They defined dress as "an assemblage of modifications of the body and/or supplements to the body,"

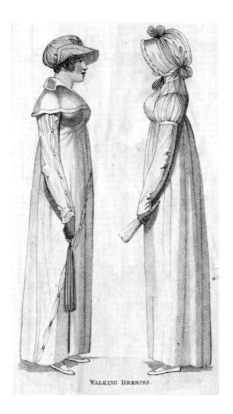

Figure 2.1 "Walking Dresses." *The Fashions of London & Paris During the Years 1804, 1805 & 1806.* Richard Phillips: London. Historic Textile and Costume Collection, University of Rhode Island. The word "dress" appears more frequently than "costume" to label outfits in this book of fashion plates.

arguing that modifications of the body include those both permanent and temporary such as scarification and makeup and that supplements to the body include such items as clothing, accessories, and handheld objects. They claimed that this definition of dress "is unambiguous, free of personal or social valuing or bias, usable in descriptions across national and cultural boundaries, and inclusive of all phenomena that can accurately be identified as dress."

In 1995, Joanne Eicher along with Barbara Sumberg extended the discussion of the term "dress" by critiquing the phrase "western dress." They claimed that "designating items as western for people who wear them in other areas of the world, such as Asia or Africa, is inaccurate" (296). Labeling it "western" privileges the West, they concluded. In an attempt to encompass the entire globe in the academic discourse on dress, they proposed "world fashion" or "cosmopolitan fashion" to describe Western fashion worn in non-Western countries (296).

"Dress" as the overall preferred term has received widespread acceptance among scholars from multiple disciplines. Titles of key scholarly works now specify dress *and* fashion, such as the Berg *Encyclopedia of World Dress and Fashion*, a ten-volume set edited by Joanne Eicher and published by Oxford University Press. This specification implies a difference between dress and fashion. The usage of the dual terms "dress" and "fashion" may be a function of the changing meanings of the words as the field develops. For some, fashion is a subset of the dominant category of dress. Yet, for cultural theorists, fashion has emerged as the preferred term. For example, the publisher (originally Berg, now Taylor & Francis) chose the name *Fashion Theory* rather than *Dress Theory* or *Costume Theory* for its new journal in 1997.

Clothing

Literally speaking, clothing is a body covering made from cloth. It is limiting to use "clothing" as a synonym for fashion in two ways. First, cloth is made from fibers, natural or manufactured, through a variety of processes, most commonly weaving or knitting. Body coverings made from skins or furs or other non-cloth material are thus (potentially) excluded in this definition of clothing. Secondly, clothing does not incorporate other body supplements such as attachments and handheld objects, or body modifications such as tattoos, or hair color and styling.

In her book *Fashion-ology*, Yuniya Kawamura distinguishes between clothing and fashion. Her position is that all clothing is not fashion. An item of clothing can become fashion, but not until it gains symbolic value. She argues that fashion has invisible elements: it is "a system of institutions, organizations, groups, producers, events and practices, all of which contribute to the making of fashion, which is different than dress or clothing" (Kawamura 2005: 43). She goes on to say that

> clothing is material production while fashion is symbolic production. Clothing is tangible while fashion is intangible. Clothing is a necessity while fashion is an excess. Clothing has a utility function while fashion has a status function. Clothing is found in any society or culture where people clothe themselves while fashion must be institutionally constructed and culturally diffused. A fashion system operates to convert clothing into fashion that has a symbolic value and is manifested through clothing. (Kawamura 2005: 44)

Fashion historian Ingrid Loschek further illuminates this perspective, arguing that adoption transforms clothes into fashion. Clothes are produced via a design and manufacturing process. Society, or a group of people, determines which clothes are accepted and thus become fashion. Her example of this transformation is the bumster pant with a bare midriff top, a look for women introduced in 1996 by Alexander McQueen. At that point, the products were clothes. She posits that the look became fashion in 2001, when young people in large cities made it visible (Loschek 2009: 133–34).

Roach-Higgins and Eicher say clothing does not include body modification, which is why they prefer their term "dress." Indeed, "clothing" has fallen out of favor as a term used in American universities as a disciplinary descriptor: former departments of "textiles and clothing" have changed their names to variants of "textiles and fashion." In 1991, the former Association of College Professors of Textiles and Clothing voted to change its name to International Textile and Apparel Association. However, its scholarly journal, first published in 1982, retained "clothing" in its title: *Clothing and Textile Research Journal.* Such changes demonstrate a disciplinary shift in the United States away from the confines of the design, manufacturing, and sale of "clothing" to more comprehensive topics. We concur that clothing is too limiting a term.

Costume

One of the most puzzling words associated with fashion is "costume." For many years, costume has been widely used to describe historic dress, or dress worn for performance, for Halloween, or other masquerade events. However, this was not always the case. Interestingly, the word "costume" in reference to everyday dress was not in general use until the nineteenth century. According to the OED, it originated among Italian artists to describe a "guise or habit in artistic representation." It was then picked up by the French and English in the early eighteenth century to mean a "manner of dressing, wearing the hair, etc., and in later times to dress." A further definition in the OED is: "the mode or fashion of personal attire and dress (including the way of wearing the hair, style of clothing, and personal adornment) belonging to a particular nation, class or period." This definition sounds much like the one Roach-Higgins and Eicher give for their preferred term "dress," except that they don't refer to mode or fashion, or thus to temporality. Roach-Higgins and Eicher opposed the use of the term "costume" as an all-encompassing and neutral term because by the late twentieth century, it referred to dress for special activities or role-play, such as performance, folk festivals, ceremonies, and rituals. They called this dress for "out-of-everyday" activities.

In surveying nineteenth-century fashion images, "costume" appears with regularity in reference to a total ensemble. The OED recognized this usage in a third definition for "costume": "fashion or styles of dress appropriate to any occasion or season; hence, dress considered with regard to its fashion or style." An example of period usage is provided: *La Belle Assemblée,* an English lady's magazine, included an "outdoor costume" in its May 1818 issue. The term

Figure 2.2 "Fashionable Costumes." *Godey's Lady's Book and Magazine,* October 1871. Historic Textile and Costume Collection, University of Rhode Island. "Fashionable Costumes," meaning contemporary fashions, was a monthly feature in *Godey's.*

was equated with contemporary fashion throughout the nineteenth century, as illustrated by Figure 2.2. The description for this image uses another synonym: "Walking dress of purple silk poplin, made with two skirts, both trimmed with a ruffle and puff of darker silk."

Numerous other examples can be given to provide evidence that "costume" was synonymous with dress in the nineteenth century. For example, Amelia Bloomer's dress reform outfit was called "the bloomer costume" in published sources at the time it was presented to the public (Figure 2.3).

Pravina Shukla, a folklorist, deliberately chose the word "costume" for the title of her book *Costume: Performing Identities Through Dress* (2015). She considers costume to be the clothing that is worn when discarding everyday identity. Shukla defines costume as the "clothing of whom we are not" (4). In this way, her understanding of costume echoes that of Roach-Higgins and Eicher, dress for "out-of-everyday" activities. She studied dress worn for Brazilian carnivals, folk festivals in Sweden, events sponsored by the Society for Creative Anachronism, Civil War reenactments, living history sites, and theatrical performances. Her goal was to investigate "how costume enables

Figure 2.3 "The Bloomer Costume." N. Currier, 1851. Lithograph. Historic Textile and Costume Collection, University of Rhode Island. Amelia Bloomer's reform outfit was introduced as a practical, everyday "costume."

individuals to perform identities that are not expressed through daily dress" (Shukla 2015: ix).

For centuries, people had worn outfits to masked balls that gave them other identities. By Victorian times, these became "fancy dress balls," which were like modern-day costume parties. For ideas about what to wear to such a ball, people turned to publications like Ardern Holt's *Fancy Dresses Described* (1887), which explained and illustrated a myriad of ideas including "Witch" and "Hornet" (Figure 2.4). It also offered outfits that drew on historical styles, for example, the

Figure 2.4 "The Witch," "The Hornet," and "Watteau." *Fancy Dresses Described; or What to Wear at Fancy Balls,* Ardern Holt, 1887. London: Debenham and Freebody. Collection of Linda Welters. Reprinted with permission. Victorians used "fancy dress" instead of "costume" to describe outfits worn to costume parties, known at the time as fancy balls.

"Watteau costume," shown in Figure 2.4. It appears that "fancy dress" was the more common term for "dress up" clothes than "costume" in the nineteenth century, a reversal of usage in the early twenty-first century.

Costume had been the word of choice when the study of historic dress began as a subject of academic interest. Early books on dress history, like Auguste Racinet's *Le Costume Historique* (1876–88), employed "costume" in the title. American universities also adopted the word "costume" for course titles; major museums with dress and textile collections also titled their departments with the term "costume" instead of "dress" or "fashion." Further, professional organizations that focus on dress history are still called "Costume Society" (of America, of Great Britain, of Nova Scotia, and of Ontario). The British Costume Society's journal is called *Costume.* To avoid confusion, the Costume Society of America, which modeled itself after the British society, named its journal *Dress*.

Only in recent decades has "costume" become an unfashionable word. Course titles are slowly changing to either "dress" or "fashion," as are names of museum collections. To wit: the Department of Textiles and Costumes at the Museum of Fine Arts Boston changed its name to Textile and Fashion Arts in 2004 upon reception of a bequest from David and Roberta Logie. The Victoria and Albert Museum no longer calls its dress gallery "the costume court"; its vast collection is now "Fashion and Textiles" instead of the former "Dress and Textiles."

The Costume Society of America debated changing its name for several years, but decided to stay with "costume." This debate affirms that language is a living thing, words go in and out of use, and meanings change over time.

Costume is no longer a synonym for fashion. We agree with Roach-Higgins, Eicher, and Shukla that costume refers to dress worn to present an identity other than that projected on a day-to-day basis.

Toilette

Another word once synonymous with fashion that has changed meaning over time is "toilette" and, as a result, has gone out of normal use. The French term appeared in the English language in the late seventeenth century, referring to the "manner or style of dressing; dress, costume," as in this 1752 observation: "Tis so long (tell Lady Caroline) since I have seen so spruce a Toylet as hers" (*OED Online* s.v. "Toilette"). Its use peaked in the 1860s. Toilette emphasized grooming behaviors, especially ones that required assistance from others or that were complex.

Apparel

Apparel is a synonym for fashion that emerged early in the English language, toward the end of the Middle Ages. The OED defines apparel as "personal outfit or attire; clothing generally, raiment, dress." It derives from the French *apparel*, also *appareil*. In 1330, the following description appeared: "fourscore armed knights, in silk appareled," which must have been quite a sight. Apparel has also been used as a verb, as in "to apparel." Today, one rarely hears someone ask, "What apparel are you wearing?" Rather, the term references the production of fashion, for example, the apparel industry.

Habit

"Habit" is one of the oldest terms in English for dress, and it derives from Latin. Not surprisingly, it is the term Cesare Vecellio used for the most famous of the sixteenth-century costume books, his *Habiti Antichi et Moderni,* originally published in Italian.

It is defined as "fashion or mode of apparel, dress." The word refers to a set of clothes or a specific garment. "Habit" has other closely related meanings such as the dress of religious orders (e.g., nun's habit) and the dress worn by ladies on horseback (e.g., riding habit).

Descriptors of fashion

Several terms associated with fashion can be considered a related group that define or name aspects of fashion. Such terms include taste, style, fad, classic, and trend.

Taste

Displaying good "taste" featured prominently in eighteenth-century discourse. The OED explains taste as "the sense of what is appropriate, harmonious, or beautiful, esp. discernment and appreciation of the beautiful in nature and/or art." Sir Joshua Reynolds, the painter, writing about taste in 1776, reflected that "taste in dress . . . is certainly of the lowest subjects to which this word is applied" ([1776] 1831: 66). The period's discourse concerning taste included philosophical examination of aesthetic value, such as Immanuel Kant's examination of taste in *Critique of Judgment* ([1790] 2007) that employs fashion as a foil for commentary on taste. Reynolds disparaged taste in relationship to dress because for him, taste was a component of creating beauty, using well-honed skills, and carefully nurtured preferences (taste) to create beauty, such as in art and architecture. Fashion, subject to change, was thus not a matter of taste in his view. William Hogarth shared this view. In 1742, he painted *Taste in High Life*, a satirical comment on the British aristocracy's obsession with fashion. It was later engraved and printed for wide distribution (Figure 2.5).

Figure 2.5 "Taste in High Life." William Hogarth, 1746. Engraving and aquatint, 1798. Courtesy of the Metropolitan Museum of Art, New York. Harris Brisbane Dick Fund, 1932. Licensed by Creative Commons. License available online: https://creativecommons.org/publicdomain/zero/1.0/legalcode. Hogarth satirized British aristocracy and their obsession with fashion in this image, which was first created as a painting and later reproduced as an engraving.

Style

The OED defines "style" as "manner, fashion," that is, "a particular mode or fashion of costume." For those who study fashion and work in the fashion industry, the word incorporates both silhouettes and details. The OED provided an example from 1860: "The dress is of the style called in Paris, the *robe Impératrice*" (meaning Empress gown), after Empress Eugenie. Another example is from 1891: "The front was all white satin, made in Empire style." Empire style specifically refers to the presence of an elevated waistline on a garment, which is placed just below the bosom and thus gives no visual emphasis to the natural waist.

However, style has come to mean something else. Coco Chanel famously said "fashion passes, style remains." Actually, she made this statement in French and used the term "mode." *La mode se démode, le style jamais* (*Chanel, Chanel* 1986). Subsequent translations substitute "fashion" for "mode." This meaning has to do with an individual dressing well in clothes, accessories, and grooming that suits their looks and personality, their age, and the occasion. In this meaning style is a personal attribute related to aesthetic skills and not to the specific attributes of a garment.

Fad

The OED does not have much to say about "fad," a relatively recent arrival to the English language. Its etymology is unknown, and it is defined simply as a "craze." It appears in the mid-nineteenth century in reference to being concerned with trifles as evidenced in this 1867 example from *The Trollope*: "She may take up some other fad now." Current usage of the word "fad" as related to dress implies a short-lived fashion adopted by a subset of a larger culture, such as the hot pants worn by young women in the early 1970s.

Classic

A classic, on the other hand, is a recurring style. It is long lived and goes through only minor modifications to reflect fashion's changes. The OED defines classic clothing as "made in simple, conventional styles that are almost unaffected by changes in fashion." An example from 1937 is provided: a company adheres "to what they call their classic blouse because it's always in demand." A contemporary example is the trench coat, a style developed for British officers during the First World War and worn since by both men and women.

Trend

OED defines "trend" as both a verb and a noun. The verb "to trend" means "to turn in some direction, to have a general tendency." The noun "trend" means "the general course, tendency, or drift." The OED's examples are from the 1960s; for example, the *Guardian* described two people as "a trendily dressed couple" in 1967. Interestingly, the rise in the usage of the word "trend" corresponds with disruptions to the mid-twentieth-century fashion hierarchy through which the fashion industries of a few European cities dictated the direction of fashion for the West. Since the decline of their dominance in the late 1960s, multiple fashion directions have appeared in cities around the globe, many created by youth who dressed in so-called street style in response to an ever-increasing network of cultural shifts.

Antonyms of fashion

The opposite of being fashionable is being unfashionable. Many in the fashion field think that the way most people dress has nothing to do with "fashion." Teri Agins, a former reporter for the *Wall Street Journal*, declared that fashion was finished in *The End of Fashion* (1999). She argued that women were dressing more like men and that they were more inspired by the street than by designers in choosing what to wear. She also observed the increasing casualization of the American wardrobe, the rise of stylish clothes available through chain stores, and the lack of risk-taking by designers in an era in which publicly owned fashion labels run the show. Yet, fashion as Agins understands it influences the way people dress: inexpensive clothing reflective of fashion trends is available through mass merchants like Target and Tesco. While Agins correctly diagnosed causes of infrastructure changes in the fashion business brought about by shifts in the dissemination and adoption of styles and trends among the public, her perspective gives little note to the desire to participate in fashion, to wear clothes that reflect the preferences of one's group or community. This is evidence of the fashion impulse at work.

Some writers view fashion strictly as the product of designers. This perspective reifies designers as creators and also attempts to secure fashion as an ideal with privileged access (Grumbach 2014). In this scenario, the doors to fashion open only to those with funds to purchase designer products. The intrusion of the masses into the practice of fashionability threatens the aura of exclusivity associated with designer-centric fashion. Would the clothing practices of the middle- and lower-income populace be called "fashion" or merely "dress"? We, the authors, observe that dress of non-elites intersects with fashion, as demonstrated in the hip-hop fashions of the 1990s. Malcolm Barnard articulates our position when he argues that "even the most 'basic' 'anthropological' or biological functions of keeping a body warm and dry cannot be immune to style, they must take some form or other. . . . Variation and cultural location are at the heart of what fashion is and therefore we must say that fashion is always with us, and that it has always been with us" (Barnard 2014: 5).

Terms that are considered to be the opposite of fashion include categories such as ecclesiastical and ritual dress as well as uniforms. Ecclesiastical dress evolved from late Roman and Byzantine forms, and has persisted into the present with little change. The Armenian priests observed by Joseph Pitton de Tournefort on his tour of the Levant ca. 1700 wore liturgical vestments still in use today (Figure 2.6). Ritual dress, such as the forms of *tallit* worn by Jews during prayer and rites of passage, stay the same from generation to generation although the materials from which they are made may change. Other types of ritual attire, like baby's christening gowns, reflect changes in fashion.

Uniforms are meant to reduce individuality in dress among a group of individuals, such as schoolchildren or flight attendants, but these too reflect shifts in fashion as seen in the nurse's uniforms in Figure 2.7. The large sleeves of the uniforms worn by these young nurses mirror fashionable daytime dresses of the mid-1890s.

Figure 2.6 "Armenian Priests." Joseph Pitton de Tournefort, 1717. Courtesy of *Travelogues*, Aikaterini Laskaridis Foundation, Athens, Greece. Available online: http://www.eng.travelogues.gr/item.php?view=43567. Ecclesiastical dress, such as the liturgical vestments of Armenian priests, remained unchanged for centuries. Thus, it has not been considered "fashion."

Figure 2.7 Studio portrait of nursing students, John H. Stratford Hospital Training School for Nurses, Brantford, Ontario, Canada, 1897. Canadian Nurses Association/ Library and Archives Canada (e002414893). The students' uniforms reflect 1890s fashionable silhouettes with their leg-of-mutton sleeves.

Recommended terminology

The common element in everybody's definition of fashion is change. A central question for us is, "How rapid must the pace of change be for fashion to come into play?" Eicher and Sumberg (1995: 299), citing Mary Ellen Roach-Higgins, argue that people need to be aware of a change in dress patterns within their own lifetimes in order for that change to be considered fashion. Thus, a second question is, "Do individuals need to be aware of changing dress habits in order for that change to be considered 'fashion' rather than simply 'dress'"? George

Sproles, in a review of fashion theory, explained the fashion cycle as the secular evolution of one style to the next. He differentiated between long-run cycles, which could occur only once in an age or once per century, and short-run cycles, which might be as short as a single season (Sproles 1981: 117). For Sproles the overriding principle was not the length of time that a style was accepted, but the historical continuity of style changes. We support Sproles's position and prefer not to put a time limit on the duration of a fashion.

In the textbook *Survey of Historic Costume*, now in its sixth edition, Phyllis Tortora and Sara Marcketti provide the example of ancient Egypt as a society without fashion, observing the static nature of dress, ultimately concluding that its dress was not fashion (Tortora and Marcketti 2015: 104). However, Egyptian dress and adornment did change over time with each political and technological shift. Although the pace of change was slow, change still occurred. For example, earrings constituted a "late addition to Egyptian jewelry" (Tortora and Marcketti 2015: 44). They also attained "popularity" in the New Kingdom (Gilbert, Holt, and Hudson 1976: 140). Gillian Vogelsang-Eastwood carefully documented the changes in Pharonic Egyptian clothing, noting that styles of dress attained increased layers and complexity over time (Vogelsang-Eastwood 1993). History of costume texts conflate changes in Egyptian dress by necessity of concision, perhaps because of giving more coverage to Western dress and to more recent fashion history. However, the apparent stasis of dress forms is an inadequate basis to conclude fashion's absence. Tortora and Marcketti continue the position held in earlier editions of this best-selling textbook, that fashion is a characteristic of Western dress, which appeared in Europe in the Middles Ages (2015: 9). Further, they exclude the "peasant" dress of Western Europe as being too divergent to include in a general survey of Western dress (2015: 10).

We argue that dress worn prior to the advance of capitalistic economies in Europe should also be considered as fashion. We propose that fashion is the preferential term for changing styles of dress, whether that change is slow or fast, in the shapes of clothes or the patterns on the fabrics, in hairstyles and colors, in cosmetic and body markings, or in permanent body modifications.

Further, if fashion is defined as changing styles of dress adopted by people at any given time and place, then the West cannot be privileged. It is more truthful to understand that the desire to embellish the human body—the fashion impulse—is the dominant reason for dress and that humans seek novelty or change; thus, fashion is endemic to human nature and is the term that we prefer over dress, clothing, costume, toilette, and apparel.

3
FASHION SYSTEMS

Fashion is a form of imitation and so of social equalization, but,
paradoxically, in changing incessantly, it differentiates one time from
another and one social stratum for another. It unites those of a social
class and segregates them from others. The elite initiates a fashion
and, when the mass imitates it in an effort to obliterate the external
distinctions of class, abandons it for a newer mode—a process that
quickens with the increase of wealth.

GEORG SIMMEL

Georg Simmel, a German sociologist, first wrote these words in 1904 to introduce his trickle-down theory of fashion (Simmel [1904] 1957: 541). At the time, the Gilded Age was still in full swing; Simmel and other academics, such as economist Thorstein Veblen, tried to make sense of fashion's hold on Euro-American society. Simmel's work was so foundational to understanding the fashion system that the *American Journal of Sociology* republished it in 1957.

In this chapter, we summarize key theories about how fashion works as a social system because the various theories affect the interpretation of the terms used in fashion discourse. Disciplines differ in their emphases or issues of concern, as will be apparent in the key fashion theories discussed in this chapter. Additional perspectives and concepts appeared with the rise of cultural studies, which are presented in Chapter 4.

Key fashion theories

The previous chapter's analysis of fashion's lexicon reveals that fashion is a social process with components of change, temporality, spatiality, and adoption by groups of people. For more than five and a half centuries, thoughtful observers from a variety of perspectives have attempted to understand or explain fashion, offering both brief and lengthy interpretations. Fashion theory anthologies attesting to the range of commentary on fashion appeared in the early twenty-first century (Barnard 2014; Johnson, Torntore, and Eicher 2003; Purdy 2004). A French essayist named Michel de Montaigne commented on the custom of wearing clothes in 1575, which may be the earliest writing that attempted to theorize fashion (Johnson, Torntore, and Eicher 2003: 15–17).

Theories explaining fashion originate from diverse disciplines including social science fields such as anthropology, economics, and sociology, as well as from business fields such as marketing and consumer behavior; and from other fields such as psychology, history, and cultural studies. Each scholarly discipline has its own foundational tenets, and each develops inquiry seeking to discover knowledge. Theory building refers to an ongoing disciplinary process that builds a framework of linked assumptions, concepts, and explanatory statements. Fresh observations put forth as propositions are tested or examined before scholars accept them as revisions to an accepted theory. Theoretical frameworks undergo constant, although often slow, development as new understandings or propositions become accepted and incorporated in the framework, or sometimes displace prior ones that are disproved.

Fashion theory, despite its apparent long history, was not a discrete scholarly field until the second half of the twentieth century. The broad field of fashion inquiry, drawing as it does upon a range of disciplines, has yet to concur on an overarching theory of fashion that comprehensively encompasses the various disciplinary perspectives. However, numerous concepts have emerged and have been incorporated into the various strands of fashion theory where contestation takes place in the field's literature.

Fashion theories attempt to explain or characterize how and why fashion occurs. The following primarily chronological discussion focuses upon theories that mark significant shifts in the perception and explanation of fashion. Starting in the 1930s, a paradigm shift in intellectual discourse within the humanities and social sciences led these intellectual fields to move away from solely positivistic analytic approaches toward analyses based on cultural interpretative processes. Examples of related academic developments include feminist perspectives, critical and cultural studies, and area studies such as those focused on identity (e.g., gender, ethnicity, social rank). The more recent theoretical developments (cultural studies) that incorporate interpretive cultural analysis are discussed in Chapter 4. In this chapter we present key foundational fashion theories up to the cultural turn as proposed by Jameson (1998). The goal is to present a broad portrayal of the earlier progress in fashion theory and to observe the points at which selected faulty assumptions took hold.

Although observations about fashion by Western essayists began in the Renaissance and continued through the Enlightenment, no one attempted a theory of fashion until the mid-nineteenth century. Indeed, the nascent status of scholarly disciplines in the nineteenth century and the constant development of knowledge must be acknowledged in a review of past developments. In the nineteenth century, knowledge had developed from observation and analysis sufficiently enough to lay the ground for the social sciences to emerge, and thus for formal theory development to proceed in the new fields of anthropology and sociology.

Change, imitation, and pursuit of novelty

In his 1854 essay "Manners and Fashion," previously unrecognized as a key work of theory, British scholar and sociologist Herbert Spencer proposed that fashion oscillates between extremes and that fashion is founded on change based in the imitation of elites and in the impetus to seek the pleasure of novelty (Spencer 1854). Thus, he presented three concepts that have continued to be discussed in fashion theory: change, imitation of elites, and pursuit of novelty. In the early twentieth century, Georg Simmel ([1904] 1957), the German sociologist quoted at the beginning of this chapter, and Edward Sapir (1931), an American anthropologist, would echo the assumption that change processes are essential to conceptualization of fashion. However, in the nineteenth century, the notion that human cultures had developed on a hierarchical scale took hold of mainstream intellectual thought. This was to influence considerations of fashion and fashion change.

Fashion theory and evolutionary theory

Charles Darwin emerged as the dominant natural scientist of the nineteenth century when he published *The Origin of Species* ([1859] 1999). He proposed the theory of natural selection that first explained speciation, which was based in part upon his observation of plants and animals in the Galapagos Islands. Darwin's theory posited that speciation was an outcome of biological adaptation to environmental context over time. This idea stimulated intellectuals to pursue discovery of human origins. The idea was also misinterpreted in applications to human differences and to their societies.

Spencer, a widely influential intellectual, promoted searching for a universal law that governed development. In his response to Darwin's work, Spencer coined the phrase "survival of the fittest" ([1864] 2002: 444). Spencer and others interpreted Darwin's theory to propose that nature progressed on a hierarchical pathway, that evolutionary processes produced succeeding improvements. The "survival of the fittest" evolutionary concept skewed Darwin's ideas, and today the phrase is not used in scientific discourse since it lacks specificity generally and does not describe current understanding of genetic adaptation. Darwin's basic assumptions regarding biological organisms' adaptations to their various environments were ignored in the theory's application to social science. The new assumption that humans and human societies develop constantly toward an improved state without understanding the relationship to environmental context implied a hierarchical ranking of humans. Likewise, societal forms were determined to have developed in constant progression. The false assumption of hierarchy in regard to human and societal development would be incorporated in theorizing fashion.

Social Darwinism, a term applied to beliefs that interpret human developments including social and cultural patterns in a hierarchical scale, took hold among many intellectuals in Europe and North America. Social Darwinism is understood to have emerged at the nexus of colonial imperialism and ongoing developments in the nascent social sciences. This historical moment was preceded by the era of European exploration, roughly from the 1400s through the 1700s, when Europeans set out on seafaring quests to expand trade, acquire natural resources, and establish colonies in distant lands. Sometimes indigenous peoples were transported to Europe by explorers, a practice that occurred over several centuries. In 1566, an Inuit woman and her daughter were taken from Labrador by French sailors and exhibited in Augsburg and Nuremburg (Sturtevant 1980). By the mid-nineteenth century, the imperial programs of European nations also included exploration for scientific research, such as Darwin's travels. Explorers and anthropologists collected artifacts of the cultures encountered, invaded, or occupied around the world. Artifacts of cultures far from the Western sphere became the basis of newly established museums. Not only were cultural artifacts displayed, but their resources, products, and people were shown at international exhibitions (Blanchard 2008; Greenhalgh 1988; Rydell 1984). From their position of power in the imperialist structure, Westerners placed their own capitalist societies at the top of the hierarchy. Conversely, the so-called primitive cultures were low on the scale and black-skinned people of African origins were the lowest.

Important to understanding fashion theory development before the late twentieth century is the acknowledgment of the confluence of social Darwinism and imperialism in intellectual thought and practice. Western capitalist societies that allowed social mobility (movement from one stratum to another) based on achievements were accepted as the pinnacle of civilization by many thinkers. It followed in this flawed logic that the dress practices of the West were also superior to those of other cultures. Fashion became associated with the cultural traits of the West. The dress of so-called primitives was outside of fashion. Several theorists set these cultures apart from fashion. Simmel claimed that "tribal and classless societies" do not have fashion (1904: 541); Sapir echoed that belief with the statement that "primitive" cultures have "slow non-reversible changes of style" and not fashion (Sapir 1931: 141). Such ideas shaped fashion theory until the last quarter of the twentieth century.

Communication, and imitation and differentiation

With focus upon their own cultures, Western observers of dress in the late nineteenth and early twentieth centuries described facets of fashion that they observed around themselves. This limitation in scope allowed several ideas to come forward. Theorists remarked upon directional flow of fashion change from one status group to another, particularly the imitation of a higher status group's fashions by the next lower stratum in social rank. Also observed was that the imitated would move on to another look or fashion once their fashion was copied. The notion that dress components or even participation in fashion were powerful communicators began to be understood.

In 1899, the economist Thorstein Veblen, who developed an interest in other social science disciplines, published the book *The Theory of the Leisure Class*. In it, he delivered a critique of capitalism. Veblen observed and analyzed the group he called the "leisure class," whose unprecedented wealth resulted from the economic benefits of the Industrial Revolution. In Western fashion history, the era is referred to as *La Belle Époque* in France and the Gilded Age in the United States, terms that evoke the luxury enjoyed by some at the top of the economic ladder. A highly visible class of elites could be seen in Western cities enjoying theater and opera, large opulent mansions, and of course, fine clothing individually handmade specifically for them. Their lifestyle sharply contrasted with that of the workers in the cities whose limited wardrobes acted as visible markers of difference from the elites. Veblen, a socialist thinker influenced by Marxist philosophy, contemplated the role of the workers and that of the leisure class in relationship to society's products.

Veblen articulated a withering critique of the leisure class for its excessive consumption and pleasure in it. He called their "pecuniary" or moneyed culture "conspicuous consumption" and pointed to its wastefulness. The conspicuous consumption of the leisure class included participation in a fashion system that demanded changes of clothes for the varied events of their day. Dressing fashionably for day-to-day social events such as lunches, teas, business events, and evening soirees entailed maintaining a fine wardrobe and staff to attend to it.

A high-society wedding served as the premier social event of the 1899 season, commanding attention to fashion details attained through extravagant expenditure. The story behind the wedding scene depicted in Figure 3.1 exemplifies Veblen's leisure class. The bride, Julia Grant, was the granddaughter of Ulysses S. Grant, eighteenth president of the United States and the general who won the American Civil War. Julia had toured Europe with her wealthy aunt, the socially prominent wife of Chicago real estate tycoon Potter Palmer. Julia met her future husband, Russian prince Cantacuzène, in Rome and they became engaged two weeks later. Their wedding took place in the fashionable resort of Newport, Rhode Island, the ultimate in Gilded Age conspicuous consumption

Figure 3.1 "Miss Julia Grant's Wedding Gown," Cover of *Harper's Bazaar,* October 7, 1899. The magazine sent a photographer to fashionable Newport, Rhode Island, to cover the wedding of the season, the marriage of Julia Grant, granddaughter of Ulysses S. Grant, to Russian prince Michel Cantacuzène.

with its grand summer cottages, where Mrs. Potter Palmer had rented the mansion "Beaulieu." *Harper's Bazar* photographed the event and reported the details because they believed it was the "most important society wedding in the United States this season" ("Miss Julia Grant's Wedding": 853). Julia wore a Paris-made gown of heavy white satin with a tulle veil (Cantacuzène 1921). An entire paragraph was devoted to describing the floral decorations at the church and the house. The magazine justified the photo spread with this claim: "This wedding . . . sets the standard and the style for the weddings that are to follow this winter" ("Miss Julia Grant's Wedding": 853).

Veblen indicated compassion for the feelings of non-elites in relation to their dress, writing that when one falls "short of the standard set by social usage in the matter of dress," "the sense of shabbiness" is keen (Veblen 1899: 168). Veblen understood that dress communicated social status and the ability to follow fashion. He also made clear that one's fashion might purposefully communicate the privilege to consume in abundance.

Key in fashion theory development is the analysis of change processes and the direction of change through a society. Georg Simmel had echoed Spencer's early statement on fashion and change, imitation, and pursuit of novelty. Simmel lived in Berlin, where he studied urban settings, and the theory he presented would have been easily observable. He articulated in his 1904 essay a theory of fashion, abstracted in this chapter's opening quotation, which held that fashion occurs in stratified societies where social mobility exists and that the lower status group emulates the fashion of the higher status adjacent group. As this process takes place, the higher status group moves to new fashions, or innovations, in order to differentiate from those who have imitated their fashions. The impetus of conforming to, or imitating, the looks of the higher status group is the basis of the trickle-down theory of fashion change. In this model of the direction of change within society, innovations disseminate from the elites downward through the status hierarchy. Simmel concluded that the dual process of imitation and differentiation present in a society of hierarchical classes compels fashion change ([1904] 1957). Since these two socially formed drives—imitation and differentiation—are widely acknowledged as prime motivations for adoption of new looks or styles, Simmel is often credited with identifying the "engine of fashion change" (Kaiser 2012: 22).

Multiple theories and models

In the search for how and why fashion occurs and changes, several models and explanations found voice in the following years of the twentieth century. In 1930, J. C. Flügel produced a discourse titled *The Psychology of Clothes* from the perspective of psychology. In the chapter on the motives to wear clothes, he discussed bodily protection and modesty as basic needs. He determined that both are affected by cultural context. The drive to decorate the self, however, he determined to be primal, noting that even in cultures with no clothing, the people are decorated with marks or supplements to the body. He called on past anthropological research by Schurtz in 1891 to declare that decoration was the "motive that led, in the first place, to the adoption of clothing" (Flügel 1930: 17). Indeed, shell beads dated to 110,000 years ago, found in 2009 in the Grotte des Pigeons at Taforalt, Morocco, are the oldest extant evidence of this urge (Barton et al. 2009). While a few beads may not be fashion, the find is telling about the human urge to embellish the body, and decorating the naked body with clothing, makeup, and other forms of alteration is an obvious element of fashion. This basic human urge equates to Craik's fashion impulse, which we introduced in Chapter 1.

When he passed away in 1934, German essayist Walter Benjamin was preparing notes on fashion. Historicism and its role in fashion change was one of the topics that was posthumously published in an edited work titled *The Dialectics of Seeing: Walter Benjamin and the Arcades Project* (Buck-Morss 1991). Historicism is a term used to describe the recycling of ideas from past fashions, or fashion history, within new fashions. Benjamin's term was *tigersprung,* or tiger's leap in English. His *tigersprung* metaphor, studied in depth by Ulrich Lehmann (2000), aptly caught the notions of energy and capriciousness of fashion change. An example of tigersprung can be found in the Dolce & Gabbana Fall/Winter 2013 collections that included tunic-shaped dresses and gowns embellished with encrusted embroideries that clearly drew upon jewelry and mosaics of the Byzantine era.

Benjamin's work on fashion has influenced many fashion theoreticians, among them Caroline Evans (2003) and Elizabeth Wilson (1985). Benjamin examined an array of fashion's aspects: the influence of the group in fashion selection, imitation, and differentiation, and the sense of contingency and possibilities in modernity that contributes to feelings of ambivalence. Benjamin also discussed shopping, using the nineteenth century as the lens. Metropolitan shopping had been transformed in the nineteenth century with the appearance of department stores and their large pane glass windows. In this discussion, Benjamin analyzed Constantin Guys's illustrations of Parisians and Charles Pierre Baudelaire's ([1863] 1964) essay "The Painter of Modern Life," which commented on Guys's works as "the painter," as well as on shopping. Benjamin was intrigued by Baudelaire's commentary on commodity culture that resonated in the 1930s and which continues today (Evans 2013). Baudelaire connected the experience of modernity to fashion. Fashion, for Baudelaire and Benjamin alike, expressed the ever-fleeting present, bringing into focus the current moment. Benjamin also played with Baudelaire's fashionable strolling couple, the *flâneur* and *flâneuse* who were envisioned in Guys's ink sketches. They walked the boulevards of Paris, enjoying the social process of seeing and being seen in their fashionable attire.

Another characterization of fashion change observed that people prefer incremental change in their fashions rather than sudden change (Brenninkmeyer 1973). Termed "historical continuity," this explanation of fashion adoption proposed that consumers experience greater comfort in choosing fashions that are similar to what they already own rather than adopting a completely new style. Consumers need time to adjust to change that is in process.

James Laver, a British writer and keeper at the Victoria and Albert Museum, expanded the theory of Western fashion's "shifting erogenous zones" first advanced by Flügel ([1937] 1945; 1969a). His inspired analysis of Western fashion over time revealed that fashion change includes a shift in emphasis from one bodily feature or zone to another and that it relates to the current ideal of sexual attractiveness. This concept is most easily observed in female fashions, but it is present in men's fashions also. For example, Alexander McQueen's "bumster" pants of the late 1990s evolved into a widely popular "low rise" jeans style for young women with the waistband resting low on the hips. When combined with tops that ended above the waist, the look revealed the belly button and bare midriff. It became the erogenous zone of the early 2000s. Belly button jewelry gained popularity and drew focus to the midriff. Young women wore this fashion whenever the weather and social context allowed. In 2008, a shift toward leggings made of stretch knit fabrics instead of denim occurred among young women. Tops became loose and tunic-like, covering the body to the hip joint. In Laver's analysis, the erogenous zone of female fashion had moved from the waist, belly button, and hips to the legs, as their shape was now nearly fully visible. The shifting erogenous zone explanation of fashion change reinforces the notion that fashion expresses the human desire for novelty that was previously acknowledged by Spencer, Simmel, and Sapir. The public had become tired of the exposed midriff and was newly pleased to focus on legs. Notably, even men's casual pants and shirts as well as suits became much more closely fitted by 2012, increasing the visibility of leg and torso contours through the clothing.

In contrast to the directional flow of fashion change described as trickle-down and posited by Simmel in 1904, fifty-nine years later C. W. King (1963) published the trickle-across theory of fashion change. The theory described a horizontal flow or simultaneous adoption of new fashions across the various class strata, or commercial price points, of fashion products. Whereas the trickle-down theory of fashion change relies upon elites, who in the original conception of the theory were the well-to-do upper class, by the 1960s the category of elites had evolved to include celebrities from entertainment and popular culture that were seen by the public in mass media. Beyond the change in the concept of elites, the new infrastructures for rapid and widely disseminated visual communication and those that further enabled mass manufacture and delivery processes provided the means for simultaneous adoption of new styles. With these elements in place, fashionable apparel and accessories could be delivered at all price points to a wide geographical spread nearly simultaneously. Furthermore, fashion influentials at each stratum could affect fashion consumption and change processes.

The next important directional flow theory of fashion change came in 1970 when George A. Field proposed the status float phenomenon as an aide to fashion marketers. He recounted observations of style adoption moving from youth cultures and "Negro subculture" into the dominant white culture (Field 1970: 46). In proposing this theory as a counter to the trickle-down theory, Field was a forerunner in understanding changes in style leadership. Also called the trickle-up theory, this direction of fashion change may be found much earlier than the 1970s, for example, in the movement of styles and behaviors in New Orleans's Storyville prostitutes that made their way into local fashion. Field mentioned cigarette smoking and using deeply colored rouge and lipstick by prostitutes as examples.

Later, in 1994, anthropologist Ted Polhemus reframed the status float concept as the bubble-up theory in *Street Style: From Sidewalk to Catwalk*. Living in London, he had witnessed the eruption of youth subcultures there that deployed fashion as a vehicle to show authenticity. In youth subculture, identity expression and thus the symbolic meaning of a look and its parts hold primacy as the members strive to style their unique visible markers of social difference. While differentiating from the dominant culture, subculture members are understood as conforming to their subculture's styles or standards. Subcultural styles also serve as inspiration to fashion designers, hence the name "bubble up," crafted by Polhemus.

Evelyn Brannon summarized Polhemus's tracing of the "path of the black leather jacket" (Brannon 2005: 100). As an academic fashion forecaster, she seeks to comprehend the fashion change process. Brannon noted that today seldom is one theory of directional flow able to explain the entire process of fashion change. She pointed out that in the case of the black leather jacket, each of the directional theories played a role. The black motorcycle jacket moved from subcultures (motorcycle gangs), where it had a functional role as protective gear, to mass fashion as a rebel look. From these groups, meanings had been attached to the style such as rebellion. Next, the style moved to other outsider groups. When Marlon Brando wore one in *The Wild One* (1953), the rebellion link was made stronger, but the jacket also became identified with a movie idol. By the 1970s and 1980s, black leather jackets were widely adopted. Numerous visible celebrities wearing the style boosted its adoption by the wider public across the decades. Some examples are The Ramones and Bruce Springsteen. Fashion designers Katharine Hamnett and Jean Paul Gaultier, who are inspired by street styles, first showed the style on fashion runways, and many designers have followed suit. The path of the black leather jacket to reach the mass market where it was enthusiastically adopted took decades. It continues to be reinterpreted by high-end fashion designers as well as at lower price points. The black leather motorcycle jacket example shows that fashion change processes in Western contexts can be slow and that they may be characterized by upward, downward, and crosswise movement in the social system.

As shown by the several sociologists mentioned above who contributed to fashion theory development, sociology played a critical role. An additional important contributor to fashion theory from the field of sociology was Herbert Blumer, a key figure in the subfield of symbolic interactionism, who is known for his preference for qualitative and interpretive methodologies, and especially for his work in collective behavior. In that vein, Blumer proposed a theory of collective selection to explain how social groups come to prefer the same idea, item, or style. According to Blumer, fashion serves by "enabling and aiding collective adjustment to and in a moving world of divergent possibilities" (1969a: 282). Collective selection functions to orient individuals toward the future and the contemporary social order (289–90). Blumer's conceptualization of fashion, in its consideration of it as a participatory process that assists the individual and the social group in adjusting to the contemporary moment, is similar to Walter Benjamin's understanding of fashion.

Fred Davis, an American sociologist, observed and wrote about fashion, notably in *Fashion, Culture, and Identity* (1992). Like Baudelaire and Benjamin, Davis associated fashion with modernity. Davis proposed that fashion is a universal social process and like Spencer, Simmel, and Sapir, he recognized that the search for novelty played a role in it.

Toward cultural meaning

Researchers working in the approach called structuralism systematically analyze relationships, and in this process, they discover and interpret meanings of cultural acts and products. Grant McCracken and Roland Barthes employed structuralism. Barthes was a French intellectual, and he decoded fashion magazine images and texts using semiotics in *The Fashion System* ([1967] 1983). Semiotics, the study of *signs* and what is *signified* (their meaning), is used to decode the underlying meaning of cultural products. Signs may be linguistic or another mode of communication, including dress (Bogatyrev 1976; Morgado 1993a,b). Barthes dissects the inter-action of clothing (the technological object) and representations of clothing (both iconic and verbal). Among Barthes's contributions to fashion theory are emphasis on the process of meaning making and recognition that a variety of meanings occur. For Barthes, fashion is not a language, such as has been suggested by Alison Lurie in *The Language of Clothes* (1981). Lurie and Barthes would agree that there is a system of communication at play within fashion.

McCracken, an anthropologist and marketing consultant with an interest in contemporary consumer culture, has also analyzed meaning in fashion items. In "Culture and Consumption" (1986), he examined the role of meaning in products as created by marketing and the consumer. In a comparative discussion, he emphasized that the instability of the meanings of the West's cultural products is due to the West's social imperative for change and its tolerance of revisions and disruptions to norms. McCracken further suggested that although clothing communicates, the process of assigning, changing, and understanding meanings of language and dress is not the same entity.

The development of fashion theory into the 1990s is diverse and complex. Many theorists looked to understand the directions of a change, but found no simple model. They looked to find the original impulse for fashion and many understood a human need for novelty, or similarly, for decoration. Others examined both the individual psychology of fashion and its role in social groups, both in the mass market and in subcultures. Some sought to understand the meaning and communication that occurs in and through fashion items. Theorists also developed concepts concerning the role of fashion in identity and in relation to social change.

Theorists, in using their own culture as their subject, misapplied the theory of speciation of organisms to human societies. In that error, ethnocentrism took hold of fashion theory. Until female anthropologists analyzed the development of anthropology and ethnography as scholarly fields, ethnocentrism was given little recognition (Baizerman, Eicher, and Cerny 1993; Eicher, Evenson, and Lutz 2008: 102–04). Until the history of fashion theory became an active topic in discourse, the mistakes of the nineteenth century continued to shape fashion theory. Fashion was understood to occur in capitalistic, socially mobile societies. An implied control of where fashion occurred dominated considerations of the definition of fashion.

4
HOW WE GOT HERE

It is very entertaining to consider the strange styles of the ancient Romans, and there is no doubt that their clothing gives us more pleasure, because of its distance in time, than does that of modern people, which we have continuously before our eyes.

CESARE VECELLIO

Cesare Vecellio wrote these words about the dress of ancient Rome in 1590 (Rosenthal and Jones 2008: 67). His book, entitled *Habiti Antichi et Moderni* (*Clothing Ancient and Modern*), was the first to present a comprehensive dress history. This chapter reviews literature from the earliest sixteenth-century costume books to the proliferation of fashion history titles today. It explains the development of Eurocentrism in the study of dress history and its recognition by dress scholars in the 1980s, reflecting the premise of Eric Wolf's *Europe and the People Without History* ([1982] 1997). The rise of cultural and critical studies and the resultant acceptance of fashion as a legitimate subject by multiple disciplines are discussed. An account of the current state of the intellectual field includes the description of a paradigm shift that has taken place since 2010. The chapter closes with a call for attention to a global fashion history.

Early writings to 1900

Historians in ancient civilizations occasionally noted the dress of other cultures, especially when it differed from their own. For example, in 98 CE the Roman historian Tacitus described the dress of the inhabitants of Central Europe ("Germania") as "the skins of wild beasts" (Owen-Crocker 2004: 18). To Tacitus, acculturated to the draped woven clothing of Roman civilization, the skins and furs of animals signified Germania's "barbarianism." But such accounts were rare prior to the invention of the printing press in Europe in 1439. All books before that time were single-issue "manuscripts," handwritten and sometimes decorated with illustrations. Termed "illuminated manuscripts" in Europe, comparable documents existed in Mesoamerica, South Asia, Far East Asia, and Islamic cultures. Illustrations from such manuscripts are used to exemplify themes in this book. These manuscripts, some of which were religious in nature, serve as a visual record of contemporary dress, but their creators offered little in the way of commentary.

Sixteenth-century costume books

Cesare Vecellio's *Habiti Antichi et Moderni* was the first *history* of dress. It came out toward the end of a long run of costume books. Approximately twelve books were published between 1562 and 1601 in multiple editions and translations (Olian 1977). The successful genre began with *Recueil de la diversité des habits* published in Paris in 1562. *Recueil* illustrated the contemporary dress of urban Italy and France as well as Turkey, Egypt, India, Persia, Africa, and Greece (Olian 1977: 22).

The costume book genre grew out of travelogues, etiquette books, and costume engravings. In 1528, Baldesar Castiglione recorded the customs and manners of Venetian court life in *The Book of the Courtier*, which was translated and reprinted for distribution to other European courts. Of the travelogues, Nicolas de Nicolay's *Navigations* was among the best. Nicolay journeyed to Turkey, Greece, the Mediterranean Islands, and North Africa as France's royal geographer, observing customs and costumes along the way. First published in Lyon in 1527, *Navigations* appeared in Latin, German, and Italian editions (Olian 1977: 25). Its sixty costume plates offered a valuable resource for other authors, who did not visit Turkey. The Ottoman Empire, which stretched from the Middle East to North Africa and Hungary during the reign of Suleiman the Magnificent (1494–1566), inspired great curiosity among Europeans. In Figure 4.1, we see Nicolay's illustration of a Turkish gentlewoman; she is in her house overlooking the seraglio. The fashionably dressed woman wears a patterned robe, striped sash, headdress, necklace, and chopines (elevated footwear). The chopines show the influence of Venetian styles on Turkish fashion. Both Venice and Istanbul were among the world's top luxury markets in the sixteenth century; fashion news must have traveled easily between these two cities.

Up until Vecellio's publication in 1590, none of the costume books investigated the dress of past civilizations. Cesare Vecellio was a Venetian, a cousin to the great Renaissance artist Titian. He made his living as an artist, printmaker, and engraver (Sherrill 2009). The first edition of *Habiti Antichi et Moderni* included 420 wood block prints of costumes from Europe, Asia, and Africa. The second edition, published in 1598, added the New World, which altered the title to read "the clothing, ancient and modern, of the whole world" and increased the

Figure 4.1 "Noble Woman of Turkey." Nicolas de Nicolay, 1580. Courtesy of *Travelogues*, Aikaterini Laskaridis Foundation, Athens, Greece. Available online: http://www.eng.travelogues.gr/item.php?view=40363. This Turkish woman is fashionably dressed in a patterned robe, striped sash, headdress, necklace, and chopines.

number of plates to over 500 (Rosenthal and Jones 2008). For the illustrations of older forms of Italian dress, Vecellio used surviving artwork as sources; for contemporary dress, he recorded what he saw in this travels. He did not venture outside Italy except for a trip to Augsburg, Germany; for the Turkish and North African plates, he copied from published sources without attribution. For example, Nicolay's "Turkish Gentlewoman" in Figure 4.1 reappears in reverse as Vecellio's "Turkish Woman" (Paulicelli 2014: 115). For the New World prints, he used sources such as John White's watercolors of North Carolina's Indians reprinted by De Bry.

Vecellio wrote the text including introductory information on fibers, fabrics, and other materials. Originally published only in Italian, the second edition (1598) added Latin so that educated people outside of Italy could read it. It was reissued in 1664. A French edition with redrawn plates appeared in 1859/60, affirming its importance as a source of information.

Vecellio happened to be in the right place at the right time with the right product. Europe's exploration beyond its borders and the widening trade with Asia and North Africa created curiosity about the world's peoples and places. Vecellio's book appeared just as Venice and the Ottoman Empire had begun to decline in power. He affirmed Italy's importance in world history by illustrating its dress, both historic and contemporary.

This detailed description of Vecellio's work is relevant for the current discussion on two accounts. First, his perspective incorporates the notion of fashion, and second, he did not restrict himself to Europe in illustrating fashionable dress. Thus, his work included fashion systems beyond Europe.

Although he used the word *habiti*, which is translated as "clothing," he commented repeatedly about the changing nature of dress, that is to say fashionable behavior, in all cultures. He cited the multiplicity of dress styles in ancient Rome and contemporary Venice. For instance, in describing the dress of ancient times, he said, "Rome was subject to changing princes and leaders, so it is no wonder that both men and women kept transforming their clothing and adopting new styles of dress" (Rosenthal and Jones 2008: 60). About Venetian women of former times, he explained: "Wearing of the style illustrated here did not last long among women, though to begin with they had liked it because they thought it was new" (Rosenthal and Jones 2008: 148).

Regarding the "habits" worn by non-Europeans, Vecellio did not distinguish them as "traditional" or "slow changing." Although both the images and the text came from other sources, his phrasing connotes the same appreciation for non-European dress as for the accoutrements of Venetians. About the American Indians, he wrote that their "extremely beautiful" feather garments were "skillfully and artfully made, in such a variety of well-matched color that for this reason and for their rarity, they can be considered the most delicate and sumptuous clothing to be found anywhere" (Rosenthal and Jones 2008: 57).

Vecellio included numerous images of the famous courtesans of Venice and Rome. Surely their stylish appearance piqued the curiosity of his readership. About the courtesan illustrated in Figure 4.2, he said, "Modern Roman courtesans dress in such fine style that few people can tell them apart from the noblewomen of that city." He described their gowns as satin and velvet trimmed with gold buttons, with "low necklines that expose their entire breast and neck, adorned with beautiful pearls, necklaces and ruffles of brilliant white" (Rosenthal and Jones 2008: 88). He also commented on their bleached blonde hair. These women had a recognizable style that situated them in time and space on the same level as the nobility despite their lower social status. With these comments, Vecellio recognized that fashion is "a market driven cycle of consumer desire and demand" (Paulicelli 2014: 96).

By the early seventeenth century, costume books had faded in popularity. European powers were establishing colonies around the world, and sailors from

Figure 4.2 "Cortigiane Moderne." Woodcut by Cristoforo Guerra, tedesco, da Norimberga. From Cesare Vecellio, *Habiti antichi, et moderni di tutto il mondo.* Venice: Presso Damian Zenaro, 1590. Beinecke Rare Book and Manuscript Library, Yale University. In the best known of the sixteenth-century costume books, Vecellio noted that Roman courtesans dressed in the latest fashions, making it difficult to distinguish them from noblewomen.

faraway places appeared in the ports of Venice, London, and Antwerp in their native garb (Olian 1977: 37). Books about foreign dress were no longer novel or interesting to readers.

Costume history books from 1600 to 1900

After the popularity of costume books waned, no significant developments in publishing dress history occurred until the eighteenth century. Engravers produced illustrations of French court fashions and masquerade costumes, but like most of the earlier publications, the emphasis was on images rather than words.

Joseph Strutt, an engraver and antiquarian, wrote the first English-language costume history book. Titled *Dress and Habits of the English People*, it was published in two volumes over the years 1796–99. Strutt drew and engraved all the images himself from manuscripts in the British Museum and the Bodleian Library, or from other original sources. Previously, he had published works on English manners, customs, and armor from which he derived some of the images for *Dress and Habits of the English People*.

Strutt's *Dress and Habits of the English People* is considered his most important work. Billed as covering dress history from the Saxons to the close of the seventeenth century, nothing preceded it. He was starting from scratch. Strutt strove for accuracy by using historical sources. He read ancient historians; he quoted from the likes of Herodotus. He did not identify the "birth of fashion." However, he established a pattern of coverage for the ancient world that would persist for centuries: he started with ancient Egypt, then moved to Assyria, Persia, Greece, and Rome before settling in on the Anglo-Saxons. A new edition was issued in 1842 demonstrating its long-lasting contribution to fashion history. It is worth noting that *Dress and Habits of the English People* has religious overtones. Strutt referenced Adam and Eve and their lack of clothing in the introduction and commented that after God clothed "our primeval parents," a "vast variety of dresses" arose (Strutt 1842: i). Christianity is another underlying factor that restricted fashion history to the West, where Christianity is the dominant religion. Thus, non-Christians were excluded from dress histories of the eighteenth and nineteenth centuries.

The nineteenth century saw increased interest in histories of costume. In 1823, James Robinson Planché, an English dramatist and antiquarian, criticized the lack of accuracy in the costuming of Shakespeare's plays on the London stage. As a result, producers hired him to research and create historically accurate costumes. In 1834, he published a history of British dress from the earliest period to the close of the eighteenth century. He wrote on other decorative arts topics, finally producing his most ambitious historical work, *A Cyclopedia of Costume, or Dictionary of Dress*, in 1879 (Figure 4.3). This two-volume work included a dictionary of costume terms starting with "abacot" (a hat) and ending with "zibelline" (sable fur). Volume 2 was a chronological history, beginning with Rome. Like Strutt, Planché consciously focused on the dress of Christian nations, subtitling his work as a "general chronological history of the costumes of the principal countries of Europe, from the commencement of the Christian era to the accession of George III."

The historicism of the Victorian era rekindled an interest in past fashion, especially that of the Gothic era. Planché's work found a ready audience with theatrical costumers, who followed his lead in designing more accurate costumes for the stage. Simultaneously, Queen Victoria and her consort, Prince Albert, began staging fancy dress balls for which the wearing of costumes representing historic English monarchs and nobles strengthened links to Britain's past. Artists who created history paintings consulted Planché. Like Strutt before him, Planché

The Dream of Life.
(Italian Costume of the 14ᵗʰ Century)
From a fresco painting by Orcagna in the Cloisters of the Campo Santo of Pisa

Figure 4.3 "The Dream of Life. Italian Costume of the 14th Century." James Robinson Planché. *A Cyclopedia of Costume, or Dictionary of Dress*. Vol. 2. London: Chatto and Windus, 1879. Planché acknowledged the source from which he took this image: "From a fresco painting by Orcagna in the Cloisters of the Campo Santo of Pisa."

sourced his illustrations from period artworks. The scene in Figure 4.3, for example, is from a fresco by Orcagna in the Cloisters of the Campo Santo of Pisa.

The English were not the only ones publishing dress histories in the nineteenth century. In France, Camille Bonnard published *Costumes des XIIIe, XIVe et XVe Siècles* (*Costumes of the 13th, 14th and 15th Centuries*) in 1829–30 in two volumes with 148 color plates by Paul Mercuri (Bonnard 2008). The painters of the Pre-Raphaelite Brotherhood are reputed to have sourced Bonnard for images of medieval and Renaissance dress. In Germany, Hermann Weiss authored *Kostümekunde* (1864) in two volumes following the usual chronology of ancient, Byzantine, and medieval dress to the Renaissance and beyond.

Why do the dress history surveys often include the ancient cultures of Mesopotamia, Egypt, Greece, and Rome to the exclusion of other great cultures farther away and others that had existed in Europe? Certainly, knowledge of the past was more limited than today due to the development of archaeology as a field in the eighteenth century and its constantly improving investigative technologies. In addition, geographical location affected the scope of coverage. Mesopotamia, bordering on the eastern coast of the Mediterranean, represented the birth of civilization itself. The Egyptian past was long lasting, well preserved, and intersected with Christianity, the predominant European faith. Imperial Rome resonated with the Age of Enlightenment and witnessed the origins of Christianity. Greek culture was considered, and still is by many, as the crucible of philosophy, geometry, and democracy, which grew in importance after 1776.

The publication of dress histories picked up toward the close of the century. In 1882, M. Augustin Challamel's *The History of Fashion in France* was translated from French into English. This book concentrated on women's attire, perhaps foretelling the twentieth century's penchant for equating fashion with female dress. Interestingly, the book deliberately used the word "fashion" in the title rather than the more usual "costume." Even the subtitle—"The Dress of Women from the Gallo-Roman Period to the Present Time"—avoids the word "costume." In defining fashion, the author described it is a "thermometer of the various infinite tastes of the day" (1882: 2). Justifying the focus on France, Challamel claimed that "at present the type of feminine dress always originates in France, into the most distant regions of Europe, and even into Asia and America" (5). Colored plates each consisting of four females dressed in fashions of the period illustrate the volume. In Figure 4.4, the women wear the styles of the early 1600s.

Auguste Racinet's *Le Costume Historique* is notable for its inclusive coverage of dress beyond the West. Its contents included sections on nineteenth-century civilizations outside of Europe as well as traditional costume of the 1880s. Originally published in France in periodical form, it was consolidated into a

Figure 4.4 *The History of Fashion in France, or The Dress of Women from the Gallo-Roman Period to the Present Time.* Augustin Challamel. New York: Scribner and Welford, 1882. Plate facing p. 113. The two figures on the left illustrate women's fashions in 1590 during the reign of Henry IV; the figures on the right display the fashions in 1614 during Louis XIII's reign.

six-volume work in 1888. It was the most wide-ranging and ambitious coverage of dress history since Vecellio, with all illustrations in color. In 2003, the art publisher Taschen reissued it in three languages—English, French, and German—a testament to its relevance in the current era of globalization.

After Racinet, the global encyclopedic approach fell out of favor. Costume histories focused on European culture and civilization after initial chapters on the ancient world.

Publications of national costume had begun prior to 1900 as a vehicle for romantic nationalism. This movement was particularly strong in Europe, where researchers traveled to villages to gather folktales and songs, study local customs surrounding births and weddings, and collect local "peasant" or "folk" dress for newly founded ethnographic museums. Presses eagerly published folk costume and regional dress titles, especially when such publications suited nationalism. An unintended result was that dress publications further split into "traditional dress" (unchanging) and "historic costume" (fashion). Even in Great Britain, the Scottish tartan was treated as traditional dress, despite the fact that it was an invented tradition (Hobsbawm and Ranger 1983).

With the emergence of anthropology as a discipline in the late nineteenth century, a new approach to dress history began. Anthropological publications contribute "scholarship that relates to understanding the place of dress in culture" (Eicher 2000: 59). Historically, the discipline explored non-Western societies. The relationship between colonialism as a program of occupation and dominance by Western nations and the nascent anthropology field, which has been discussed in Chapter 3, at first allowed a divide based on an assumed cultural hierarchy. The geographical divide between European-based cultures and indigenous cultures perpetuated the distinction between Western and non-Western dress.

This pattern of Eurocentrism, the practice of viewing the world from a European perspective with the implication of the superiority of its own culture, was well established by the eighteenth century. The above discussion shows how entrenched Eurocentrism became embedded in the costume history field. The emphasis was soundly on civilized Europe and its real or perceived heritage in ancient Mediterranean and near eastern cultures. Further, the dress of rural peoples in Europe was treated as a separate branch of inquiry, and in this way, fashion was separated from nonurban dress practices.

Twentieth and twenty-first centuries

Books from 1900 to 1960s

By the twentieth century, the perspectives of the various disciplines with an interest in dress influenced histories of dress. Theatrical costumers needed references to design period costumes for the stage and the emerging cinema. Museum professionals in departments of costume and textiles, or those working with ethnographic collections, needed detailed works to help them identify objects. Educators, particularly in the United States in what became known as the home economics field, needed accurate references and textbooks for teaching design.

Max Tilke, a German artist and ethnographer, was among the first to focus on dress as an object. Acknowledging expanding interest from artists and fashion firms, he realized that something was missing from previous publications: the dress itself, meaning the cut, construction, and embellishment. To remedy the problem, he gathered patterns on garments he encountered on his journeys through North Africa, Spain, the Balkans, and the Caucasus. He also visited museum collections. The result was *Orientalische Kostüme in Schnitt und Farbe* (*Oriental Costumes in Cut and Color* (1923)). His publication coincided with the height of international interest in the "Orient," a vague designation that covered North Africa and most of Asia.

Tilke made careful renderings of garments from the places he visited, plus China and Japan. The garment in Figure 4.5, drawn from the original in the Museum für Volkerkunde (Ethnological Museum) in Berlin, is a *tobe* from a colonial region called at that time "French Soudan." It features narrow cotton fabrics woven on strip looms sewn together and embroidered in silk. His illustrations of flattened garments off the body, showing seams and ornamentation placement, were a novel approach. Tilke's book met with great approval, and he went on to publish multiple costume titles in several languages.

Figure 4.5 A *tobe* from colonial French Soudan. Plate 13, Max Tilke. *Orientalische Kostüme in Schnitt und Farbe*. Berlin: Verlag Ernst Wesmuth A-G, 1923. Special Collections, University of Rhode Island Library. Tilke's illustrations showed garments off the body, flattened to show seams and decoration. He emphasized garments from non-Western cultures like this *tobe* from the colonial region called French Soudan.

Although many nineteenth-century dress history books were bound with chromolithographs, the advent of photography in 1839 made media other than "faithful drawings" possible. However, fashion publications did not use photography to display fashion until the 1910s. Even then, fashion photography vied with fashion illustration for decades at fashion magazines and in fashion history books. Thus, it is not surprising that it took until the twentieth century for photography to be fully exploited in fashion history publications, especially color photography.

The English and French have been leaders in chronicling the history of Western fashion, joined by Germans and Americans. Notable authors include the prolific Cecil Willet Cunnington and Phillis Cunnington, who wrote many books based on their personal collection of English women's fashion now housed in Manchester, England, at the Gallery of Costume, Platt Hall. Together and individually, they wrote over two dozen books about fashion history, most of which were originally published in the 1950s and 1960s. The Cunningtons focused on everyday dress and undergarments. They illustrated their books with drawings and occasional photographs. James Laver, former keeper of prints, drawings, and paintings at the Victoria and Albert Museum in London, also penned many books including a general survey entitled *The Concise History of Costume and Fashion* (1969b). As discussed in Chapter 3, he promoted the "shifting erogenous zones" theory of fashion change (Laver 1969a).

In Germany, Emma von Sichart edited Karl Köhler's 1871 German costume book, scrapping his historical introductions and modifying the illustrations and patterns. She added photographs of people modeling original garments as well as reproductions and theatrical costumes. It was published in English in 1928 as *A History of Costume.* Dover released an unabridged edition in 1963 (Köhler 1963). The value in Köhler's work was that he looked at garments, or their reproductions in art, and drafted patterns, although Sichart modified them. It was a popular textbook for historic costume classes, especially in theater.

In the United States, theatrical costume designer Millia Davenport collected thousands of photographic images for her 1948 *The Book of Costume*. The book covered Western fashion from ancient Egypt until 1860. She prefaced her work with the comments that books illustrated by the author are "terrible" and that the best books are the ones "with the most pictures" (Davenport 1948: ix). Thus, her work includes a whopping 2,778 black-and-white photographs with extensive captions. It was reprinted in 1964. This book remains a valuable reference.

In France, François Boucher's *20,000 Years of Fashion* appeared in 1965 and was reprinted in 1987. It had 1,188 illustrations, many in color, with no redrawings. Boucher's book was outstanding in this regard; it is still used as a college textbook. The author used the terms "costume" and "fashion" interchangeably starting with fourteenth-century dress, despite the promising title.

Fashion history publications from 1900 through the 1960s had several elements in common. First, their coverage was decidedly Western. Many books followed the pattern established in previous centuries by examining the ancient world to the modern in Europe and its diaspora, reflecting the model in art history scholarship. Second, they were primarily descriptive. Interpretive examinations would come later. Third, many of them were based on sound academic research, which explains the many reprints of these classic texts.

Most of the titles use the word "costume" rather than "fashion." Costume was seen as the all-embracing term that included ancient and medieval dress as well as fashion. Costume did not have the dress-up connotation that it has today. Yet, although the word "costume" was broad enough to cover the ancient and medieval eras, the dress of non-Western cultures was largely ignored as it was outside the parameters of interest. Only Tilke and Planché looked beyond the usual geographical boundaries.

Costume history textbooks

Costume history has been taught in American colleges and universities since the early twentieth century. The courses were part of the home economics curriculum, which had begun a half-century earlier when social reformers applied scientific principles to homemaking. The movement received a boost in 1862 when the US Congress passed the Morrill Act, which established land-grant universities in every state. Home economics was considered a field appropriate for women.

At the 1910 American Home Economics Association meeting, Jane Fales advocated for a course in historic costume so that students (mostly female) would understand artistic design and develop originality (Fales 1911). Such a course was meant to serve as an inspiration for designers and dressmakers. As it was, dressmaking ranked third in employment for women in the United States in 1916 (Allinson 1916). Thus, a costume history course was justified. The proposed syllabus surveyed the dress of ancient Egypt, Greece, Rome, ancient Gaul, the Franks, and modern France from the Merovingians to the French Republic. Interestingly, America was not included; Fales stated, "In America, we have no past" (Fales 1911: 244). Home economics units evolved, and separated into textiles and clothing departments, which were renamed to include design and fashion merchandising; through all these organizational changes, costume history courses remained part of the core curriculum. Although some professors in American universities called for a less Eurocentric viewpoint in costume history classes, little has changed (Jasper and Roach-Higgins 1987).

In the beginning, there was no textbook. Faculty members assigned background reading from general histories and collected fashion plates for illustrative purposes. Eventually the previously discussed books by Köhler, Davenport, Boucher, and Laver served as textbooks.

Blanche Payne, a professor at the University of Washington, wrote one of the first comprehensive histories of Western dress intended as a textbook. Published in 1965, it treated men's and women's dress equally, stopping at 1900. Payne traveled to museums in the United States and Europe, where she made pattern drafts from extant garments and sourced original artwork to accompany her text. She also researched folk dress in the former Yugoslavia in the 1930s; she produced a manuscript on Yugoslavian dress, but did not secure a publisher. Payne's *History of Costume* was the most widely used textbook for decades. Twenty years after her death it was revised and updated (Payne, Winakor, and Farrell-Beck 1992). A challenger with a similar temporal and geographical scope appeared in 1989 in Phyllis Tortora and Keith Eubank's *Survey of Historic Costume*. It became the dominant textbook. It is now in its sixth edition with a new author, Sara Marcketti, replacing Eubank (2015).

Theater costume classes for many years used Lucy Barton's *Historic Costume for the Stage*, published in 1935. Focusing on styles frequently used in theatrical productions, it was accompanied by pattern drafts for specific garments. Douglas Russell's *Stage Costume Design: Theory, Technique, and Style* replaced it upon its publication in 1973.

All of the textbooks trace the history of dress as it reflects Western civilizations, with varied attention to ancient cultures of the Near East and Mediterranean. Tortora and Marcketti (2015) have responded to the need for a global perspective by including boxed features called "global connections." Cross-cultural influences on Western dress are incorporated into coursework. Although some universities offer courses in ethnic dress, global fashion history courses are rare.

Daniel Hill took on the monumental task of writing about the history of world dress (2011). He attempted to be comprehensive, and he avoided privileging the West. At about the same time, Oxford University Press and Berg Publishers released the ten-volume *Encyclopedia of World Dress and Fashion* (2010). These are important resources. Yet, there is no uniform agreement on how to build a global framework into existing courses. What remains to be written is a world fashion history textbook appropriate for undergraduate courses.

In Europe, by the 1960s, the history of dress was a subject taught in theater design and in art and design schools offering fashion diplomas. Not until the latter twentieth century and the acceptance of cultural history as a scholarly endeavor did fashion history courses and degree programs appear at European universities.

Journals/periodicals

The formation of societies devoted to the study of historic dress resulted in meetings and symposia for the purpose of presenting research. The Costume Society of Great Britain was formed in 1964 and published their first journal *Costume* in 1967. *Costume* publishes articles from a broad chronological period and with a worldwide remit, emphasizing the social significance of dress.

The Costume Society of America formed in 1973 and began publishing its journal *Dress* in 1975. It publishes peer-reviewed scholarship on dress in art, social history, anthropology, and material culture. It also invites work on fundamental concerns such as theory and research methods

The journal titled *Fashion Theory* appeared in 1997 aimed at a more critical analysis than what typically appeared in either *Costume* or *Dress*. As stated inside the cover, *Fashion Theory* "takes as its starting point a definition of 'fashion' as the cultural construction of the embodied identity." It publishes works on both historic and contemporary dress.

More recently, Intellect Publishers has entered the arena with a host of titles focusing on fashion. These include *Fashion, Style & Popular Culture*, which is dedicated to fashion scholarship and its interfacings with popular culture. *Critical Studies in Men's Fashion* focuses on the many dimensions of men's appearance. *Clothing Cultures* takes a semiotic approach to dress studies, making a distinction between "clothing" and "fashion." While clothing covers the body, "fashion alludes to the glamorous, the ephemeral and the *avante garde*." The *International Journal of Fashion Studies* aims to bring the fashion scholarship of non-English-speaking authors to English-speaking audiences by providing translation services after peer review. While all of Intellect's journals emphasize current fashion discourse, historic topics are included.

A variety of other journals ranging from *Winterthur Portfolio* to *Textile: Cloth and Culture* publish research on the history of dress. As will be discussed later in this chapter, interest in fashion history has expanded into many disciplines, enriching the many perspectives to be considered. Journals from the disciplines of history, anthropology, geography, and more have published peer-reviewed scholarship on dress history topics.

Museum exhibitions/catalogs

Curators in museums work with objects to illustrate themes about art, culture, and history. Museums mounted increasing numbers of costume exhibitions starting in the 1970s, when the history discipline embraced its social and cultural dimensions. Art and design museums soon followed. More recently, museum curators in non-fashion departments have been including dress and textiles in thematic exhibitions.

Many museums in North America have departments of costume/fashion. In New York, the Metropolitan Museum of Art's Costume Institute began mounting annual exhibitions in 1972. These exhibitions, always accompanied by a catalog, have grown into major fundraisers for the museum. The openings (e.g., the Met Ball) have become fashion spectacles of their own, with much-photographed celebrities in designer fashions. The exhibitions have raised the profile of fashion history immeasurably. The Museum at the Fashion Institute of Technology, in

New York's garment district, regularly features exhibitions and catalogs. The Rhode Island School of Design Museum of Art, the Los Angeles County Museum of Art, the Museum of Fine Arts in Boston, the Cincinnati Museum of Art, the Canadian Museum of Civilization, and the McCord Museum in Montreal have all contributed to fashion history scholarship in North America.

In London, it is the Victoria and Albert Museum that regularly mounts fashion exhibitions. In Paris, it is the Musée de la Mode. In Japan, it is the Kyoto Costume Institute. This list could go on, but suffice it to say that many historical museums and art museums across the world have produced exhibitions and catalogs with long-lasting relevance.

The early focus of costume exhibitions was on stylistic analysis of elite fashions. Simple chronologies are no longer enough. Instead, curators employ postmodern frameworks to explore themes across time and space (Crawley and Barbieri 2013).

Encyclopedias and other reference works

The new millennium saw an uptick in the publishing of encyclopedias for reference works in many fields. Fashion did not escape this development. One of the first was Valerie Steele's three-volume *Encyclopedia of Clothing and Fashion* (2005), which has 640 essays focusing on the emerging field of fashion studies. It was advertised as featuring "multidisciplinary critical insights into history and contemporary experience of clothing and fashion." A plethora of encyclopedias on dress and fashion have appeared since 2005 (Condra 2013, Snodgrass 2014, Lynch and Strauss 2015).

Most ambitious was the ten-volume *Encyclopedia of World Dress and Fashion*, edited by Joanne Eicher. It is especially important for a history of world fashion because the coverage is comprehensive. There is more depth in the topics from 1700 forward. Arranged geographically, it does not favor the West. It is billed as the first single reference work to explore all aspects of dress and fashion globally, from prehistory to the present day.

The future of printed encyclopedias is in question as the knowledge base moves to digital platforms. Leaders in the field of reference works, like the *Oxford English Dictionary* and the *Encyclopedia Britannica*, no longer publish printed editions. The *Encyclopedia of World Dress and Fashion* is available online as part of the Berg Fashion Library, which also includes over seventy electronic books and exclusive online articles (Eicher 2010).

The digital age has created a new window of opportunity for fashion research. Nearly all academic journals are available digitally; some do not have print versions anymore. Academic services like Digital Commons make self-published scholarship accessible to anyone with internet access the world over.

Another valuable digital resource is the information on museum websites. Museums and universities with fashion departments are posting images and catalog information online. Students and scholars can do object research without leaving home. Some sites have essays accompanying selected objects. The Metropolitan Museum of Art's Heilbrunn Timeline of Art History includes essays on specific objects. The Victoria and Albert Museum's website features detailed descriptions for specific fashion objects.

The new fashion history

In the 1980s, the "new" fashion history emerged. Valerie Steele was among the first to use this term in the preface to the *Encyclopedia of Clothing and Fashion* (2004). The new fashion history embraced the developments taking place in related disciplines; hence, the phrases *interdisciplinary* and *multidisciplinary* took on new relevance. While appreciating the groundwork laid by object-based fashion historians, the new fashion history strove for interpretation and cultural context. Significantly, the new fashion history embraced those who had been left out of the old costume history.

At this point, we have discussed the early writings on fashion as a system (e.g., "Key Fashion Theories" in Chapter 3) and the development of fashion history literature (prior sections of the current chapter). As we have seen, much of the early writing in fashion history has concentrated on elites in the West. Now we will briefly describe theoretical developments in related fields that have intersected with the work of scholars interested in textiles and dress, giving rise to fashion studies.

Rise of cultural and critical studies

The emergence of the new fashion history hinged on changes in the objectives and analytic approaches in the social sciences and humanities, and especially as occurred in sectors of the related fields of sociology, cultural anthropology, archaeology, history, literary studies, and linguistics. The shift toward interpreting culture included turning away from structuralism. Post-structuralist and post-positivist critiques blossomed in mid-century, and the emerging fields of cultural studies and social critical theory grew in influence. They turned attention to power relationships and cultural identity, and thus questioned metanarratives of privilege such as Eurocentrism.

The shift toward interpretive non-positivistic methods had already begun in German sociology in the 1930s; Georg Simmel was among those who rejected positivism in the study of societies (Levine 1971). Critical social theory had already been formed in Germany's Frankfurt School in the 1930s with a foundation in Marxist theory. Among that group, Walter Benjamin (see Chapter 3) contributed to fashion theory through his conception of modernity, understood in part to mean experiencing and adjusting to the "now" through fashion participation.

Post-structuralist scholarship in history, cultural anthropology, and sociology provides focus upon the meanings of cultural forms, whether social or material, and upon how those meanings are created, transmitted, and interpreted in everyday life. The *cultural turn,* as this shift in analytic methods and objectives is often called, created new or alternative points of departure for scholarship (Jameson 1998). Understanding previously marginalized groups and issues surrounding marginalization gained a central role in intellectual discourse. Studies related to identity—race and ethnicity, gender and sexuality, social status, and place— increased. The effects of economic power and of the processes of production and consumption that intertwine with identity also received increased scholarly attention. Interdisciplinary or multidisciplinary scholarship grew in importance as multiple perspectives or cross-disciplinary research skills were needed in order to address topics of concern.

Literary theory was crucial in the development of the cultural turn and new scholarship. French literary critic and philosopher Roland Barthes was also a semiotician and he used that technique in *The Fashion System* ([1967] 1983). Similarly, critical literary theory, often based in the hermeneutical method, was developing detailed and nuanced understandings of a text. This methodology, which first developed for written texts, can be applied to any "text" or cultural form, such as the corset. The corset has been variously interpreted as deforming women's bodies, disciplining women's bodies, impeding conception, and stimulating eroticism (Davies 1982; Steele 2001).

The field of cultural studies engages social and political consciousness to examine power relations inherent in cultural systems; it aims to produce change. Following its inception at the Birmingham School of Cultural Studies in the 1950s, the influence of cultural studies spread in the second half of the twentieth century. Led by Stuart Hall, the early work examined white working-class youth subcultures. The ethnographic work of Dick Hebdige (1979) provided insights into British youth subculture and inspired fashion scholars to further consider the dress of non-elites as important sites of inquiry. The rise of cultural studies as a disciplinary field stimulated scholars to bring forward the voices and stories of the marginalized.

Important thinkers that contributed to the cultural turn include Clifford Geertz and Pierre Bourdieu. Geertz was an American anthropologist whose development of the ethnographic analytic technique called *thick description* influenced many dress scholars (Geertz 1973). For example, Gwen O'Neal used Geertz's methodology to support the argument that an African-American aesthetic of dress has its roots in West African culture (O'Neal 1998).

Pierre Bourdieu's contributions include the concept of *habitus*. Habitus is an individual construction encompassing both the formation of and the reaction to social constructs such as race and gender. It extends to how one chooses to dress oneself. Habitus reflects location within a society, including one's taste and preferences (Bourdieu 1977, 1990). Maurice Merleau-Ponty, a French philosopher, identified the body and the way it experiences the world as the primary force in one's perception of the world (1976). This theory, known as *corporal schema,* countered the prevailing philosophy that perception develops in the mind.

Bourdieu, it should be noted, also employed structuralist techniques and relied on statistical data analysis for his important work *Distinction: A Social Critique of the Judgment of Taste* (1984). The project outlined how those with cultural and social capital, for example, a university degree, set taste standards, and that in this way the production of taste exemplifies the reproduction and sustainment of cultural dominance. In order to find acceptance, people in lower class groups must sublimate their own preferences and conform to the tastes of the dominant classes in possession of cultural capital.

Judith Butler, an American feminist philosopher, theorized gender, identity, and performativity (1988, 1990). Her theory of *gender performativity* proposes that categories of gender, such as the normative concept of masculinity in a male, are socially constructed. In the case of normative masculinity, an array of bodily movements and behaviors that are constructed and perceived as masculine constitute the masculine gender identity, but the particular bodily movements and behaviors are not in themselves a specific gender. Butler understands such socially constructed gender norms as a means of control. Butler's work has influenced gender and identity studies, and has proven applicable to fashion studies, as dress is often a primary component of gender presentation.

We cannot leave the discussion of cultural studies without mentioning the philosophical concepts of *deconstruction* and *postmodernity*. Deconstruction is a philosophic critique proposed by Jacques Derrida during a period of social upheaval in the West (1967 [1978]). It questioned the power structures and hierarchies of existing cultural institutions in order to include the marginalized and forgotten peoples within history. Postmodernity was characterized by French philosopher Jean-François Lyotard in *The Postmodern Condition* (1979) as the period after modernity, that is, after the devastation of the Second World War, in which attainment of a single truth and of progress ended. He described postmodernity as a rupture between modernity and the next historical era. Multiple truths and the end of beliefs in metanarratives mark postmodernity. The postmodern condition, that is, the experience of postmodernity, includes feelings of ambivalence in the experience of postindustrial society infused with technologies and in the face of the end of progression toward truth. In postmodernity, the barriers or boundaries of society exhibit permeability or even breakdown. The philosophies of deconstruction and postmodernity share the position that a single historical narrative no longer holds and that, instead, multiple and diverse human experiences are present. Fashion as it has been occurring since the late 1960s is recognized as an expression of postmodernity.

Marshall McLuhan observed the multiplication of imagery in his famous book *The Medium is the Massage* (1967), which became a catch phrase of the 1970s. He prophetically identified the circulation and recirculation of imagery as a critical component of the culture of that time and increasingly in the future. He made these observations decades before the arrival of the internet, the personal computer, the tablet, and the smartphone. The contemporary proliferation of images intersects with the notion of *simulacrum*. *Simulacrum* is Latin for "likeness," but in recent philosophical discourse its meaning has expanded. Jean Baudrillard expounded on the complexity of imagery, and of images made from or of other images, and complications related to the real or original and the simulacra or copy ([1981] 1994). He argued that in postmodernity, symbols of real things such as events, places, and objects, rather than the things themselves, shape reality. Consider an animal-printed fashion piece such as a scarf; it represents the animal, yet was drawn from an image of an animal or a print of an artwork of an animal, and was then created as a printed textile in an industrial setting. An actual animal has little or no relationship to the scarf. Baudrillard's analysis provides fashion scholars a rich theoretical basis to examine fashion practice in relation to image proliferation and simulacrum; he drew attention to the postmodern breakdown of borders and boundaries between cultural forms, between the actual and its image. Simulacrum is also involved in contemporary reflexivity, flush with selfies and online posts, and in historicism in fashion wherein the historical is reimagined, styled, photographed, and broadcast repeatedly.

Taken in sum, the perspectives discussed in this section may be assessed as foreshadowing the need for a global and inclusive view of fashion history. They provide openings for inquiry into the dimensions and occurrences of fashion among non-elites, non-Western cultures, and in varied power or economic structures. They also suggest to the fashion discipline that critical questions and analyses are needed in order to amplify the understanding of power relations related to fashion and the production, consumption, and practice of fashion. This book, *Fashion History: A Global View*, is a product of these perspectives. Through examination of the symbolic concept "fashion," it critically analyzes the historical formation of the meaning of fashion as a term and as an expression of privilege; that is, this book investigates the problematic heritage of Eurocentrism including Imperialism and Social Darwinism, in the conceptualization of fashion.

Rise of fashion studies

Developments in related fields affected by the rise of cultural and critical studies, especially linguistics, anthropology, sociology, feminist studies, geography, art history, history, languages, and comparative literature, aroused interest in the history of dress. Beginning in the 1960s, fashion gradually emerged from the shadows to become an accepted topic of academic study in the new millennium.

Linguistic interpretations were among the first to theorize fashion. French cultural critic and linguist Roland Barthes published *The Fashion System* in 1967 in which he deciphered words and images in French fashion magazines. He focused on the silent communication of the printed fashion magazine page to readers. He did not study actual garments or accessories; rather, he studied words and images. *The Fashion System* raised awareness of alternatives to object analysis and study of art representations. Semiotics, the methodology he used, is a structuralist method of analysis, but Barthes transitioned to a post-structuralist position as his work continued. He found that there might be multiple interpretations of a written text. It cannot be overemphasized how much his work affected dress studies in that it opened up a new interpretation of dress as a form of silent communication. The concept has been applied to ethnographic costume and textiles from Central and South America in *Costume as Communication* (Schevill 1986), as well as to American fashionable dress in *What Clothes Reveal: The Language of Clothing in Colonial and Federal America* (Baumgarten and Watson 2002).

In the field of anthropology, the emphasis was on theorizing material culture. Two major works appeared: *The Fabrics of Culture: The Anthropology of Clothing and Adornment* (Cordwell and Schwarz 1979) and *Cloth and Human Experience* (Weiner and Schneider 1989). These works looked at dress and textiles as a system, whereas anthropologists had mostly ignored dress before these publications. Later research focused on identity formation. Anthropological studies were among the first to succeed at merging materiality with theory.

Sociologists extended identity formation to its social expression through fashion. Fred Davis, who was influenced by Herbert Blumer and symbolic interaction theory, published *Fashion, Culture and Identity* in 1992. He argued that clothing is encoded with meanings in cultural context. Joanne Entwistle, drawing on the concept of habitus, coined the term *embodied practice* in her landmark book, *The Fashioned Body* (2000). She proposed that the dressed body and the experience of dressing mediate the individual to the social world.

Among feminist authors, Rozsika Parker's *The Subversive Stitch* (1984), Elizabeth Wilson's *Adorned in Dreams* (1985), Angela McRobbie's *Feminism and Youth Culture* (1991), and Caroline Evans's *Fashion at the Edge* (2003) are notable for advancing the discourse as it relates to feminism. Parker argued that women's embroidery was relegated to craft status rather than art status.

Elizabeth Barber expanded on the relationship of women to textile work in the widely read *Women's Work: The First 20,000 Years* (1994). Wilson's work drew attention to fashion as an expression of modernity; she observed that scholars of fashion repeatedly had to justify their choice of topic. Apologies were no longer needed by the time Evans published her postmodern analysis of fashion in the new millennium.

Geographers, embracing the cultural turn, developed a branch of the field termed "cultural geography" that included exploration of fashion as it relates to space and place. This strand of scholarship produced works that explored fashion and the city such as *Fashion's World Cities* (2006) by cultural historian Christopher Breward and cultural geographer David Gilbert.

Fashion historians have had a long relationship with art history. In fact, the field of dress history paralleled that of art history with its prior emphasis on chronological development of high art in the West. Art historians did not pay much attention to dress, however, until Anne Hollander published *Seeing Through Clothes* (1978). She demonstrated to art historians and fashion historians the ways in which clothes represented in art idealized the human body. In England, the postgraduate studies program at the Courtauld Institute of Art brought art historians to the table by training students to analyze dress in painting and prints. The program was started in 1965 under the direction of Stella Mary Newton, who wrote numerous well-regarded books on dress history such as *Health, Art and Reason* (1974), *Renaissance Theatre Costume* (1975), *Fashion in the Age of the Black Prince* (1980), and *The Dress of the Venetians, 1495–1525* (1988). Aileen Ribeiro assumed leadership of the program from 1975 to 2009. Ribeiro has authored many books and articles on the history of dress in art, such as *The Art of Dress* (1995) and *Ingres in Fashion* (1999).

In the history discipline, the arrival of the "new history" in the 1970s turned scholarly attention toward cultural history and social history. Dress and fashion became an acceptable subject of inquiry, especially after French historian Daniel Roche published *The Culture of Clothing: Dress and Fashion in the Ancien Régime* (1994). Roche examined inventories of different social classes in seventeenth- and eighteenth-century France, concluding that a clothing revolution occurred by the end of that time. He thought that clothing, more than any other commodity, reflected social values. Roche called for a more holistic study of fashion systems, encouraging others to explore the production and consumption of clothing. Some historians have followed his lead, for example, Beverly Lemire in *Fashion's Favorite: The Cotton Industry and the Consumer in Britain, 1660–1800* (1992), Giorgio Riello in *A Foot in the Past* (2006), and John Styles in *The Dress of the People* (2007).

Scholars in languages and comparative literature have embraced the study of fashion, some with a global scope, others with a regional focus. Eugenia Paulicelli, a professor of Italian, along with dress scholar Hazel Clark, edited *The*

Fabric of Cultures: Fashion, Identity and Globalization (2009), which explored fashion as it shapes the identity of cities and nations within a global framework. Contributors to that volume focused on recent examples. Meanwhile, Regina Root, a professor of languages and Hispanic studies, has taken a historical approach to her research. Addressing her own Latin American sub-area, she declared that "scholars will need to assess carefully and push forward definitive Latin American fashion histories in the future . . . . The stories remain, for the most part untold" (2013: 403).

All this newfound attention to fashion resulted in an explosion of research. Dress historian Lou Taylor stated that since the late 1990s, "our field has broken its banks and flooded into a fertile plain of new approaches and methodologies" (Taylor 2013: 23). Taylor captured the state of the field well in her books *The Study of Dress History* (2002) and *Establishing Dress History* (2004), in which she outlined the development of various methodological approaches to dress history as well as the history of the field itself. Taylor coined the phrase the "Great Divide" in reference to a chasm between the two sides whose main area of research interest was fashion in the early twenty-first century. One side included traditional fashion historians interested in the object/artifact (e.g., material culture), whereas on the other side historians embraced interdisciplinary scholars who employed theory (e.g., cultural studies). An example of an object-based historian is Janet Arnold, who contributed greatly to the field with her pattern books, which are enormously useful to museum curators and costumers (Arnold 1964, 1966, 1985). An example of cultural studies scholarship is found in the work of Christopher Breward, who wrote one of the first general histories focusing on the cultural meanings of fashion: *The Culture of Fashion: A New History of Fashionable Dress* (1995). The Great Divide was apparent at a 1997 conference in Manchester, England, entitled *Dress in History: Studies and Approaches*, selected papers of which were published in *Fashion Theory* (1998). According to Lou Taylor, in recent years the old divides have collapsed as museum curators and theorists work together to investigate problems in fashion history (2013: 28).

This interdisciplinarity is evident in a number of collaborative works. The previously mentioned encyclopedias are one example. Others include the numerous fashion readers and handbooks that have appeared in recent years: *The Fashion Reader* (Welters and Lillethun 2007, 2011), *The Men's Fashion Reader* (Reilly and Cosbey 2008), *The Men's Fashion History Reader* (McNeil and Karaminas 2009), *The Fashion History Reader* (Riello and McNeil 2010), and *The Handbook of Fashion Studies* (Black et al. 2013). Also influential has been the Dress, Body, Culture Series edited by Joanne Eicher. The inaugural title was *"New Raiments of Self": African American Clothing in the Antebellum South* (Foster 1997), a postmodern history of dress of a marginalized people. In addition to the readers and handbooks focused on fashion history, volumes primarily focused on fashion theory have appeared. Among them are *Fashion Foundations* (Johnson, Torntore, and Eicher 2003), *Fashion Classics* (Carter 2003), *The Rise of Fashion: A Reader* (Purdy 2004), *Fashion Theory: A Reader* (Barnard 2007), and *Dress History: New Directions in Theory and Practice* (Nicklas and Pollen 2015).

For this present work, it is crucially important to distinguish between fashion in cultural studies and fashion in history. While the field of cultural studies appreciates history, it has not drawn attention to the need for a global approach to fashion history. Cultural studies scholars who research contemporary fashion are already global in their perspective. For example, Jennifer Craik in *The Face of Fashion* (1994) rejected the viewpoint that fashion is unique to capitalistic culture. She argued that fashion systems operate globally and that non-Western dress has been shortchanged by labeling it "traditional" (Craik 1994: 4). She later elaborated on this viewpoint: "Fashion is not a phenomenon that has existed since the fourteenth century. Nor has it been confined to Europe" (Craik 2009: 21). Recall from Chapter 1 that Sandra Niessen had appropriated Wolf's phrasing to point out that scholars have been thinking of fashion history as "Europe and the People Without Fashion" (2003). Some researchers absorbed this commentary; Susan Kaiser, for example, lists as one of her key assumptions that fashion is now transnational, not just Western or Euro-modern, in *Fashion and Cultural Studies* (2012). She wrote that at the end of the twentieth century, the accepted narrative of fashion beginning in the West in the fourteenth century did not ring true anymore as cities around the world were vying for attention on the global fashion stage.

We interpret the developments described above to suggest that those in the field seek to better understand its intellectual history, which this book aids in addressing. We also acknowledge that some scholars have already questioned the long-standing theoretical frameworks of the field that have defined fashion as a product of Western capitalism.

A paradigm shift

Given the new intellectual developments from several fronts concerning locating fashion in human experience, we observe a paradigm shift under way. The term *paradigm shift*, initially conceived by T. S. Kuhn (1962) in regard to scientific inquiry, has many definitions. For our purposes, a paradigm shift is a change in the theory or practice of a particular science or discipline. A change such as the fashion discipline is undergoing, in the altering of its foundational concepts and in research methods, reshapes understanding and knowledge. Fashion scholarship is continuing to expand beyond image descriptions, object analysis, texts from historical records, experiments, and quantitative data to contextualization and multidimensional approaches.

The paradigm shift in fashion history, which has yet to fully occur, places the need for a global fashion history in the foreground. In 2012, we articulated the need for a radical change in how fashion history is conceived. We noted the movement to an inclusive framing of fashion that acknowledges fashion as "global and diverse in its development, occurrences, and dimensions" (Lillethun, Welters, and Eicher 2012: 77–78). This constitutes a change in ontology, in the underlying assumptions about knowledge within the discipline. The paradigm shift in fashion history is reshaping what is known about past fashion systems and processes; previously unexamined questions and groups now receive attention, and prior conclusions and interpretations are reexamined.

We are not alone in our appeal for a global history of fashion. Among the earliest to recognize problems with the former rigid definition of historical fashion have been anthropologists. Jane Schneider observed that the history of dress in courtly societies of non-Western cultures demonstrated the same fundamental elements of a fashion system—changing styles and stylistic influence of elites—as did the court fashions of Europe, although they "stopped short of the perpetual mutation" that took hold in the courts of Italy's mercantile cities during the Renaissance (Schneider 2006a: 208). Joanne Eicher has been an important proponent of our position. Recognized for her scholarship in dress and fashion, she trained as an anthropologist and conducted fieldwork in Africa. In the introduction to National Geographic's *The Fashion of Dress*, she explained that "change happens in every culture because human beings are creative and flexible" and that humans "enjoy change" (Eicher 2001: 17, 19).

In the new millennium, a few established scholars in traditional disciplines have attempted broad histories of dress. Robert Ross, a historian, wrote *Clothing: A Global History* on sartorial globalization of dress from the sixteenth to the twenty-first century. He reviewed an admirable range of literature, but ultimately stuck with existing definitions of dress, clothing, costume, and fashion; he associated fashion with the upper circles of society who used it to exclude those below on the social scale who could not follow sartorial changes fast enough (2008: 6). Robert DuPlessis, also a historian, focused his work on the clothing trade in the Atlantic during the period of colonization. His understanding of fashion incorporated change and novelty, but did not go so far as to limit it to the upper echelons of cultures (DuPlessis 2016: 18, 28). His view that clothing is never static reflects our thinking. The field needs more comprehensive studies like these.

A handful of scholars have gone deep in a single country, observing fashion in what had formerly been considered "traditional" dress systems. Antonia Finnane, in *Changing Clothes in China*, claims that "the fact remains that little is known in the English-speaking world about changes in material culture in non-Western societies" (Finnane 2008: 8). Toby Slade, writing about Japan, hoped to "demonstrate that there are other modernities, and different fashion histories beyond the canon of European and American dress narratives, which dominate nearly all interpretations of the practices, styles, institutions and hermeneutic structures of clothing in the modern age" (Slade 2009: 1). Penelope Francks noted that fashion operated in elite circles in China, India, and Japan from at least as far back as the eighteenth century. She further argued that fashion cycles occurred not in the cut of Japanese clothing, but in the fabrics (e.g., background colors, type of pattern, and overall design), an observation that we explore further in chapters 6 and 7 (Francks 2015).

These are examples of studies that will move the global history of fashion forward. We have noted that senior scholars who possess broad and deep knowledge have accomplished some of the best studies in the new fashion history. Achieving a global history of fashion will encounter challenges: language barriers restrict access to research studies, reports, and books for many researchers, thus affecting cross-cultural exchange; lack of evidence limits the understanding of the dress of past cultures; the scholarly talents needed are diverse; the idea faces resistance in the teaching profession due to embedded beliefs and classroom time restraints for topics. However, a global fashion history movement will provide richer knowledge of humanity with understandings not yet known. By displacing fashion history of privilege as the dominant format with a multivalent fashion history, the global fashion history will provide for more truthful and integrative teaching and learning about human history. This objective is transformative.

PART TWO

OUTSIDE THE CANON: ALTERNATIVE FASHION HISTORIES

5

FASHION SYSTEMS IN PREHISTORY AND THE AMERICAS

Fashion, in some sense, has characterized human culture since the first adornments of the Upper Paleolithic. Although the processes of fashion comparison, emulation and differentiation are more noticeably apparent in the rapid changes that characterize systems of industrial production, the same processes are observable or at least inferable in most cultures.

AUBREY CANNON

With these words, Canadian anthropologist Aubrey Cannon introduced the notion that fashion exists in all cultures across time and space (1998: 23). He argued that the universality of fashion is evident in its definition as style change. Cannon understood fashion as a process driven by the human need for self-identity and social comparison, and by the desire to set oneself apart visually. Narrowing the definition of fashion to a continuous process such as that found in Western industrial societies, he claimed, excludes the systematic style changes that occur in all cultures, including indigenous ones. Cannon explained that anthropologists and ethno-historians typically attribute short-term and long-term changes in small-scale nonindustrial societies to external forces rather than internal processes. He pointed out that small-scale societies might have systematic style changes only sporadically in response to a specific set of circumstances; nevertheless, they constitute the same process as fashion in Western cultures.

Cannon noted that style change is rarely documented in indigenous societies, but that accounts of the North American fur trade are an exception to the lack of documentation. Fur traders recorded in detail the changing demand for cloth and items of adornment, especially beads. They regularly updated the types of beads and colored cloth in current demand by Native Americans. Beads became less valuable when markets were saturated. In some instances, tastes changed in as little as a year or two. Cloth color also exhibited style change. Native Americans could even be said to have their own style leaders whom they emulated. For Cannon, the frequent changes in native tastes as well as the existence of style leaders exhibited the criteria for fashion.

Jennifer Craik supports Cannon's stance, claiming that "fashion is *not* exclusively the domain of modern culture and its pre-occupations with individualism, class, civilization, and consumerism" (Craik 2009: 19). As explained in Chapter 1, Craik used the phrase "the fashion impulse" to express the universality of the human desire for novelty and change. In this chapter, we take Cannon's position in arguing that change in dress and appearance is a universal human behavior that is evident in the fashion impulse among prehistoric peoples and indigenous societies in the Western Hemisphere. We begin with the fashion impulse as found in the archaeological record.

Archaeology as a source of evidence

Sources of information on the dress of indigenous cultures in the past are extremely limited until contact with Europeans. This section discusses what can be deciphered through archaeology, the study of human culture through evidence discovered by excavation. Archaeological evidence is partial evidence. Much dress evidence is lost due to decay of the materials used, and what is recovered is usually fragmentary and degraded. The two elements of survival and discovery, each often of tenuous circumstances, must converge for the possibility to document, recover, and study evidence of the past.

Archaeological evidence of dress that can be dated with a degree of confidence captures a moment in time, allowing us to interpret through inference and deduction what was worn, or part of what was worn, at a specific time and place. Synchronic evidence such as a single grave or deposit must be compared to other finds in order to assess change. However, grave goods buried with an individual can indicate status when compared to other individuals from the same stratum of a site.

Knowledge of climate and geographical context is critical in archaeological research since in preindustrial times weather patterns and natural resources determined the availability of materials for creating dress and accessories. Inherent cultural contact that results from trade or exchange patterns may be revealed by the presence of a resource not found locally.

While textiles are sometimes found in archaeological contexts, their prior presence can also be detected. These may occur as an impression in clay, mud, or plaster, and as a pseudomorph, which is "a physical trace remain of a former fiber, thread, or textile." In the strictest sense a pseudomorph contains only the "chemical breakdown products" of the textile. Variants are a "negative hollow of the fibers in casings of metal salts, much like a fossil cast," and a combination of the two prior types can also occur (Good 2001: 215). Examples of pseudomorphs that show evidence of textile knowledge have been found in North America as early as 8000 BCE. Cordage and fabric impressions on prehistoric ceramics from eastern North America reveal knowledge of how to spin and ply fiber into yarns and to construct twined fabrics; archaeologists use fiber type, cordage, and twining to infer changes in technology and arrival of new cultural groups in geographical areas (Petersen 1996). Through these types of artifacts, change can be documented, if only intermittently.

The types of sources used and the questions asked by archaeologists are similar to those used by researchers of more recent historical periods. When examining textile evidence, an archaeologist studying textiles and dress seeks answers to questions such as: What fibers were used? Were they locally available or traded? What spinning technology was used to make yarns? Did the culture make objects with netting, twining, matting, or basketry techniques? Did they make felted textiles? Did the culture weave and, if so, using what type of loom? Similar questions would be applied to non-textile materials used for dress and accessories. These include shells, pottery, stones, metals, and animal resources such as hides, sinew, bone, and teeth.

Grave finds in which the body, clothing, and accessories have survived the ravages of time are optimal discoveries, since the placement of the body supplements can be observed. The materials, garment shapes, and techniques may be analyzed. Sometimes dried or mummified skin will disclose body modification such as tattoos. However, usually only partial remains survive. The chemical context of a grave will affect what materials survive. Acidic conditions favor protein materials such as animal fibers and hides, while alkaline contexts favor the survival of cellulosic (plant) materials. Increasingly, the application of analytic technologies is providing new information for consideration of remains, even in reference to artifacts found centuries ago. One example is the extraction analysis of DNA from wool textiles found in Danish Bronze Age bog finds from the nineteenth century (Brandt 2014). A second example is the study of dyes and dyed fibers dating to the first and second millennia CE found in Chile's Atacama Desert that showed textile dyes were imported from neighboring areas, implying trade (Niemeyer and Agüero 2015).

Evidence applicable to decipherment of the dress of lost cultures extends well beyond garments and accessories found with human remains. Evidence of technologies and materials such as pottery, metals, and glass plays an important role. Representations in two-dimensional and three-dimensional forms offer much information. Cave and rock art depicting humans may suggest clothing forms, such as the indications of garment silhouettes on human figures in the Sahara at Tassili n'Ajjer (ca. 6,000 BCE). Sculptures of humans may reveal garments as well as technological information; the Stone Age Venus figurine (ca. 23,000 BCE) from the late-Gravettian culture found at Lespugue, France, depicts "the first clear evidence for fiber string" in the figure's string skirt, according to Elizabeth Barber (1994: 54).

Tools such as stone blades and loom weights and needles of various materials allow insight into crafting and making techniques. Evidence of human work patterns can inform knowledge about dress; for example, the identification of a location as a site where dyeing occurred may provide information about textile processing and the extent of labor devoted to textile coloration, as well as information about dyes used.

Written evidence discovered at an archaeological site, such as laws, taxation records, notations of tribute, and contemporary accounts, may include references to textiles or dress and thus provide valuable information. They may attest to value, preferences, exchange, and quantities related to materials used for dress. The glyph texts on the architectural monuments of the Mesoamerican Mayan culture are an example. Glyphs at multiple sites, exemplified by those at Bonampak (580–800 CE) in Chiapas, Mexico, describe tribute as "heaps of textiles or neat packages that contain green feathers" accompanied by chocolate beans and shells (Houston 2000: 173).

All of the types of evidence described above and more are important in the study of dress in archaeological contexts. When scant or no extant garments and accessories, or parts thereof, survive, every type of evidence that bears potential information is utilized. Surviving garments and accessories from as recently as the seventeenth century are rare. In cases of more recent finds, such as accidental discovery of nineteenth-century paupers' graves—where the cloth has disintegrated, but metal buttons with patent dates remain—written forms of evidence such as patent records may survive in libraries and other places of safekeeping, rather than in archaeological contexts.

Beads and tattoos

Some of the earliest surviving evidence related to dress and adornment is shell beads, that is, shells that humans turned into beads by piercing holes to enable wearing them on a strand or by attaching them to garments or hair. Figure 5.1 shows the skeletons of two females estimated to be between 25 and 35 years of age from the Téviec site in France. Restrung shell bead jewelry—necklaces and bracelets (which are out of the picture frame)—adorned the skeletons that now reside at the Museum of Toulouse. Téviec is a late Mesolithic Era site dating to between 5500 and 5110 BCE based on radiocarbon dating of content in the marine shell midden that also served as the inhabitants' cemetery. The site, which was first excavated in the late 1920s and 1930s, lies on an island in the Atlantic Ocean off the southwest coast of Brittany. Twenty-three skeletons were found in ten graves at Téviec and Hoëdic (Schulting 1996).

The husband and wife team Marthe Péquart and Saint-Just Péquart discovered Téviec and Hoëdic, a similar island site in the local region. The grave finds include shells, shell beads, and bone pins (Péquart et al. 1937; Péquart and Péquart 1954; Taborin 1974). The ubiquity of cowrie, periwinkle, and other shells in the grave goods at Téviec has been interpreted as symbols indicating prestige, especially since the shell species would have been of low importance in the inhabitants' diet; the midden and study of historical resources point to available red deer, wild boar, and a wide range of marine life for the resident hunter-gatherers to eat (Schulting 1996). Cowrie shells were located often in adult male graves and periwinkle shells in adult female graves. Distribution patterns of the pierced shells led to the inference of shell necklaces and wrist bracelets, such as with the women in Figure 5.1 and in other graves. Shell headwear was suggested by the patterns of shell beads in some graves at the site (341). While no significant difference in the "artefact richness" of adult male and female grave goods is present, male graves contained higher numbers of

Figure 5.1 Two women's skeletons, protected by antler. Tomb of Téviec. Recovery in 1938 restoration 2010. Didier Descouens, photographer. Museum of Toulouse. Licensed by Creative Commons. License available online: https://creativecommons.org/licenses/by/4.0/. The grave goods include funeral jewelry made of marine shells drilled and assembled into necklaces, bracelets, and anklets.

utilitarian items (342). With shells, the other most common grave goods were flint blades and bone pins (like a stick pin). Burials containing bone pins and abundant grave goods such as cowrie and periwinkle shells, shell beads and flints, and situated with antler structures as seen in Figure 5.1, belonged to high-status individuals.

Schulting explained that clothing is "one of the earliest-appearing and most effective means of communicating differences in status" (346). Clothing at Hoëdic and Téviec is inferred through the presence of single bone pins approximately five inches long "found placed on the chest in a manner suggesting garment fasteners" in burials with rich grave goods (346). No fibers or fragments of clothing survive; however, the long pins could have held a garment closed around the body. Dress also serves as a marker of group identity, a function facilitated by the distinction of the bone pins at each location; bone pins at Hoëdic were created from red deer antler and at Téviec they were crafted of wild boar bone (348). At Téviec, the abundance of shell beads attested to status distinctions among the twenty-three burials there, and also indicated distinction in the symbols associated with adult males and females.

While fashion demonstrated by change cannot be assigned to the late Mesolithic Era culture in Brittany with the limited evidence available, the fashion impulse may be assumed. In the pierced shells and their distribution patterns (by the skull, neck, and wrists) we recognize the urge to embellish the human body with shell bead jewelry. In the divergent materials used for the bone pins at Téviec and Hoëdic we recognize distinction of one group from another. The processes of comparison, emulation, and differentiation noted by Cannon to be present in most cultures were in place.

The earliest evidence of modern humans creating decorative elements to wear, of the urge to decorate the body, comes from Africa in the form of shell beads. As noted in Chapter 3, a cave find of Nassarius shells at the Grotte des Pigeons at Taforalt in Morocco pushed the date of human-pierced shell beads, and thus of human symbolic behavior in personal ornamentation, to approximately 110,000 years ago (Barton et al. 2009). The trove of pierced shells resembles at least four other similar but more recent finds in Morocco as well as a find with the same shell species in South Africa, indicating a wide dispersal of modern humans at this time (University of Oxford 2009).

The oldest beads in the Middle East, also pierced shells, were found at Ksar Akil in Lebanon, and date to 41,000–35,000 years ago. This date range matches the date of the arrival of modern humans in Europe and therefore holds importance in tracing human movement out of Africa (Douka et al. 2013). The find at Ksar Akil includes ten pierced snail shell beads and one larger clamshell-like Glycymeris shell that is pierced at the shell's hinge edge. Together the shells create a necklace with the Glycymeris shell as a pendant centered between the ten snail shells. The composition indicates a fashion impulse—a composition that moves beyond a series of the same shell as at Taforalt—that indicates change in style over time. The necklace, found near a young female skeleton, affirms the urge to decorate the body 30 millennia prior to the date of the Téviec shell jewelry.

In addition to their role in understanding human movement out of Africa, beads are significant as evidence in the development of techniques used to make things. Humans certainly had already made beads or jewelry from many other natural materials besides shell. Nuts, seeds, flowers, and fruits are good materials for jewelry, if temporary ones. Since these materials are highly perishable, little evidence survives of such ornaments. An exception is Egyptian floral collars (1320 BCE) that provide insight into the ways jewelry can be crafted from plant materials (Winlock and Arnold 2010: 58–63, 73–74). Even before these Bronze Age examples of plant-based jewelry, humans created beads from ostrich shells, stones, clay, glass, and eventually metals. Each subsequent material reflects advancement in technology, and the composite materials attest to increasing knowledge (Liu 2010). New bead materials that arrive to a locale by trade and exchange provide groups with novel colors and texture and in this way stimulate the desire for fashion change. For the archaeologist, beads that are not locally made serve in the tracing of cross-cultural contact.

An important find in bead history is the graves at Sungir, Russia, dated to 32,050–28,550 BCE (Trinkaus et al. 2014). Mastodon tusk beads laid with the skeletons of an adult male and two adolescents in three graves number over 13,000. The beads lay in patterns that implied garment shapes, for example, leggings or trousers and sleeves or arm covers. The clothing had been highly embellished with the handcrafted ivory beads. While this isolated find cannot attest to fashion change, the beads demonstrate a drive to decorate that resulted in time and material investment.

Marking the body with tattooing or scarification may be as old as shell beads jewelry, but the record does not provide reliable and direct evidence dated before approximately 3200 BCE. That is the date of Otzi the Iceman found in the Alps in 1991 in a thawing glacier. While his discovery captured the world's attention, tattoos on his mummified skin stimulated much discussion in popular imagination. Experts interpret his body markings—lines and dots on his back and knees—as therapy for strains and sprains. Prior to his discovery, the oldest known tattoos were those adorning female mummies in the tomb of priestess Amunet from the Egyptian Bronze Age (ca. 2000 BCE). Their tattoos, located on their thighs and abdomens, are associated with fertility and childbirth according to Joanne Fletcher (Lineberry 2007).

Many of the known prehistoric tattoos are interpreted similarly, that is, to serve an amuletic purpose such as protection or empowerment through the placement or pattern of the tattoo. Body marking including temporary designs made with media such as clay, pollen, and minerals probably preceded clothing. Some of the earliest indications of tattoo practices come from tools that survive, such as stone and bone reservoirs for marking media and associated sharp needles for penetrating the skin. Examples of these were found by the Péquarts in the Pyrenees at Grotte du Mas d'Azil dating to the Upper Paleolithic Era. The find included types of sharp bone needles, some with eyes for non-tattooing uses and others without eyes and with a longitudinal groove to hold the marking media; ochre, also found in the cache, could have been the media used with the grooved needles (Péquart and Péquart 1960). The impulse to decorate the body in prehistoric times extended globally: tattoos are attested across Asia, Europe, North and South America, and the Pacific (Gilbert 2000). Despite the lack of evidence, we assume that decorating the body with temporary and permanent markings was a universal human urge. Some textile specialists believe that tattoos moved off human skin and onto cloth by way of embroidered designs to protect certain parts of the body believed to stimulate fertility (Paine 1990: 7).

We are not alone in linking archaeological finds to the fashion process. Diana DiPaolo Loren studied archaeological material culture along with archival sources to determine how Americans framed their identities in colonial times. In her analysis of sartorial expression, she used the word "fashion" to explain the mixed dress styles evident in her sources. She argued that colonization of the Americas did not result in straightforward adoption of European fashion by indigenous groups, but rather in creation of mixed or hybrid dress styles (Loren 2012: 109). Individuals, she explained, created their own "colonial identities at the intersection of taste, fashion, and sumptuary laws" (Loren 2010: 32).

In the following sections, we offer examples of fashion systems among indigenous peoples in the Americas before and after European colonization. Examples include Native Americans of southern New England and the indigenous peoples of Meso- and South America. Loren's argument for interpreting post–Contact sartorial expression as hybridization rather than wholesale adoption of Western dress is germane to the discussion.

Fashion systems among southern New England's Native Americans

Tribes in northeastern North America existed apart from Europe's fashion system prior to the sixteenth century. The Contact Period for southern New England spans the years after Europeans made the first documented contact with New England's tribes until King Philip's War began in 1675. The Florentine explorer Giovanni da Verrazzano was the first to provide a written account of the customs and habits of the Native Americans he encountered along the Atlantic coastline from Maine to North Carolina in 1524 (Wroth 1970). It is probable that European fishermen had traded with New England tribes prior to that date, although no written documents exist (Brasser 1978).

This brings us to the issue of documentation. Historians rely on written documents for evidence. For sources about the Indians of New England, this includes explorers' accounts from the sixteenth century when European monarchs sponsored expeditions to the New World; merchants' records such as those of William Pynchon, who operated a trading post in present-day Springfield, Massachusetts; and early English colonists' ethno-historical writings whose detailed descriptions were meant to interest others in emigrating to New England. Natives, on the other hand, depended on oral histories that are not written down; they are transmitted from generation to generation by tribal elders. This is problematic for historians, who favor the written word over legend. Another problem is that organic materials from which apparel is constructed do not survive in archaeological contexts, that is, unless they are in a microenvironment that allows preservation (e.g., near metal). New England's extreme temperature and moisture changes from the cold winters to wet summers are inhospitable to textiles.

Few images of northeastern North America's indigenous peoples from the early Contact Period exist. The most reliable are John White's watercolors of the Algonquian-speaking tribes of North Carolina. Painted in 1585, they are invaluable records of the appearance of Native Americans in the early Contact Period. Theodore de Bry as well as Cesare Vecellio later copied these images.

Some burials accidentally discovered in New England have been excavated, which provides evidence beyond the written descriptions of the aforementioned European explorers and early colonists. One of the authors of this book, Linda Welters, has been involved in analyzing textiles from two Contact Period Native American burial grounds and a third post–Contact Period site (Welters et al. 1996; Welters and Ordoñez 2004).

The first site is known as RI-1000, a Narragansett burial ground located in North Kingstown, Rhode Island. The excavation of the remains and associated grave goods of fifty-six individuals took place in 1982 after accidental disturbance by a bulldozer prior to retail development. Based on the analysis of the grave goods, the site was dated 1650–70, decades after trading posts had been established in the area, but prior to the Great Swamp fight in 1675, which decimated the Narragansetts' numbers.

The second site, another burial ground, is called Long Pond. It is located on the Mashantucket Pequot reservation, which was established in 1666. The site, consisting of twenty-one individuals, was accidentally discovered in 1990 while digging a house foundation near Ledyard, Connecticut. The date range assigned to the site is 1670–720. After analysis, all remains and grave goods were reburied.

The third site is in Mashpee on Cape Cod in Massachusetts, home to Wampanoag Indians. The undated remains of two individuals were discovered in fill dirt from house construction in 1990. Welters and her colleague Margaret Ordoñez were contracted to analyze the many textile fragments associated with the burials and to suggest a possible date.

It is challenging to decipher fashion systems among the indigenous groups in New England because the chronology is not continuous, just as Cannon and Craik observed. Gaps in knowledge exist, resulting in dependence on accounts by early explorers and colonists, who viewed Indians as uncivilized. Some of these writers spent much time with Native Americans, so their accounts are considered reliable despite their prejudices.

Here is what we do know. When Europeans arrived, the tribes of southern New England wore "skins of beasts as deer, moose, beaver, otters, rackoons, foxes, and other wild creatures" (Gookin [1792] 1970: 17). They processed skins by scraping the flesh and softening them with oils. The hair was sometimes left on, particularly when the skins were intended for use during the winter. Natives were very particular about the deer tails being left on, as they considered "defaced" any skin with a missing tail (Morton [1637] 1969: 30). The skins and pelts were not cut or tailored to the body as were the fashions of the Europeans; this inspired comment and comparison to the "wild Irish" and other people considered "primitive" and "uncivilized" because they did not tailor (e.g., cut and sew) their apparel. Native Americans also revealed parts of the body that Europeans covered up. This prompted use of descriptors such as "naked" and "nude," or as William Wood put it, they dressed "only in Adam's livery" ([1635], 1977: 82).

Europeans loved furs, and made good money trading beads and cloth for furs. However, the furs and skins worn by Europeans were always tailored or manipulated in some way so that the end product did not resemble the source. Beaver pelts were processed by shaving the fur and mixing it with wool for the fashionable beaver hats worn by kings as well as commoners. Constance Snow's beaver hat, dated 1615–40, is material evidence of the popularity of these hats among the Pilgrims; it is housed in the Pilgrim Hall Museum in Plymouth, Massachusetts. Furs were used to line coats and trim garments in Europe, which contrasted with the untailored furs worn by New England's indigenous peoples. Samuel de Champlain commented that "you can see the flesh under the arm-pits, because they have not the ingenuity to fit them better" ([1604–18] 1907: 55). The Indian footwear known as moccasins did involve sewing. Some styles were ankle height while others were knee high, similar to leggings, which provided protection while walking through underbrush. Sometimes they were decorated. Europeans admired Indian footwear because it was comfortable, noiseless, and could be wrung out and "hang'd up in their chimney" to dry (Williams [1643]

1936: 120). In contrast, European cobbled shoes squeaked and creaked in the forest, and did not lend themselves well to hours of walking through the woods.

Adult men and women always wore a breech clout, an apron-like garment that covered their "secret parts" (Gookin 1970: 17). Young girls wore them too, but boys did not don them until puberty. Natives wore skins or pelts over one or both shoulders; they also slept under them. Some skins intended for mantles were decorated with embroidered or painted borders. Thomas Morton described how the painted borders were made, which he likened to the "lace set on by a Taylor" . . . "in workes of severall fashions very curious, according to the severall fantasies of the workemen, wherein they strive to excell one another" (Morton [1637] 1969: 29). Here we see something akin to a cohort of artisans creating designs from their own imaginations rather than being bound by tradition.

One curiously worked garment that Native Americans esteemed as much as Europeans valued velvet was the turkey feather cloak (Williams [1643] 1936: 119). Two references mention these as fashioned for children (Josselyn [1674] 1988; Ward 1699). Older men and women made turkey feather coats, "which they weave together with twine of their owne makinge, very prittily" (Morton [1637] 1969: 28). These short capes were worn over the shoulder and under the arm.

Europeans commented on the Indians' adornment of body and hair with great interest. Samuel de Champlain, who visited Cape Cod in 1605, saw "a girl with her hair very neatly dressed, with a skin colored red, and bordered on the upper part with little shell beads. A part of her hair hung down behind, the rest braided in various ways" (Champlain [1604–18] 1907: 73). Indians' dark hair was oiled and carefully dressed on a daily basis. Sometimes it was dyed. William Wood gave a detailed description that incorporates Craik's fashion impulse: "Sometimes they wear it long, hanging down in a loose, disheveled womanish manner; others tied up hard and short like a horse tail, bound close with a fillet. . . . Other cuts they have as their fancy befools them, which would torture the wits of a curious barber to imitate" (Wood [1635] 1977: 83) (see Figure 5.2). While some styles marked affiliation with a particular tribe or signified status within a tribe, the descriptions reveal that hairstyles were personal choices and that quite a few people displayed pride in their individual appearance. Indeed, as Roger Williams observed: "Pride appears in any colour" ([1643] 1936: 165).

Native men painted their faces before entering into battle, but both men and women used face paint as decoration. They had several colors to choose from for cosmetic use: red, yellow, white, and black. They applied animal fat to their bodies to ward off mosquitoes in summer and to add a layer of warmth in the winter, which must have provided a good base for application of powdered pigments. They wore ornaments as pendants around their necks and on their ears in the form of "birds, beasts and fishes, carved out of bones, shell and stone" (Wood [1635], 1977: 85). Tattooing was practised, as noted by Wood,

Figure 5.2 "Native American Sachem," ca. 1700. Artist unknown. Oil on canvas. Photography by Erik Gould, courtesy of the Museum of Art, Rhode Island School of Design, Providence. Gift of Mr. Robert Winthrop. This sachem (leader) of a southern New England tribe demonstrates the Native American male's interest in hairdressing and personal adornment. He wears a wampum headband and shell jewelry. His breech clout and mantle, fashioned from imported woolen cloth, contrast with his locally made deerskin leggings.

who described portraiture of animals on the cheeks of higher-ranking individuals as well as geometric designs on the arms and breasts.

A change in materials preferred for ornament occurred during the Contact Period (Marten 1970: 11). The early explorers commented on brass and copper breastplates, necklaces, and bandoliers fashioned and worn by indigenous people along New England's coast prior to colonization. But after the Pilgrims landed, shell jewelry replaced copper and brass. Dutch traders had introduced shell ornament known as wampum to the indigenous peoples around Plymouth in 1627 as a form of money. It had been in common use further south among the Indians of Long Island and quickly became accepted throughout New England as both currency and ornament. Coastal tribes, especially the Narragansett, became skilled at manufacturing tubular beads from local quahog (clam) shells. Numerous ethno-historical accounts describe the process of drilling the white and purple beads, and then stringing them on Indian hemp for necklaces. To make their bandoliers, belts, and headbands, Indian women strung sinew on small portable looms, then inserted strings of wampum, sometimes in decorative patterns. A belt owned by the Wampanoag chief Metacomet, known as King Philip, was nine inches wide and many feet long and worked in "various figures and flowers, and pictures of many birds and beasts" (Church [1675–76] 1975: 170). King Philip had owned a similarly designed headband. Wampum in the form of headbands was found at Long Pond and as beads in the RI-1000 site, documenting the observation that brass and copper ornament had gone out of style in favor of shell bead ornamentation by the mid-seventeenth century. Figure 5.2 illustrates how wampum and a neck ornament were worn at the end of the seventeenth century.

Glass beads, of course, were traded from the very beginning. Verrazzano noted in 1524 how much the Narragansetts desired blue crystal beads to wear as jewelry, while ignoring the proffered fabrics of silk and gold, which they considered worthless (Wroth 1970: 138). Beads and other ornaments eventually were strung on hemp strings, or sewn onto skins and cloth.

By the middle of the seventeenth century the supply of furs and pelts had been depleted because of exports to Europe. Natives began wearing woolen cloth, much of it a thick, fulled woolen cloth called duffles, trading or trucking cloth. Cloth came from English, Dutch, and French traders until England issued the British Navigation Acts in 1651 restricting trade in England's American colonies to Great Britain. Cloth was sold in 1 ½ to 2 yard lengths and used for mantles, blankets, and breech clouts. The sachem in Figure 5.2 wears a red woolen breech clout and a woolen mantle along with deerskin leggings.

Wool cloth was not a simple substitution for fur. New England natives liked certain types and colors of woolen cloth; Roger Williams wrote that the Narragansetts with whom he traded preferred "a Mantle of *English* or *Dutch* Cloth before their owne wearing of Skins and Furres, because they are warme enough and lighter" ([1643] 1936: 160). Natives throughout North America had definite color preferences that varied regionally (Becker 2005). Traders could not unload colors that were not fashionable. In 1704/5, Thomas Banister, a merchant in Boston, ordered predominantly "blews." "Next the blews the red sells best and next the Red the purple"; later, Banister wrote: "Leave out the purple. Those no body Chuses to buy" (Montgomery 1984: 159). Suppliers were asked to pay attention to the selvages, about which some Indian consumers were very exacting: they wanted striped selvages (Wilmott 2005). A red woolen cloth dubbed "strouds" (made in Stroudwater, England) found acceptance all over North America (Wilmott 2005).

The color preferences listed in the ethno-historical accounts are supported by the finds at Long Pond, where red wool fabrics dominated, along with green. At another Rhode Island site, called Burr's Hill (1650–75), a white Hudson Bay style blanket with striped selvages was recovered (Dillon 1980).

Ready-made English clothes were gifted or traded to Native Americans early on, even prior to the establishment of Plymouth Colony. In 1602, eight Indians in a small boat visited Bartholomew Gosnold's ship anchored in a New England harbor: "One of them appareled with a waistcoat and breeches of black serdge, made after our sea fashions, hose and shoes on his feet" (Brereton [1602] 1966: 11). Cloth coats were a regular gift item to sachems. Reactions were varied. Some accepted them with pride and wore them when trading with the English; others passed them on to underlings, not able to tolerate the tight fit of a tailored coat. But at least one tribal leader, Chickatabot, so admired them that he had Governor John Winthrop's tailor make a suit of clothes for himself (Winthrop 1908). Ready-made English clothes seemed to be popular further west, at William Pynchon's trading post in Springfield, where Indians stole ready-made coats and petticoats from his storehouse (Thomas 1979). English wool cloaks may have been gifted too. Fragments of a fine wool fabric, possibly camlet, were found in a grave associated with a high-status male at the RI-1000 site. A cloak of similar wool camlet is in the collections of the Rhode Island Historical Society. It belonged to Richard Smith, who operated a trading post near the RI-1000 site.

By the later seventeenth century, shirts and other European garments and trims had been adopted in combination with native-made articles of dress. These were not always worn or used as intended. A metallic trim from the Burr's Hill site—a fancy edging called a galloon made of silver wrapped around a silk core—was found in a grave not attached to a textile, but rolled up as it would have been acquired from a European source (Dillon 1980). By the later 1600s, Native American males had readily accepted shirts. These were made of Holland linen, but possibly also cotton. Three fragments of cotton were preserved at the RI-1000 site, which may have been part of a shirt. Cotton was a relatively new commodity in the seventeenth century after being introduced to English markets via the East India trade. An account by Mary Rowlandson, a captive of the Wampanoag prior to King Philip's War, described how the sagamore Quanopin wore a linen shirt with laces trailing from the shirttails (Rowlandson [1682], 1981: 66). An engraved print from 1710 illustrates how a Mohawk sachem, Etow Oh Koam, wore his shirt (Figure 5.3). He had been brought to London along with two other tribal chiefs. His illustration shows the shirt worn like a tunic along with moccasins, wampum belt, mantle, and ear ornaments. His face was tattooed

Figure 5.3 "Etow Oh Koam, King of the River Nation." John Simon after John Verelst, 1710. Mezzotint. Courtesy National Gallery of Art, Washington, D.C. When visiting London in 1710, this Mohawk sachem wore an outfit consisting of shirt, moccasins, wampum belt, sword, mantle, and ear ornaments. His face bears tattoos.

with bird motifs. This demonstrates acceptance of shirts, but not wholesale adoption of English male dress, which would have been the coats, waistcoats, and breeches fashionable in London at the time.

Further south, in Delaware, a curious fashion for what can be described as parti-colored coats developed. In the 1650s, Swedish settlers traded coats with "one side of the breast and back, red, the other side, blue, likewise on the arms, as the clothes of orphan children in Stockholm are made" (Becker 2005: 741–42). High-status sachems liked these coats very much, supporting the concept of fashion leadership in a small-scale society.

In the post–Contact Period, after King Philip's War, the Narragansetts who survived were placed on reservations or sold into slavery. The Mashantucket-Pequots had already been relegated to life on a reservation in 1666. So too were the Mashpee Indians, who were of Wampanoag heritage. The English had pushed hard to Christianize the Native Americans, thereby "civilizing" them and getting them out of their scanty attire and into English clothes. These Christianized Native Americans became known as praying Indians. The Indians at Mashpee were early to convert, and Mashpee became known as a praying town. There the Indians lived in English-style houses instead of wigwams. They learned to spin and weave and to cut and sew. The accidental discovery of the two individuals during excavation for house lots revealed Christian burials evidenced by coffin nails and bodies extended rather than flexed as in pre-Christian New England burials. Many fragments of wool cloth survived with these two individuals, revealing remnants of English-style clothes. There were seam allowances, cloth buttons, appliqués, a knee-band from breeches, and fragments of a stocking. Reverend Gideon Hawley, a minister to the Mashpee, wrote in 1802 that the women were good spinners and weavers and clothed themselves and their families in homespun (Hawley [1815] 1968). Interestingly, many woolen fragments were preserved by a metal headband, a holdover from the old way of dressing, revealing that individual choice remained, even in dressing for life after death.

The dress history of the Native Americans in southern New England demonstrates that fashion systems existed in pre–Contact, Contact, and post–Contact periods despite the relative scarcity of evidence. As the documentary sources and archaeological record suggests, Craik's fashion impulse was alive and well among indigenous groups in New England.

Fashion systems in Mesoamerica

Mesoamerica is an area that includes present-day Mexico and Central America. It is a cultural zone whose pre-Columbian heritage is characterized by a succession of highly sophisticated societies beginning around 1000 BCE. Mesoamerican civilization reached a pinnacle under the Aztecs, who were in power when Hernan Cortés conquered the Aztec Empire in 1521 for Spain (Anawalt 2007).

The Aztecs and their predecessors had a well-developed dress culture. It has garnered scholarly attention, mostly from anthropologists, who offer interpretations of Mesoamerican dress as an expression of identity, gender, ethnicity, and status. See, for example, a recent edited volume entitled *Wearing Culture: Dress and Regalia in Early Mesoamerica and Central America* (Orr and Looper 2014). Less frequent are studies that incorporate fashion into the analysis, and these tend to focus on post-Conquest dress (Root 2005; Scheinman 1991). Our purpose here is to take a broad look at Mesoamerican dress in terms of fashion, for if a culture was as sophisticated as that of the Aztecs, it follows that its sartorial expressions would display elements of a fashion system.

The available evidence limits our knowledge of change in Mesoamerican dress practices in the centuries before Cortés's arrival. However, the dress worn just prior to, and immediately following, the Spanish Conquest is known because of surviving pictorial books that include many images of gods and people. The Mesoamericans who produced these books, known as *codices*, used a Mayan system of hieroglyphics to record aspects of religion, economy, agriculture, and everyday life. One researcher estimated the number of surviving codices at 434, although most are fragmentary (Anawalt 1981). The Aztec culture is the best documented. A particularly detailed compilation of Aztec culture was completed under the supervision of a Franciscan friar named Bernardino de Sahagún in the second half of the sixteenth century. It is known as the *Florentine Codex* (World Digital Library 2016). It found its way to the Biblioteca Medicea Laurenziana in Florence, Italy, where it was discovered in the nineteenth century. A page is reproduced in Figure 5.4.

The pictograms in the codices illustrate basic garment styles as well as fiber- and fabric-processing techniques. Cotton, which is native to Central and South America, was considered a prestige fiber; therefore, it was reserved for use by elites in Mesoamerica's stratified societies. Common people wore garments made of agave, yucca, or palm fibers. The backstrap loom was used to weave fabrics; it produced cloth of rectangular proportions that had selvedges on all four sides. The Aztecs used the cloth as it came off the loom either in single units or sewn to other units to make larger pieces of cloth. Cloth usage was similar across Mesoamerica: a single rectangle made a man's loincloth; two or more rectangles joined together made a man's tie-on cape; two or more joined pieces made a woman's wrap skirt. Women's upper body garments consisted of webs of cloth sewn together in such a way as to result in a poncho known as *quechquemitl* or a blouse known as *huipil*. Both words come from the indigenous Nahuatl language. In some regions, a single length of cloth had multiple uses in the female wardrobe: shawl, baby carrier, or head cloth. Of uncertain origins, it became known as a *rebozo* after Spanish colonization (Chico 2010: 60–61).

The upper section of Figure 5.4 shows a seated male wearing a cape. The middle illustration is a trio of huipiles, and the bottom illustration shows six wrap skirts in different patterns. While the skirt designs varied according to age and occasion, the different designs of the huipiles imply at least some individuality. Both sexes wore headdresses and accessories. Mesoamericans showed status in their appearance through beads and other ornaments, cloth made of cotton, cloth with surface decoration, featherwork, and copper and gold jewelry (Orr and Looper 2014: xxviii). Regulations were in place to restrict the wearing of certain styles and materials to the upper classes.

Anthropologist Patricia Anawalt completed a detailed study of twenty-eight Mesoamerican codices, categorizing the pre-Hispanic dress depicted therein into six groups based on geographical region (1981). Anawalt's detailed charts lay out the garment types and where they were worn, but not changes over time. She does discuss inconsistencies in data and offers a "fashion-follows-

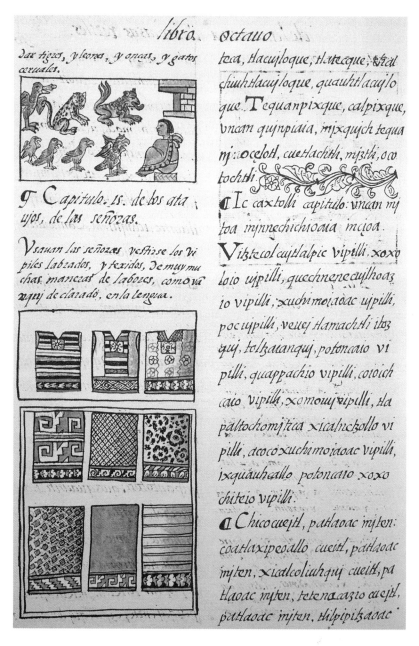

Figure 5.4 "The Clothes of Noblewomen with Embroidered Huipil Blouses." Facsimile of the Florentine Codex by Friar Bernardino de Sahagun, *Historia general de las cosas de Nuevo España*. Nahuatl, mid-sixteenth century, Mexico. Templo Mayor Library, Mexico. Gianni Dagli Orti / The Art Archive at Art Resource, NY. In the upper section, a seated male wears a cape. The middle section shows three huipiles (blouses). The bottom section illustrates six wrap skirts in different patterns.

power" explanation as well as the influence of the missionaries (215). The very existence of sumptuary regulation suggests the desire of non-elites, such as the artisan and merchant classes as well as victorious warriors, to wear prestige styles; emulation of the class above an individual's station is a basic feature of the trickle-down theory of fashion. Researchers acknowledge the skill and inventiveness of Mayan weavers; it follows that while the garment forms might have remained constant, the patterning and accessories embraced innovation. Further, traveling merchants introduced new materials, which elites must have adapted for their garments and accessories. Indeed, some researchers have stressed that Mesoamerican dress was never static (Schevill 1991: 6).

After the Spanish Conquest, the indigenous population endured dramatic changes. Not only did their numbers drop precipitously, but the Spaniards attempted to Christianize those who survived by putting rules into place that required them to cover more of their bodies. Men were ordered to wear Spanish peasant attire consisting of white pants and shirt. Native women fared better as their wrap skirts and upper body garments were deemed modest enough. The Spanish also introduced the treadle loom, which produced longer and wider pieces of cloth that needed to be cut before assembly into clothing.

As the Spanish settled in and intermarried with the indigenous population, a new social order emerged. A caste system developed in the eighteenth century that classified people according to bloodline. Spanish citizens born in Spain were at the top of the social hierarchy, while Spanish born in Mexico were slightly lower in status. Both of them were termed *espanole*. Indians, or *indios*, represented a lower rank followed by *negros* (Africans). Children born to Spaniards who married Indian women were known as *mestizos*, while children of Spaniards and people of African descent were *mulattos* (Earle 2001: 181)

Casta paintings, a panel of which is illustrated in Figure 5.5, documented the various racial combinations. These paintings also illustrated the rules for how the different ranks were expected to dress (Voss 2008). The Spanish elite wore European styles in luxurious fabrics along with the appropriate accessories. Not-so-wealthy Spaniards and people of mixed heritage also wore European styles, but they were often depicted as plain, even a bit disheveled. Only purebred Indians wore indigenous styles such as huipiles and rebozos. Some of the more prosperous *indios* used fabrics intended for European styles, but made up in indigenous styles. Figure 5.5 illustrates an Indian woman in a fine gauze huipil worn over a wraparound embroidered skirt; the huipil is so fine that her corseted torso can be seen underneath. She wears a folded rebozo on her head instead of the mantilla accorded to Spanish women. The overall silhouette reflects elite European women's fashion of the eighteenth century. Her husband, who is Spanish, is dressed in a European coat, waistcoat, and breeches accessorized with a tricorn hat. Their child, of mixed blood, is attired in European dress like his father.

Figure 5.5 "De Español è Yndia, Mestizo." Anonymous, eighteenth century.
Copperplate painting (48 x 36 cm). Museo de América-Coleccion, Madrid, Spain. Album
/ Art Resource, NY. This *casta* (caste) painting illustrates how people of different racial
combinations were expected to dress in Spanish Mexico. The Indian mother wears a
huipil blouse and a rebozo on her head. Her Spanish husband and mixed-race son dress
in European styles.

As trade with Europe and beyond commenced, silk was introduced to Central
America (Duan 2016). Spaniards imported black mulberry trees and silkworm eggs
into Mexico in 1536 in an attempt to develop a silk industry. Common people wore
this novel (to them) fiber despite attempts by the Mexican government to control
who wore silk. Domestic sericulture faded away after the Manila galleon trade
brought Chinese silks to Mesoamerica in 1573. Subsequently, Spanish Americans
developed a partiality for silks despite the warm climate for which the indigenous
cotton would have been more practical. Although people of Spanish extraction
wished to distinguish themselves through their dress, mixed-race groups were
quick to take up "new goods, styles, and practices" (DuPlessis 2016: 224).

Fashion systems in South America

The New World's other great ancient civilization was the Andean civilization. The
area south of Mesoamerica that now includes contemporary Columbia, Ecuador,

Peru, Bolivia, northern Argentina, and northern Chile has been occupied since at least 9000 BCE, with increasingly complex societies after 1000 CE (Meisch 2010). The last pre-Hispanic culture that ruled this large area was the Inca, who gained control in the 1460s. Andean geography varies from dry coastal areas adjacent to the Pacific Ocean to the high plains and peaks of the Andes mountain range. The north coast of Peru receives some rainfall, but the larger central and south coastal areas are very dry. Given that Peruvians buried their dead in layers of clothing, this desert-like climate allowed for excellent preservation of cloth and clothing. Likewise, sacrificial burials found in the frozen highlands include textiles. Some areas such as Ecuador are wetter, and less is known about their pre-Inca dress. However, textile and dress historians have a plethora of information about stylistic change in pre-Conquest Andean cultures on which to base their investigations (Anawalt 2007).

Cotton is native to the lowlands while the highlands are home to wool-bearing camelids: the alpaca and vicuña, which grow fine fibers, and the llama, which grows coarser fibers. Andean cultures were also in proximity to the Amazon River basin with its colorful birds that supplied feathers for garments and headgear. Archaeological finds provide evidence that Peruvian cultures enjoyed a robust trade network between the coastal regions, the highlands, and the tropical regions of the continent.

Ancient Andean cultures were highly advanced in weaving and other textile constructions. They used several types of looms, including backstrap looms, to create woven clothing. Like the Mesoamericans, they planned their weaving so that the fabric that came off the loom had an intended purpose and was used without cutting. Some sewing of panels of cloth was employed to make large mantles and garments. Men wore loincloths, *uncu* (tunics), mantles, and various types of headgear. Inca women wore a one-piece dress consisting of a rectangle that wrapped around the body called an *aksu* (also *acsu, aqsu, acso, anaku*, and other variants). It was either pinned at the shoulder with a long stickpin, a *tupu*, and belted, or partially sewn (Meisch 2010; Rowe 1995–1996). In Ecuador, women had worn a wrapped skirt and mantle prior to the Inca period, but adopted the full-length wrapped dress under the Inca regime (Rowe and Meisch 2011).

Like Mesoamerica, the basic garment shapes did not change significantly, but the materials and motifs did. Scholars can categorize and roughly date textile types by designs and techniques. A very wide range of textile techniques has been identified including twining, plaiting, knotting, looping, sprang, plain and twill weave, tapestry, double-sided tapestry, gauze weave, embroidery, and ikat dyeing (Meisch 2010). (Ikat fabrics are created by resist dyeing yarns prior to weaving, resulting in patterned areas with hazy edges.) Andean cultures produced tapestries with very high thread counts; for example, the Huari culture (ca. 400–700 CE) created finer tapestry cloths than Europeans did centuries later, weaving over 200 weft threads per inch (Rowe 2005). The concept of fashion is applicable in terms of broad changes over time that occurred in basic garment styles as well as patterns woven or embroidered into the cloths, or in the fabric structures.

Ann Pollard Rowe, who has researched textiles and dress in South America for decades, wrote in the preface to *Costume and History in Highland Ecuador* that she realized a historical context was necessary "to make even the simplest statements" in discussing the dress of Ecuador's indigenous peoples (Rowe and Meisch 2011: xi). Change came to pre-Hispanic dress practices with the Inca conquest, and then again when the Spanish arrived.

Peru's Chimu culture (ca. 800–1532 CE) created matched sets of clothes with loincloth, tunic, and headdress in coordinated styles that are datable to specific periods (Rowe 1984). Like pre-Columbians before them, they worked with feathers, tying colorful quills onto base cloth to create tunics and impressive headgear. Figure 5.6 illustrates a feather tunic from the Chimu culture of Peru.

Figure 5.6 Feather tunic, Peru. Chimu culture. Plain weave with paired warps (cotton), with applied feathers. The Textile Museum, Washington, D.C., 91.395. Acquired by George Hewett Myers in 1941. Pre-Hispanic Peruvians produced highly sophisticated textiles and featherwork, often in matched sets, which are datable to specific cultures.

The feathers in the background are yellow while the feathers of the bird motifs are turquoise; the other small figural elements use feathers of red or green.

In 1528, the Spanish arrived on the Pacific beaches of the Peruvian north coast. Four years later in 1532, Conquistador Francisco Pizarro led the expedition that conquered the Inca Empire, which extended from Ecuador in the north to Chile in the far south. The Spaniards laid claim to the empire's riches of gold and silver, decimating the culture, just as they had done to the Maya in Mexico. Following the execution of Inca Emperor Atahualpa, Pizarro married Atahualpa's consort, a child bride. She received a Spanish name and bore Pizarro two mestizo sons. The marriage of Nusta (indigenous noblewoman) Beatriz Clara Coya, the niece of the deceased Incan emperor, to Martin Garcia de Loyola also merged the Inca royalty with the Spanish conquerors. Beatriz's European-style wedding attire is depicted in a painting as having bands of Inca geometric iconography called *tukapu* (also *tocapu*) (Leibsohn and Mundy 2005). Tukapu signaled social status and role (Meisch 2010). Just as in the viceroyalty of New Spain that reached from Panama to California, in the viceroyalty of Peru, which covered most of South America, marriage between ethnicities led to hierarchical classifications of the children of the couples. The practice of delineating the various couplings and assigning their children a type—as depicted in the casta paintings, which originated in Mexico—apparently held less sway in Peru. Only one extant casta painting from Peru survives (Bagneris 2013: 167).

Throughout the viceroyalty, Inca elite women continued to wear the aksu and the anaku; both terms referred to a wrapped dress (Rowe and Meisch 2011). Their dress marked by tukapu bands announced their high status to other natives as well as to the Spanish. While an aksu or anaku worn by an elite woman continued to include a tukapu band, another motif band might display indigenous feminine iconography such as birds and flowers (Bagneris 2013: 190–93). The tukapu reflecting the continuity of the Inca culture contrasted with the motifs in the metal tupu (stickpin): an elite woman's tupu, which might be fifteen inches long and include a terminus, or head, of three to six inches in width, reflected style change. Emblems in the terminus of extant silver tupu incorporate both European metal-smithing techniques and iconography (Bagneris 2013: 191–93). Inca men's attire also reflected the influence of European material culture. A man's seventeenth-century unku (Brooklyn Museum #86.224.51) includes embroidery that apparently occurred in three stages. The tukapu band around the bottom edge, embroidered in wool, is considered original. On one side of the tunic above the tukapu band were added stylized human figures that portray Inca royal events, but on the other side of the tunic, the band added above the tukapu presents non-Inca imagery, techniques, and materials. Worked in linen and metallic thread, this band includes European-style heraldic lions and shields. The incorporation of European iconography, techniques, and materials into elite Incan material culture may be viewed as a choice that purposefully targeted making their "status legible to the Spanish," a goal that could ensure status privileges (Bagneris 2013: 193). Yet, such changes also comply with our understanding of fashion in which a group adopts a style, in this case European-style motifs simultaneously worn with Inca motifs. A strategy for communication through dress and accessories is compatible with fashion.

Travelers to Peru in the seventeenth and eighteenth centuries remarked upon the dress they observed there, emphatically commenting on the luxurious textiles (Earle 2001: 182, 188). The high quality of the clothing and currency of the fashions of lower classes incited comments of disbelief (Earle 2001: 182, 188). Peru was a leading trade center. Chinese traders delivered fine patterned silks, and from Europe arrived the favored Flemish laces and fine linen. In the urban Pacific ports such as Trujillo and Lima (the seat of the viceroyalty), and far away in the cities of today's Ecuador, Bolivia, and Chile, consumers ignored restrictions on "stuffs" to indulge their preferences to the extent that they could afford (Earle 2001), and the underground market in fine textiles and trimmings thrived. Watercolors painted in Peru in the late eighteenth century in the folio volumes of Bishop Baltazar Jaime Martínez Compañon's *Trujillo del Peru* (Madrid, Biblioteca Nacional) illustrate numerous examples of women who displayed a variety of fashions and tastes in trimmings and accessories. These included a cummerbund, an apron of fine linen and lace, and colorful stockings and garters. Flat slip-on shoe styles prevailed, often in open-toed styles (Guengerich 2013).

The painting *A Merry Company on the Banks of the Rívas River* (ca. 1790–1800, Figure 5.7) portrays the distinctive *pollera* ensemble as worn by Peruvian Spanish elite women and their black and mulatto servants in the late eighteenth century. The image presents a family and friends outdoors accompanied by servants. A black harp player in the center of the group provides music. The wealth of the Spanish family, signified by the distant estate house on the left, extends to the dress of the Spanish men and women, and to the servants. However, on the left, in plain clothes and sandals, an indigenous woman enters the scene, perhaps to sell flowers. The men in the party of revelers are dressed in current late eighteenth-century European fashions, and the black male servant reflects the same European style.

The pollera ensemble that developed and became fashionable in viceregal Peru, and thus was worn from current Ecuador to Argentina, diverged from the dominant eighteenth-century European women's fashion. The skirt, with its several trims and petticoats, ended well above the ankle instead of at the ankle or shoe top. The skirt was dome shaped rather than elliptical. The upper body was not corseted and no gown or bodice covered the voluminous *camisa* (chemise) embellished with lace and embroidery. At the Costume Society of America annual symposium in 2014, James Middleton proposed an alternative to the widely accepted concept that the look developed solely from historical Spanish fashion. In Spain, a women's at-home dress consisted in part of a wrapped skirt

Figure 5.7 "A Merry Company on the Banks of the Rímac River," ca. 1800. Lima School. Oil on canvas, 26 x 35 ½ in. (66 x 90.2 cm). Brooklyn Museum, Gift of Lilla Brown in memory of her husband, John W. Brown, by exchange, 2012.41. The women, servants and elites alike, wear the distinctive *pollera* ensemble of late-eighteenth to early-nineteenth century Andean culture. The fashion diverged from the dominant European silhouette of the time, instead presenting a regional hybrid style.

called *faldellin*, a camisa, and a jacket with open sleeves called *jubón*. According to Middleton (2014), this Spanish at-home attire and the wrapped skirts and dresses of elite Inca women each contributed to the distinctive pollera ensemble style. The wrapped Inca dress (aksu, anaku), which the Spanish initially would have perceived as falling short of proper public dress, was eventually understood as appropriate dress as worn by Inca women. In this context, the intersection of the two wrapped dress forms provided the opening for *creole* (European born in the colonies) Spanish women to wear their own culture's relaxed style in public, according to Middleton. A pollera ensemble with a wrapped skirt seldom appears in the eighteenth-century visual record. Regularly shaped folds, such as those made by cartridge pleats, a centuries-old European pleat technique, seen in the skirts in Figure 5.7 and in the *Trujillo del Peru* watercolors, are more common in surviving images. Thus, we conclude that the pollera, as described by Middleton, is a hybridized style.

In the cities and remote villages of the Andean region today, Aymara and Quechua women wear localized pollera ensemble fashions. As with the eighteenth-century style, the modern Andean styles reflect hybridity resulting from a confluence of influences and cultural selections. The Andean fashions continue to reflect colonial heritage, ethnic traditions, and new impulses from the modern global context. In La Paz, Bolivia, a bowler-style felt hat, long associated with the pollera style, is commonly worn; elsewhere other styles that shield the eyes from the sun are worn. Blouses with lace or embroidery, reminiscent of the lace-embellished linen *camisas* seen in Figure 5.7, are worn; in cold regions, layers of sweaters are seen. In some locations, a snuggly fitted wool jacket covers the blouse. A wrap or shawl woven of local alpaca fibers often drapes the shoulders. Shawls may have fringed ends or include macramé-fringed edges on all sides. A carrying cloth woven with native symbols continues the ancient heritage. The dome-shaped skirt, created by multiple petticoat layers topped by a woven skirt, has many variants. Skirt styling ranges from wrapped to gathered to pleated, including the previously mentioned cartridge pleats. Flat slip-on shoes, low-heeled lace-up boots, or sandals protect the feet. Colors, textiles, embroidery, jewelry, and shoes provide opportunity for style options. Elayne Zorn, for example, documented an autonomous fashion system in highland Bolivia "where tens of thousands of members of an indigenous ethnic group are passionately concerned about fashion, but with the difference that they design and produce almost all of their clothing themselves" (Zorn 2005: 115). Loren's (2012) interpretation of historical dress processes in the Americas, the selection and adaptation of fashion, applies to the modern context; the contemporary Andean pollera ensemble is both an identity construction and a statement of fashion as the style preference of a group even as the fashion may be specific to a small locale.

Mexico, Central America, South America, and the Caribbean offer rich opportunities for research connecting dress to fashion systems among indigenous peoples. This applies to the pre-Conquest period, the era of colonization by Spain and Portugal, and the current age of independence. Scholars have tended to see the dress of this large geographical area as either traditional, hybrid, or Western, with fashion applying only to the latter. It is time to follow Diana DiPaolo Loren's lead in North America and consider how indigenous groups in Meso- and South America fashioned their own identities by selectively adapting Euro-American styles while retaining parts of their heritage. As Regina Root has stated, "Latin American fashion design and history has long been overlooked" (2013: 393). She concluded that "scholars will need to assess carefully and push forward definitive Latin American fashion histories in the future" (2013: 403).

6

FASHION SYSTEMS AND TRADE NETWORKS IN THE EASTERN HEMISPHERE

The market-town of Muza is without a harbor, but has a good roadstead and anchorage because of the sandy bottom thereabouts, where the anchors hold safely. The merchandise imported there consists of purple cloths, both fine and coarse; clothing in the Arabian style, with sleeves; plain, ordinary, embroidered, or interwoven with gold; saffron, sweet rush, muslins, cloaks, blankets (not many), some plain and others made in the local fashion; sashes of different colors.

THE PERIPLUS OF THE ERYTHRAEAN
SEA: CHAPTER 24

An unnamed Greek-speaking ship captain based in Alexandria (Egypt) wrote these words in the first century CE. *The Periplus* documented distances, coastal landmarks, and harbors along the Red Sea, the Persian Gulf, and the Indian Ocean as a guide for other seafaring merchants. He reported that fashion goods such as ivory, tortoise shell, and copper for bracelets and anklets could be obtained in ports along the eastern coast of Africa. In towns on the Arabian Peninsula, like the above-mentioned Muza, goods imported from the Arabian interior could be sourced. The navigable routes across the Indian Ocean reached ports on India's West Coast, where Indian muslins, figured linens, "thin clothing of the finest weaves," and "bright-colored girdles a cubit wide" were available (*The Periplus*: Chapter 49). Around the tip of India and up to the mouth of the Ganges River traders could acquire raw silk, silk yarn, and silk cloth brought over great distances by foot. Notable in the above quote is the emphasis on Arabian style, with *sleeves*. Artfully draped garments had signified the height of civilization to the Greeks and Romans in the first century, but their introduction to new materials and styles such as sleeved garments from Persia and silk from China was about to usher in a new world of fashion.

This chapter presents examples of fashion that relied upon Eurasian land and sea trade routes forged in ancient times. Trade disseminates materials and processes as well as ideas and concepts. As sites of novelty, new materials and processes play important roles in fashion systems; desire for novelty, the so-called fashion impulse, serves as an impetus to fashion. Bronze Age luxury trade, Silk Road commodities, textiles and dress of selected Eurasian courts, and the Malaysian archipelago's *kebaya* serve as examples of the nexus of trade and fashion in selected regions in Eurasia.

Luxury trade in the Ancient Near East

Luxury goods circulated in the Ancient Near East as early as the Bronze Age, supporting our argument that the fashion impulse was at work long before previously acknowledged. The geographical area known as the Ancient Near East includes an east-west span from the eastern Mediterranean into the Iranian Plateau and a north-south span from the Black and Caspian Seas to the Arabian Sea at the southern edge of the Saudi Arabian Peninsula. Ancient cultures of the region include, among others, the Minoan and Mycenaean, Canaan, Assyrian, Hittite, Sumerian, Babylonian, Median, Elam, and the Egyptian Kingdoms. Connections with farther distant regions existed, especially with cultures in the extended geographical ranges in Africa, and central and south Asia.

Trade networks emerged in the Neolithic Era connecting Western Europe with eastern Asia. By the fourth millennium BCE during which urban organization advanced considerably, trade in the raw materials copper and tin intensified and spread. Combining tin and copper creates bronze, a much harder metal suitable for improved tools and weaponry. This discovery ushered in the Bronze Age, the chronology of which varies by region. In Western Europe it began around 3300 BCE.

Roads to facilitate trade caravans between the Levant and Mesopotamia were established by the second half of the third millennium BCE. Settlements or way stations about every twenty kilometers, or the distance of a day's journey, offered rest to the merchants who traveled the routes. Prestige materials moved along routes from one commercial center to the next; exchanges occurred at commercial centers such as Byblos and Qatna rather than through direct contact between kingdom emissaries (Al-Maqdissi 2008; Casanova 2008).

In Egypt and Mesopotamia, beliefs that blue represented prestige and power meant that the hard blue stone lapis lazuli held value. Mined in Afghanistan and the Central Asian Pamir Mountains, evidence of working lapis lazuli has been found in archaeological contexts dated to the fourth millennium BCE in Egypt and the seventh millennium BCE in Mesopotamia and Iran (Casanova 2008). It was used as a pigment in art works, as a precious material for carving and inlay, and for personal adornment.

Beads of lapis lazuli might be used in necklaces, earrings, or bracelets. A hidden trove of beads, gold items, and cylinder seals associated with the palace in the Mycenaean settlement at Thebes attests to the lapis lazuli trade reaching central Greece in the Bronze Age. The lapis lazuli beads in this treasure may have come to the palace area in the thirteenth century BCE via trade centers in the Syrio-Levant or Cyprus. The blue beads had been combined with locally sourced beads (Aravantinos 2008). Lapis lazuli survives as inlay in gold items: for example, in the funerary treasures found in King Tut's tomb. In addition to such prestige contexts, at the ancient sites Sarazm (in Tajikistan), Mundigak (in Afghanistan), and Shahr-I Sokhta (in Iran), where the stone was imported, "the craftsmen adapted their work to meet local demand" (Casanova 2008: 60). Thus, the blue stone that moved from Afghan mines to elite contexts apparently was enjoyed more widely in some locations than others. Workshops making products adapted to local demand suggest the presence of the fashion impulse.

A shipwreck found in 1982 off the southwest coast of Turkey near Uluburun and dated to the late fourteenth century BCE revealed a large cargo of tin and copper ingots. Luxury items present attest to their trade. The precious cargo included thousands of beads and flat decorative items made of glass and faience, such as may be sewn onto textiles. Smaller numbers of beads of amber, agate, faience, and ostrich eggshell were recovered. The disc-shaped eggshell beads had traveled African trade networks starting deep in the continent before reaching the ship, which circulated the eastern Mediterranean before it sank. These smaller groups of beads "may have been for the personal adornment of those aboard the ship" (Pulak 2008: 296).

Anastasia Dakouri-Hild (2012) studied the production and consumption of the ornament industries for jewelry, furniture, and elaborate weapons in Thebes (Greece) from ca. 2000 to 1050 BCE. The data was drawn from remains of workshops, storage contexts, and mortuary contexts. Changes in details and complexity occurred across the approximately 950 years, particularly toward simpler styles in the later years. The materials used in jewelry included imported lapis lazuli and lazurite, among others. According to Dakouri-Hild, the emphasis in production was on "dress items and furniture, the distant origin of materials . . . [and] manufacture, assemblage, and transformation of parts into composite, elaborate goods" such as a necklace of amethyst, carnelian, faience, and gold (474). The wider society reflected a taste for materially complex personal ornaments and emulated the elites; the differentiation process present in many fashion systems was evident already at this early date. In this process the higher-status group differentiated with a newer fashion when the lower status group copied the higher status group's older fashion.

Despite meager fashion evidence in the Bronze Age, other scholars have echoed Dakouri-Hild's interpretation that a fashion process was present in the wider society. Jack Phillips examined the repair, replacement, recycling, and reshaping of jewelry parts or elements in the Bronze Age Aegean, concluding that fashion played a crucial role in the choices of jewelry owners even as they sought to reuse chipped, marred, or old jewelry elements. Phillips (2012) remarked on this clearly individualized process of reuse claiming that the Aegean jewelry owners "were aware of, and attempted to follow the latest fashion" (490).

Luxury trade on the Silk Road

The Silk Road refers to a network of trade routes in Eurasia in use from the second century BCE to the fifteenth century when maritime trade expanded during the onset of the European Age of Exploration. The network linked the far distances of the continent in all directions by land and sea, allowing long-distance trade to occur. The overland rest stops grew as commercial trade increased; the controlling governments levied taxes on sales and tariffs on passage. Of course, conflicts and internal events sometimes temporarily closed trade routes, tribal groups might expect payment for passage, and banditry occurred. Across the vast space of Asia the cultural forms varied from tribal nomadic to pastoral herding, to agricultural settlements, to urban centers often built around an oasis. By the third quarter of the first millennium, the Eastern Hemisphere trade networks were connected; the old routes in Africa linked to those in Eurasia. Important to consideration of fashion, trade goods, as noted above in *The Periplus* documents, included silk skeins, woven textiles, garments, and precious and semiprecious stones. The cultural contact also brought motifs and metal working techniques to the sphere of exchange.

Amber (fossilized pine resin) from the Baltic Sea was one of those valued commodities. It had been traded as early as the Neolithic period and was used in antiquity for pendants and perfume containers. From the tenth to the twelfth centuries, large amounts of amber traveled across the Silk Road to China, where it became desirable for personal ornaments and fragrance-related accessories (So 2013).

We call the network of routes the Silk Road because silk was a key commodity traveling East to West. In China, the Shang dynasty (ca. 1600–1046 BCE) restricted silk to the court, and successive dynasties attempted to maintain a monopoly on both the raw material and finished goods. However, Chinese silk reached Germany by the mid-sixth century BCE and Greece by the late fifth century BCE (Barber 1991). Greek and Roman women expressed their desire for silk; in the early first century, Seneca the Younger condemned it as too revealing of the body as worn by some Roman women. Silk was clearly fashionable. The distance from eastern China to Damascus and connections farther westward is about 5,000 miles over often harsh trails, and the Han Dynasty pressed for the routes west to be open so that they could acquire horses and glass. Thus, Roman blown glass became a key commodity traveling west to east. The routes between Xi'an and Central Asia diverged into a north and a south trail around the Taklamakan Desert and Tarim Basin. At Xi'an in the east, connections to eastern China, Japan, and Korea, as well as to Southeast Asia, were made. From the western trade hub of Central Asia, connections were made to India, Pakistan, Afghanistan, and eastward to the Levant and Mediterranean. The sea routes continuously gave access to goods from far distances: in the ports, cargo was off-loaded and exchanged for new cargo from interior networks.

During the first third of the fifteenth century, the Ming Imperial Court sent Zheng He (1371–1433 CE), the intrepid Muslim sea captain, on seven voyages southward and westward from Nanjing to gain control of the seas. Zheng He's armadas included numerous support vessels to accompany "treasure ships" reported to be a colossal 450-feet long. The impressive show of Chinese power throughout the Indian Ocean and beyond was underscored by the approximately 27,000 men on board as crew, soldiers, and specialists. Zheng He's westernmost reach was Mecca on the northern Red Sea. In concert with statecraft, Zheng He engaged in commerce. The cargo for sale included "bronze jewelry . . . fans, umbrellas, embroidered velvet and taffeta . . . thread and needles, clothing, dyes, glass beads" (Finlay 2008: 337). Among the tribute goods carried back to China that could be used in fashionable products were "precious stones, ivory, ebony . . . deer hides, coral, kingfisher feathers, tortoise shell . . . rhinoceros horn . . . and safflower (for dyes and drugs), Indian cotton cloth, and ambergris—which the Chinese knew as 'dragon's pittle' and used for making perfume" (337).

Colorful feathers, noted in Chapter 5 as important among Maya, Chimu, and Andean cultures in Western Hemisphere fashion systems, were a long-lasting fashion in China. The iridescent blue kingfisher or halcyon feathers appear in Chinese imperial court ornaments in the Han Dynasty (206 BCE–220 CE). Later, Zhou Daguan, a Chinese diplomat for Mongol Emperor Chengzong of Yuan, visited the Khmer kingdom in Cambodia in 1296 and 1297. In about 1312 he wrote the only eyewitness account of the Khmer court titled *A Record of Cambodia: The Land and Its People*, in which he noted that the kingdom exported kingfisher feathers to China (Kindseth 2009). In the fifteenth century, they continued to be in demand at the Chinese court. Apparently the Cambodian kingfisher feathers were highly prized even though the birds were native in southern areas of China: Admiral Zheng He's vessels garnered additional Cambodian kingfisher feathers in the early fifteenth century to satiate the demand in China (McCarthy and Chase 2003).

Feathers of the various kingfishers display a range of brilliant iridescent blues from lapis to turquoise. They were used in a technique called *tian-tsui* to create art works and personal ornaments at first only for the court and performers, and later for other elites. The feathers were desirable by ladies of the court for "headdresses, hairpins, hair combs, earrings, and other types of personal ornament" (McCarthy and Chase 2003: 15). The taste for kingfisher feather ornaments spread as non-elites emulated the elites and by the "late nineteenth century jewelry decorated with kingfisher feathers was available more widely in China" (McCarthy and Chase 2003: 14). The tian-tsui technique involved adhering tiny sections of feathers to silver metal or silver-colored paper in a manner similar to enamel cloisonné: metal partition walls of silver wire enclosed each space while on paper, string or folded paper did the job (McCarthy and Chase 2003). Design motifs included dragons, phoenixes, butterflies, and flowers embellished with pearls, colored glass beads, and bits of other bird feathers in violet, green, and white (Clark 2013; McCarthy and Chase 2003).

When the Silk Road trade burgeoned in the first century, settlements also thrived along the routes fringing the edges of the vast Taklamakan Desert in the center of Eurasia. Due to the dry conditions, textile artifacts have survived at various sites there dating from the Bronze Age to 1000, often with mummified human remains. Within Xinjiang, or "New Borders," lie the archaeological sites at Yingpin, once a town on the southern rim of the Tarim Basin, and its cemetery at Niyä. The sites yielded evidence of both Indian and Chinese influences in contact with those of the Sogdians, dated to ca. 300 to 500. The grave of Yingpin Man (in Tomb No. 15) held a decomposed body, but well-preserved and sumptuous clothing. His ethnicity is officially undetermined, but reports of his facial features and brown hair suggest he was Caucasoid.

Yingpin Man's burial is unique among those at Xinjian. He was wrapped in textile strips and held in place by wooden armatures inside a finely made wooden coffin. A silk shroud covered his body. His clothes portray an extremely wealthy man and they also reflect a confluence of cultures. His silk and wool knee-length kaftan opens on the right in the Chinese fashion, but its cut—narrow-sleeved, closely fitted waist flaring to a wide hem—indicates a horseman's attire, despite the fine textile. The wool brocade of the kaftan has a red ground with rows of yellow pomegranate trees, pairs of naked males fighting with swords and pairs of abutted goats, a design reflective of Graeco-Roman motifs (Sheng 2010). A wide silk sash encloses his waist and a bag for aromatics is attached. His deep maroon-red wide-legged silk trousers are embroidered in wool yarns of blue, green, and yellow in lozenges composed of dots, stars, and floral shapes. Silk boots decorated with gold foil and wool embroideries, made expressly for the burial, shod his feet. Sets of miniature clothing made of spun silk accompanied his body. His grave goods included a glass bowl assumed to be from Syria, part of the late Roman Empire (Jager and Mair 2010; Sheng 2010). All of these attributes led Ulf Jager and Victor Mair to propose that Yingpin Man was a "wealthy traveling trader" and, as a Caucasian, he may have been a Sogdian

(2010: 57). Sogdians originated in Central Asia and were Iranian. Without their own kingdom or homeland, they allied with others as skilled traders and expert craftsmen.

Elizabeth Barber remarked on the "riot of color" in the textile finds at Xinjian, especially mentioning the finely patterned silk brocades created by Chinese weavers (2010: 77). The Sogdians used the samit weave to create "variations of a striking Sassanian design called the *pearl roundel* . . . in which a ring of pearl-like circles surround a central design" (2010: 78). The pearl roundel became a favored design in the Tang Dynasty in China. In this way textile techniques and patterns traveled the Silk Road and were adapted as new designs, reflecting the fashion impulse.

Indeed, Central Asian coats with long tight-fitting sleeves and overlapping front closures were excavated at Antinoë, a trading town in Middle Egypt that connected the Nile Valley to the harbors on the Red Sea. Made of sheep's wool, some had tablet-woven borders, while others had silk appliqués (Evans and Ratliff 2012). They date to the fifth and sixth centuries, roughly the same period as Yingpin Man. This example illustrates the wide circulation of new styles over large geographical areas. As Cäcilia Fluck articulates, trade and cultural exchange brought new fabrics and garment forms to western regions including North Africa, "where they were adopted alongside local traditions, still heir to the Roman styles" (2012: 160).

Fashion systems in the Byzantine Empire

Most costume histories include Byzantine dress, but coverage is scant for an empire that lasted over a thousand years. There is much more to the study of Byzantine dress than the mosaics of Justinian and Theodora at the San Vitale Basilica in Ravenna, Italy. Scholars have begun addressing the complexities of Byzantine dress, notably Jennifer Ball (2005) and Timothy Dawson (2006). Further, two New York City institutions recently displayed rare dress artifacts in exhibitions from the early and middle Byzantine periods; both treated dress as a changing form of material culture subject to the vagaries of fashion. A full-color catalog accompanied each exhibition (Evans and Ratliff 2012, Thomas 2016).

Byzantium came into existence in 324 CE, when Constantine, the emperor of Rome, founded a second capital in the eastern part of the empire, which was not so vulnerable to attacks from the so-called barbarians (people who did not speak Greek or Latin) as Rome was in the west. When Rome finally fell in 476, the new capital, called Constantinople in honor of its founder, grew in importance. The city enjoyed a premium location on the Bosporus Strait, which divided the Eurasian continents into Europe and Asia while at the same time connecting the

Mediterranean to the Black Sea. Over time the Eastern Roman Empire became known as Byzantium after the small town upon which Constantinople was built. Byzantium embraced Christianity, which perhaps contributes to why its dress is included in Western costume histories while the dress of its Islamic neighbors to the east is not.

For over a thousand years, Byzantium was the most advanced political, cultural, and scientific civilization in the West, and its style influence was felt as far away as eastern China and northern Europe. Byzantine styles dominated the wardrobes of the elite in Europe. The women of Charlemagne's court (768–814) wore Byzantine dress as did Otto II in an ivory dated 982, as well as the Norman Roger II when crowned king of Sicily in the twelfth century (Ball 2005). The Byzantines "were extremely interested in creating, borrowing, and wearing fashionable dress" (Ball 2005: 1). Not only the courts but also ordinary citizens participated in the fashion system. Charioteers, for example, were reputed to have dressed well. While proscriptions for court regalia were recorded for posterity in *The Book of Ceremonies*, no such restrictions existed for non-court dress.

Until the seventh century, the empire included four great cities: Rome, Constantinople, Alexandria (in modern Egypt), and Antioch (in modern Turkey). Although the spread of Islam reduced the size of the empire in the seventh and eighth centuries, it rebounded to experience a golden age in the tenth and eleventh centuries. The Crusades, ostensibly intended to recover the regions that had fallen into Muslim hands, weakened the Byzantine Empire so that by 1204, the empire was little more than the city itself. A reduced Byzantium finally succumbed to the Ottoman Turks in 1453.

Constantinople was the Paris of its era. The city housed the palace, imperial workshops, a magnificent Christian church, and entertainment venues. Over the course of its long history, the Byzantines changed dress styles multiple times, reflecting cultural influences from both inside and outside the empire, as well as from its border areas. Initially, in the fourth century, residents wore the same general styles as the rest of the Roman Empire. This consisted of a tunic—knee length for men and children, and long for women—and an outer wrap called *chlamys*. Women also wore shawls and headscarves (Dawson 2006). The many tunics recovered while excavating Christian burials in Egypt reveal that their structure and decoration underwent continual change and innovation (Thomas 2016). The tunic "developed into a vehicle for decorative elements placed at the neck, shoulders, and sleeves, vertically along the torso and following the alignment of the legs (*clavi*), extending to the ankles, and along the lower edge" (Thomas 2016: 43). These decorative elements, in use since Roman times, were colorful squares (*segmentae*) or circular designs (*roundels*) in addition to vertical stripes. Patterning on tunics, along with hairstyles and jewelry, offered plenty of room for individual expression. The basic tunic had close-fitting sleeves. In the tenth century, an over-tunic with wide sleeves came into use; it was termed *dalmatic* in period sources (Dawson 2006).

The Constantinople of Justinian's time (527–565) supported an open social system in which it was possible to elevate one's social standing. Justinian himself was the son of a farmer. His wife, Theodora, had been an actress and a courtesan, the lowest class of society. Justinian had to change a law to marry her. Life in the capital offered excitement. The hippodrome and amphitheater were a vital part of urban life, with chariot racing the leading sport. Special factions, designated by color, organized the teams of charioteers. The Blues and Greens became the most powerful, functioning like a local militia. Procopius, a Byzantine historian of the sixth century, wrote a sarcastic, vitriolic volume titled *The Secret History* ca. 550 that describes infighting between the Blues and the Greens. The following extract shows that the Blues followed the same motivations as any twenty-first-century subculture by setting themselves apart from the dominant Roman culture and aiming for shock value in their appearance:

> First the rebels revolutionized the style of wearing their hair. For they had it cut differently from the rest of the Romans: not molesting the mustache or beard, which they allowed to keep on growing as long as it would, as the Persians do, but clipping the hair short on the front of the head down to the temples, and letting it hang down in great length and disorder in the back, as the Massageti do. This weird combination they called the Hun haircut.
>
> Next they decided to wear the purple stripe on their togas, and swaggered about in a dress indicating a rank above their station: for it was only by ill-gotten money they were able to buy this finery. And the sleeves of their tunics were cut tight about the wrists, while from there to the shoulders they were of an ineffable fullness; thus, whenever they moved their hands, as when applauding at the theater or encouraging a driver in the hippodrome, these immense sleeves fluttered conspicuously, displaying to the simple public what beautiful and well-developed physiques were these that required such large garments to cover them . . . . Their cloaks, trousers, and boots were also different: and these too were called the Hun style, which they imitated. (*Procopius of Caesarea*: Chapter 7)

This passage reinforces the fact that fashion in Byzantium was not monolithic across time and space. Styles were introduced in the capital and from regions far from the center. The fashion for turbans, for example, came to Constantinople from Cappadocia in the twelfth century (Ball 2005). Further, regional preferences developed. Citizens living in the western part of the empire during Late Antiquity wore the Roman-influenced tunic and chlamys, while those in the eastern section were more likely to wear the front-opening robes that derived from the coats of the nomadic herdsmen of the Central Asian steppes.

Trade allowed goods to move through the empire. People with the resources could pick and choose from among a range of products to fashion a unique look. For instance, in the mid-twelfth century, David Komnenos, governor of Thessaloniki (a city in modern Greece), was chastised by a bishop for wearing tight pants held up by a knot in the back, "new-fangled shoes," and a red Georgian hat (Ball 2005: 58).

Ball (2005) studied the dress of what she called the "borderlands" of Cappadocia (in modern Turkey) and Kastoria, then part of Bulgaria, but now part of modern Greece. She found that the Cappadocians wore a *kavadi*, translated as "kaftan" or "coat." Worn over a tunic, it opened in the front. The kavadi was sometimes decorated with *tiraz* (embroidered bands). It evolved from the robes of honor first worn during the Sassanian period in Persia (224–651), made of patterned textiles. Nearly a thousand miles away in twelfth-century Kastoria, wealthy women wore long draping sleeves with points that nearly touched the floor, like those popular in Western Europe. Kastoria was a trading hub occupied briefly by Normans, and it was also near an area settled by Armenians and Georgians who had fled their homelands. Thus, residents of Kastoria wore both European-influenced tunic styles with long pointed sleeves and Central Asian coat styles.

As the western parts of the empire were lost, Byzantium looked east for style innovation. The ceremonial robes worn in Central Asia gradually displaced tunics. The patterned silks that constituted a major commodity along the Silk Road were often destined to be sewn into Byzantine robes. These patterned silks were woven in Sassanian Persia and China. Later, Byzantium became famous for its own magnificent silks, the best of which were produced during its Golden Age in the tenth and eleventh centuries. It did not start out that way. When Justinian came to power in the mid-sixth century, silk fabrics were in great demand in Byzantium. Most fabrics were imported from the East, from the Sassanians, who exacted high tariffs. Byzantine weavers had mastered draw-loom weaving (first developed in China), but they needed silk yarns to weave their own cloth. Silk was sometimes not available during Byzantium's frequent conflicts with Persia. Justinian was looking to sidestep these problems.

According to Byzantine historians, the practice of sericulture was introduced to Byzantium during Justinian's reign. Procopius related a story about two monks who obtained silkworm eggs from eastern destinations along the Silk Road, hiding them in hollow bamboo canes for the trip back to Constantinople. Upon arrival, the eggs hatched and were fed mulberry leaves. "Thus began the art of making silk from that time on in the Roman Empire," observed Procopius. Scholars question the veracity of this story because sericulture already was known in Sassanid Persia in the third century and Syria in the fifth century. Regardless, sericulture and silk weaving picked up speed in Byzantium in the following centuries. Peasants cultivated mulberry trees, fed the leaves to the silkworms, collected the cocoons, and sold them to a cartel, which in turn sold them to Byzantium's weavers and dyers. Byzantine workshops produced a wide variety of silk textiles, and silk became an important sector of the economy by the tenth century (Laiou and Morrisson 2007).

Workshops in Constantinople, Syria, Egypt, Tyre, and Beirut produced patterned silk twills, often with roundel motifs. Fabrics were patterned with rows of paired animals, hunting scenes, or charioteers. Favorite animals included lions, eagles, and griffins enclosed in roundels. Purple was the imperial color; known for over a thousand years in the eastern Mediterranean, it was obtained from the glands of a shellfish, and large amounts were needed to dye even a small amount of silk. Embroidery was another technique employed to create patterned textiles, with gilt and silver metallic threads predominating.

The silk business was tightly controlled through a guild system, as spelled out in the *Book of the Prefect*, a historical source that describes five separate guilds. The emperor got the first pick of the purples from the imperial workshops, but often he needed more and purchased them from private workshops, who sold their wares in stalls and at fairs (Laiou and Morrisson 2007). Byzantine silks were prized in the Latin West, particularly Italy, but also in Russia and Bulgaria. They were sent as state gifts, and some have survived in European church treasuries where they wrapped remains of saints or relics associated with saints.

As the above discussion reveals, fabric was important, and this is an area where innovation occurred. Jewelry was another status indicator, and many fabulous pieces survive. Crowns, earrings, necklaces, rings, cuffs, and bracelets attest to the skills of Byzantine artisans. The portrait of a splendidly dressed family who donated funds for an eleventh-century church in Kastoria shows the wife wearing large basket-shaped earrings and no fewer than fourteen rings on her fingers (Ball 2005).

Both men and women concerned themselves with personal appearance in Byzantine times, especially the hair and face and personal aroma. They dyed their hair, applied ointments to prevent hair loss, removed unwanted facial hair, and used a variety of cosmetics to reduce wrinkles and accentuate features. Physicians concocted hair dyes, face creams, and perfumes for patients' use. Much of their knowledge came from Roman sources, particularly the work of Criton, who wrote a four-volume tome called *Cosmetics* in the second century, which every respectable home owned (Lascaratos et al. 2004).

Recipes for various ointments included such pleasant sounding ingredients as maidenhair (an herb) and anemone flowers as well as some not-so-nice substances needed to produce the desired chemical reactions, such as dried animal dung and urine, which also figured in recipes for finishing cloth. Hair dye was a popular product according to the physician Alexander of Tralles, who wrote in the sixth century: "Many great personalities desire to change the color of their hair not only to dark but also to red, blond, or white and sometimes oblige us to provide dyes" (Lascaratos et al. 2004: 399).

Byzantine empresses were expected to have a pleasing appearance to go along with their rich purple mantles and cloth-of-gold gowns. One empress became involved in making her own perfumes and ointments. Her name was Zoe, and she lived a fascinating life. She was "born to the purple" in 978, meaning she was a member of the imperial family. She was betrothed to the German king Otto III when she was 22, but he died while she was on her way to Italy for the wedding. She had to wait until age 50 until another appropriate marriage could be arranged. Her first husband died a few years into the marriage, purportedly with her help, and she went on to wed twice more, enduring many intrigues in the process.

According to the Byzantine chronicler Michael Psellus, Zoe was considered more beautiful than her sisters with golden hair, large eyes, and dark eyebrows. Even in her later years,

> there were few signs of age in her appearance: in fact, if you marked well the perfect harmony of her limbs, not knowing who she was, you would have said that here was a young woman, for no part of her skin was wrinkled, but all smooth and taut, and no furrows anywhere. (Psellus Book 6, chapter 6)

Psellus tells us that she had a cosmetics lab in the palace:

> The thing on which she spent all her energy, was the development of new species of perfumes, or the preparation of unguents. Some she would invent, others she improved. Her own private bedroom was no more impressive than the workshops in the market where the artisans and the blacksmiths toil, for all round the room were burning braziers, a host of them. Each of her servants had a particular task to perform: one was allotted the duty of bottling the perfumes, another of mixing them, while a third had some other task of the same kind. (Psellus Book 6, chapter 64)

Zoe obtained exotic plants from India and Egypt to make her concoctions. While scholar Carolyn Connor (2004) suggests that this production may have been used for church offerings, Zoe managed to retain a youthful aura into old age. Psellus, who had seen her himself, stated that "although she had already passed her seventieth year, there was not a wrinkle on her face. She was just as fresh as she had been in the prime of her beauty."

One image of Zoe survives—a mosaic in the church of Hagia Sophia in Istanbul—which depicts her as having a round face, prominent eyes and eyebrows, and an aquiline nose (Figure 6.1). Mosaic artists did their best to achieve realistic portrayals of their subjects and their clothing. Regal in her imperial attire, Zoe, who died in 1050 at the age of seventy-two, was the epitome of Byzantine beauty.

Figure 6.1 Empress Zoe (1028–50) holding the deed from the endowment of the church, Byzantine mosaic, eleventh century. Hagia Sophia. Erich Lessing / Art Resource, NY. The Byzantine Empress Zoe had her own personal cosmetics lab in the palace.

To form advantageous political alliances, Byzantine emperors sent their daughters as brides to foreign courts, as evidenced by Zoe's engagement to Otto III. For the same reason, foreign brides emigrated to the capital. Irene of Hungary (1088–1134) was one of those brides. Her mosaic at Hagia Sophia features a much different style than Zoe's, although it was created less than a century after Zoe's (see Figure 6.2). Most obvious is that she wore her thick red hair in braids, a hairstyle seen in the West on female figures on the portals of French cathedrals ca. 1200. The fact that she did not cover her hair, as Zoe did, represents a change in fashion. Another new feature is her long trailing sleeves, not the older closed sleeve worn by Zoe. Her sleeves bear decorative bands, not the pearl roundels seen on Zoe's gown. Irene's image is the first to show a Byzantine woman in the capital wearing such a dress (Ball 2005).

As the Byzantine Empire declined, Italian city-states advanced in the luxury market. Italian textiles borrowed motifs and techniques from Byzantium and points east, not to mention the workers themselves through forced removal

Figure 6.2 Empress Irene, a Byzantine mosaic in the interior of Hagia Sophia, Istanbul. 1118–22. Photograph and © by Anthony McAulay. 2011 / Shutterstock.com. The Hungarian princess Irene married into the Byzantine Komnenos family in 1104 and became an empress. Her Eastern European braids became fashionable in Constantinople.

from weaving centers in Greece. Venice became a wealthy city, and their traders commanded respect on the Silk Road. Marco Polo (1254–1324) was one of those traders. He accompanied his father and uncle on a return trip to China and visited the court of the Yuan dynasty emperor Kublai Khan. Marco entered his service for seventeen years. After returning to Europe, he dictated a romanticized version of his travels while in a Genoese prison titled *The Travels of Marco Polo*. His book received wide readership and reportedly kindled European interest in exploring sea routes to east Asia (Tortora and Marcketti 2015).

Ottoman style

The growing power of the Ottoman Turks, who had settled in Anatolia, finally toppled what was left of the Byzantine Empire in 1453. Mehmed II, the Conqueror, set out to reshape the crumbling city. Christian Constantinople became Muslim

Istanbul. The great Byzantine church built by Emperor Justinian in the sixth century, Hagia Sophia, was converted to a mosque. The mosaic portraits of Zoe and Irene were plastered over, not to be rediscovered until the mid-nineteenth century. Mehmed II constructed the Grand Bazaar, a covered shopping area, in the merchant quarter; he built Topkapi Saray, the sultan's palace, on a promontory overlooking the Bosporus. Here are preserved the robes of all of the Ottoman sultans, from the rule of Mehmed II (1451–81) to that of the last sultan, Mehmad Reşad (1909–18) (Tezcan 2012). Kaftans and other clothing belonging to the sultans, sultanas, and their children were wrapped and labeled with the wearer's name. The approximately 1,550 artifacts in the Topkapi Palace have been regularly inventoried, cleaned, and rehoused over time, even after the palace was no longer the residence of the sultans (Tezcan 2000).

The over 500 kaftans in this collection show little change in structure from century to century. Worn over an inner shirt and a type of trousers called *salwar* or *salvar*, they demonstrate remarkable adherence to tradition. Yet, despite the constancy of form, it is the fabrics that demonstrate changing tastes expressive of fashion.

The Turks inherited Byzantium's textile workshops, but they immediately shifted production to appeal to Ottoman tastes. In the late fifteenth century, the workshops under Mehmed II and his immediate successors initially utilized designs long established through Silk Road trade, such as Chinese-inspired elements, arabesques, and geometric patterns. An Istanbul-based artist named Baba Nakkaş was the chief practitioner of this so-called international style (Denny and Krody 2012: 17). Popular in the fifteenth century were crescent and star patterns as well as çintemani designs, which consisted of two wavy lines and three balls. The latter design was possibly acquired from contact with Timurid Persia (1370–1507) (Tezcan 2000).

When Süleyman I (1520–66) came to power, the Ottoman Empire entered a classical phase during which it enjoyed economic, political, and military dominance. This period saw fast-paced stylistic innovations in court workshops, which culminated in a distinct Ottoman style. First, a court designer who had emigrated from Tabriz, named Shah Kulu, created the *saz* style of undulating leaves, rosettes, lotuses, and mythical Chinese animals. Then rapid growth saw the state workshops divided into two branches, one populated by Anatolian designers, the other by non-Anatolian (mostly Persian) designers. Out of the Anatolian workshops emerged a talented young man named Kara Memi. He eventually headed all state workshops. He is credited with creating a highly original style based on floral designs around 1550 (Denny and Krody 2012). Its vocabulary consisted of tulips, carnations, hyacinths, rosebuds, and honeysuckle. Variations on this floral style soon appeared in ceramics and bookbinding as well as textiles. The floral style became enormously popular: supply could not keep up with demand. Production spread to weaving and embroidery workshops in other urban centers. From these outlying workshops, its diffusion continued to small towns and villages throughout the Ottoman Empire and beyond, as far away as Hungary, Russia, Egypt, and Persia, where it was incorporated into clothing and household textiles. It is an example of a style that moved horizontally across higher status consumers and vertically through layers of social strata (Denny and Krody 2012).

Figure 6.3 is a section from a late-sixteenth-century garment, probably produced in Istanbul. The characteristic Ottoman layout features medallions in a lattice of ogives on a dark red ground. The medallions are filled with carnations, rosebuds, and tulips, making it a rare early survival of this uniquely Ottoman style.

The sultans' kaftans illustrate shifting tastes in textiles. In addition to Ottoman fabrics, kaftans were made of velvets from Venice and Genoa as well as silks from Persia and China. Style influence moved in both directions: Venetians wore

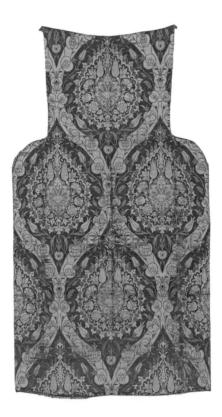

Figure 6.3 Fragment of a floral *serenk* from a robe, probably Istanbul, late sixteenth century. The Textile Museum, Washington, D.C., 1.57. Acquired by George Hewett Myers in 1951. The floral style seen in this fragment appeared in the Ottoman court in the early sixteenth century, and can be attributed to a single artist. It eventually became popular throughout the Ottoman Empire.

garments made from Turkish velvets as evidenced in Renaissance portraits (Denny and Krody 2012).

Ottoman style continued to evolve in subsequent centuries. Suraiya Faroqhi (2004) argued that the principle of fashion change was present in Ottoman dress as did Charlotte Jirousek (2004). During the eighteenth century, distinctions blurred between servants and their masters and mistresses because of the greater availability and variety of cloth and the lively secondhand clothes market. By the nineteenth century, French and English merchants reported color preferences and "that traders had to be on the alert in order to make timely responses to changes in demand" (Faroqhi 2004: 30).

Westerners found Turkish dress fascinating. Nicolas de Nicolay traveled there in the sixteenth century and included illustrations of Turkish men and women in his costume book *Navigations* (Figure 4.1). Subsequent authors used his images to illustrate their own costume books. In the eighteenth century, Lady Mary Wortley Montagu (1689–1762), the wife of the British ambassador to Turkey, wrote letters home describing her experiences at the Ottoman court. While in Istanbul, she wore Turkish dress. When she returned home in 1719, she sat for several portraits wearing Turkish dress. This inspired European and American artists to paint their sitters in Turkish dress, known as *turquerie* (Peck 2013).

Over the course of the nineteenth century, Turks gradually adopted Western dress. The Ottoman Empire dissolved in 1918 after being defeated in the First World War, and the modern Republic of Turkey emerged in 1923. Its first president, Mustafa Kemal Atatürk, undertook modernization efforts including sumptuary laws banning religious-based clothing such as turbans, hats, and veils. Western hats for men replaced the fez, which was banned in 1925. This short history of Ottoman dress and textiles illustrates how the fashion can be in the fabric.

The Ottomans and the Persians: A shared heritage

The Ottomans shared a common heritage with other peoples who settled in the Middle East, notably in Persia. That heritage originated on the Central Asian steppes with the Seljuqs, one of the nomadic Turkic tribes. They moved west in the eleventh century in search of better pasturelands, eventually reaching Anatolia. As horse riders, their clothing consisted of layers that fitted the body closely, unlike the draped garments of the ancient Mediterranean world or the loose robes of China. Both men and women wore coats over shirts and trousers. The coats fitted closely to the torso and flared at the hip. Some extant examples show coats that fastened on the right in the Tatar style (*aqbiya tatariyya*) while others buttoned on the left (*aqbiya turkiyya*) (Canby et al. 2016).

The Seljuqs were a very cultured society of nomads, who lived in tents next to their cities. Their society revolved around hunting, but they believed in pomp and circumstance, feasting, music, and dancing. Clothing and jewelry mattered, and so did having a pleasant aroma. Thus, public baths and attendant rituals had a prominent place in Seljuq settlements. Instruction manuals, such as one titled *Mirrors for Princes*, advised sultans and their retinue how to dress. Another manual called *Book of Elegance and the Elegant* devoted substantial attention to attire. It was mainly through gold jewelry and silk garments that a sultan displayed his position. Household slaves dressed to match their master's status with gold bracelets and anklets.

The few surviving garments reveal motifs on textiles derived from multiple production sites—Spain, Italy, China, and eastern Islamic sources—testifying to the dynamic trade patterns during this time period. The coats are made from elaborately patterned silks with roundel motifs similar to those found elsewhere in the areas where they traded: trees, hunters, birds, harpies, and double-headed eagles. Other artifacts show dress habits too. Bowls depicting musical scenes show women with earrings, diadems, tattooed hands, and patterned robes (Canby et al. 2016).

Originally believers of animism, the Seljuqs absorbed Islam before migrating to Persia, present-day Iran and Iraq. Islam had arisen in the seventh century in Saudi Arabia, and with it came the proscription in the Quran for women to cover their hair. Thus, the veil that was already in wide use became affiliated with Muslim women. Men adopted the turban, again already in use in the Middle East, to signify their religious affiliation.

Coats are Central Asia's gift to the contemporary wardrobe. Judging from archaeological discoveries in the Tarim Basin, the sleeved coat is much earlier than the Seljuqs. A rare coat was recovered in Xinjiang at Pichan that is dated to the fifth to the second century BCE (Mair 2010). The coat, of cream-colored wool, has a center front opening, a stand-up collar and narrow sleeves. The body silhouette differs from the coats of Yingpin Man and others from the region dated to the second to the eleventh centuries with silhouettes of close-fitting waists. The rare wool coat is straight in the body except for two triangles of cloth inserted under each arm in the side seam. The transformation of the cut of the coat from loose to more fitted as documented in the Xinjiang finds shows that the shape of men's dress in ancient Central Asia changed over time, while reflecting shifts in taste for textiles from plain cloth to brocade and other pattern weaving (Mair 2010).

Safavid Persian style

Safavid Persian decorative arts have received scholarly attention from textile historians but not from fashion historians. In textbooks, Persia and the cultures that preceded it are mentioned in early chapters as wearers of sleeved coats and trousers during ancient times. While we know now that trousers originated on the Eurasian steppes by 1300 BCE to accommodate horse riding, in the textbooks the first ones presented are on the guards at Persepolis (518–460 BCE). Fast forward to the great Safavid Empire (1501–1722 CE) and we see the same technical capabilities as the Byzantines and Ottomans for textile production. As noted above, Persian textiles were considered more highly developed than Ottoman textiles in the sixteenth century, and they served as a design source for other production centers.

Miniature painting, practised at court workshops in Persia as well as Ottoman Turkey and Mughal India, provides one of the best sources for the study of Safavid dress. Not as much material culture is available as for the Ottoman Empire. The Persian capital moved several times—from Tabriz to Isfahan to Shiraz to Tehran—and as a consequence not much has survived. Manuscript illumination began in the thirteenth century, developing into various schools by the fifteenth century, with the objective of illustrating literature (Scarce 1987).

These miniatures show men and women dressed in garments made of lavish textiles. Men wore a knee-length belted tunic over loose leggings or trousers tucked into calf-length boots. This ensemble was worn over a wide area ranging from Syria to Central Asia and northern India. Indoors, women wore a long belted robe over trousers. The robe had long tight sleeves embellished with contrasting borders. They wore their hair in long thick braids with wisps pulled forward to frame the face. Ornaments often embellished the hair; filmy veils appear, ready to disguise if needed. Makeup accentuated arched eyebrows, and black beauty spots embellished the face and neck (Scarce 1987). Small heart-shaped red lips were admired, as evidenced in Persian poetry. When outdoors, women wore a white body-encompassing veil called a *chadar* with a separate face veil of horsehair (*picheh*).

Enjoyment of miniature paintings picked up in the sixteenth century, and they reveal changes in women's fashion. Necklines changed to a V-shape. Robes became longer and showed numerous variations. The upper-class woman pictured in Figure 6.4 wears a fine gauzy yellow underdress with tight-fitting sleeves. It shows at the neck and arms as well as through the slits in the skirt of her overdress. The overdress is light purple brocaded with figures of hunters chasing rabbits amid vegetation. It is tightly fitted at the waist and belted with a cord. The skirt slits are fastened with brooches. The overdress sports an unusual square-shaped neck. Many others at this time have a deep V neckline. The closures are rows of flat silk braid joined with a button and loop. The overdress sleeves are wide, reaching the elbow, and are held with the same brooches as the skirt. Her hair is gathered in a topknot and bound with a light veil. Some hair is brought forward with side curls. A shawl or veil flutters from her shoulders. Around her neck she wears what looks like four necklaces, possibly three of pearls, which were highly valued in Persia. She wears slippers with pointed toes instead of boots. All of this attention to the details in this outfit signifies a love of fashion.

The Safavid Empire included the Georgian homeland, but the Georgian and Persian ethnicities remained distinct. Today, Georgia borders the Black Sea in the west, the Russian Federation in the north, and Turkey, Armenia, and Azerbaijan in the south. It was through Turkey, Armenia, and Azerbaijan that Georgia was contiguous with the Persian Safavid Empire. Guests and travelers came to Isfahan, the centrally located Safavid seat of power, from Europe and Asia. Armenian and Georgian elites lived in Isfahan among Persian high society. The cosmopolitan and refined social environment included art collecting, such as painted manuscripts and miniatures (Figure 6.4), which were examined intimately, and in the late seventeenth century a taste developed for large-scale

Figure 6.4 "Young woman giving water to her dog," late sixteenth century. Safavid Persia, gouache miniature, Shah Abbas School. Free Library of Philadelphia. Scala / Art Resource, NY. The elite Safavid woman wears a gauzy underdress and an overdress of fine brocade depicting hunters pursuing rabbits. The overgown's unusual square neckline implies fashion innovation. Jeweled brooches hold the skirt of the overgown and sleeves in place.

murals displayed in high-ceilinged galleries within palaces and elite homes. Michael Chagnon (2013) investigated five surviving works and among them is the opulently dressed Georgian woman in Figure 6.5.

The Georgian woman presented in the oil-on-canvas painting, a medium that arrived from Europe, wore a robe with a tightly fitted bodice and flared skirt over trousers. A mauve-colored shirt, revealed at the neck, is fastened with a golden

Figure 6.5 "Young Woman in Georgian Costume," second half of the seventeenth century / early eighteenth century. Iran. Oil on canvas. New York City. Private Collection. The nearly life-size image represents the dress of a Georgian woman in Safavid Persia. Her attire incorporates fine Safavid silk brocade textiles into the Georgian fashion of flared coat and trousers.

button. Applied across the bodice lay three horizontal frogged braid fastenings. Each braid included a center front button closing the bodice. The robe's sumptuous scarlet textile was emblazoned with floral sprays in tones of dark olive and orange, and silver metallic thread. The design of the sinuously arranged floral sprays reflected Persian influence while the flared shape of the robe's skirt echoed the silhouette of Central Asian coats. A floral border edged the skirt center front and hem edges, and the sleeve hems. Her trousers of a deep plum-colored cloth ended with cuffs of a floral and geometric striped textile. Wrapped around her hips is a sash woven with floral designs in the border and along the edges. Her hat with a wide upturned black brim had a pointed crown covered by a floral textile. Gold earrings dangled from her ear lobes. Leather high-heeled mule-style shoes covered her feet. Her ensemble broadcast a hybrid fashion specific to Persia's Georgian community.

The nearly life-sized paintings portrayed human types rather than individual people and Figure 6.5 was not a portrait but a symbol of Georgian ethnicity. The murals depicted the "social communities who inhabited Isfahan" yet may have been based upon artistic models from etchings (Chagnon 2013: 258). They represented one "dialect" of "a broader visual language developed for the description of cross-cultural encounters throughout the Early Modern world" (Chagnon 2013: 263). The visual language of depicting human diversity was rooted "in an Enlightenment-era (pseudo-)scientific curiosity about racial development and difference" (Chagnon 2013: 263). The Spanish culture's casta paintings and Europe's sixteenth-century costume books also engender this curiosity and broad visual language. European visitors perceived the murals as depictions of the costume of diverse cultures, while members of the Persian empire who admired them as "pleasing" and "wondrous" must also to some degree have understood the murals as signals of the power of the empire (Chagnon 2013: 258).

Like the Ottomans, the Persians influenced Western dress when in 1666 the English king Charles II adopted the Persian vest and coat, which historians regard as the forerunner of the modern three-piece suit. Samuel Pepys recorded the event in his diary, noting its subsequent rapid adoption by the English elite. The Safavid dynasty came to an end in 1796, followed by the Qajar dynasty. It fell in 1925, ushering in the modern Pahlavi era which itself came to an end in 1979 with the Iranian Revolution.

Kebaya fashions in Java

By the later fifteenth century, elite Javanese women had adopted a loosely fitted jacket called a *kebaya* that was worn with a *kemben*, a chest-wrapping cloth, and a wrapped skirt, which could be a tubular sarong or a *kain panjang*, meaning a "long cloth" (Gittinger 1979). The word "kebaya" is derived from the Persian or

Arabic languages with variants *cabie* and *cabbay* (OED 1989 s.v. kebaya). This case study explores the strands of trade and influence that produced the kebaya as worn in Java and elsewhere in the Malay Archipelago. Figure 6.6 shows a Javanese woman in the early twentieth century wearing a kebaya sarong ensemble.

Java is the capital island of Indonesia, a nation of thousands of islands, whose government formed in the mid-twentieth century based on the boundaries of the colonial Dutch domination that lasted from the seventeenth to the twentieth century (with brief interregna). As a crossroads between the Indian and Pacific Oceans, and proximate to the southeast coasts of Asia, Indonesia's culture reflects many influences prior to the arrival of Portuguese ships in 1512. When the Portuguese tried to assume control of the spice trade in Indonesia, some women on Java already wore a kebaya on their upper body. In 1602, the VOC (the Dutch East India Company) gained control of the islands, allowing the Muslim sultanates to continue, subject to the Dutch trading company's overview.

How the kebaya came into use in Java remains unclear since several cultures were potential contributors to the transfer of the style to the island. Indonesians traded with societies in India and China by the middle of the first millennium, and perhaps much earlier given the proximity to their coasts. Some trade records survive from the late first millennium. A document written in stone and dated to 929 limited the amount that was imported without a levy. The text indicated active trade in textiles and clothing: "Those who carry their trade *pikul* (shoulder pole)—such as vendors of clothing . . . transporters of cotton (*kapas*) . . . [they shall be allowed up to] 5 *bantal*-weight per person" (Christie 1998: 370–71). Since the garments are not described, whether the clothing was cloth or sleeved jackets cannot be known. Chinese and Indians wore sleeved garments by this time, as did all of Eurasia. Such garments may have been imported, but surviving art works do not show Javanese men or women wearing them.

From shores farther to the west, Arab and Persian trade ships reached Java by the mid-seventh century (Donkin 2003). They brought a new faith—Islam—to Java, as did Muslim Chinese merchants who converted to the religion. The religion was firmly established in Java in the fifteenth century. Perhaps the kebaya served to provide body coverage to court women and other elites in reaction to the Islamic strictures for covering the body; apparently for this reason the Majahapit court (1293–1500) was the first to formally adopt the kebaya (Chavalit and Phromsuthirak 2000). When Zheng He visited the Majahapit kingdom in 1413, Ma Huang served as the voyage recorder. He described the court in detail noting that the men were bare chested and that the women wore a cloth wrapped around their chest and a wrapped skirt. All other garments worn by ethnic locals used uncut lengths of cloth wrapped, draped, or tied on the body (Ma [1433] 1970).

Ma Huang further noted that the people inhabiting the island included locals, Chinese and Arab merchants (Ma [1433] 1970). Arabs dressed in sleeved robes and, as noted previously in *The Periplus*, trade in sleeved garments was in

Figure 6.6 Portrait of a woman in sarong and kebaya with child. Dr. W. G. N. van der Sleen (Fotograaf/photographer). 1929. By permission of the Collection Nationaal Museum van Wereldculturen. Coll. no. TM-10027458. Reproduced by permission. The *kebaya* for women has roots in sleeved garments introduced through Chinese and Arabian traders before 1512. This jacket style continues today in fashionable women's dress in the Malay Archipelago.

place along the Arabian coast for centuries. Sleeved garments may have been exported to Java whether from China, India, or Arabian states. Alternatively, sleeved garments may have been sewn locally within the respective Arab and Chinese communities where they were worn.

Wearing the kebaya was established by the arrival of the Dutch; however, the style was not widespread among the native population. Many women continued to wear only a sarong or kain panjang, others added a kemben when that fashion spread beyond the court elites. Most of the female population also wore a *slendang*, or shoulder cloth, used for carrying items. Whether by emulation of the elites or by the influence of Islamic and Christian moral codes or both, by the late eighteenth century, the kebaya was widely adopted and became a site of fashion variation.

Rens Heringa (1997) called the kebaya and sarong combination a mestizo style as worn in the Pasisir, North Coast of Java in the nineteenth century. The North Coast was the location of entrepreneurial innovation in the batik industry for kain panjang (further discussed in Chapter 7). However, the multiple strands of influence present suggests that the concept of hybridity was deeply embedded in fashion as a whole and this played a part in the eventual role of the kebaya through the colonial era and into modern styling. In the nineteenth century the various ethnicities and strata had unique style concepts for their kebayas. The Javanese court and elites preferred velvet or patterned silks. Other Javanese wore sateen and various cotton cloths. In the Paranakan Chinese community, women learned embroidery, which they used to embellish their kebayas (Heringa 1997). Among the *Indisch*, or Dutch, kebayas were made of linen imported from Belgium with fine lace or other needlework trims.

Thin, delicate fabrics and lace or embroidered trims gained in fashionability. The Javanese woman in Figure 6.6 wore a typical kebaya and sarong fashion of the early twentieth century. Three brooches pinned the front of her kebaya closed, as had been typical in the court. The front edge of the sheer jacket and the hem and sleeve cuffs were embellished with embroidered trim to provide a fashion statement. In the twenty-first century, designers of kebaya sarong elaborate on the themes of delicate textiles and needlework as they continue on the long path of kebaya fashions.

This chapter surveyed evidence across nearly three millennia indicating that the fashion impulse is part of human nature. Changing tastes took place in jewelry, cosmetics, and grooming. Innovations occurred in textile production and garment styles. Initially adopted by elites, new fashions diffused throughout the social strata. It was through trade and cross-cultural exchange that new ideas about dress and appearance spread across the Eastern Hemisphere.

7

FASHION SYSTEMS IN EAST, SOUTH, AND SOUTHEAST ASIA

In China with these women, the hair is done once or twice a week. With a view to avoid injuring the elaborate coiffure during sleep, the lady supports the nape of her neck upon a pillar of earthenware or wood, high enough to protect the design from being damaged. In our land this device would imply a sacrifice of comfort, and here and there a case of strangulation would ensue; but no very grave objections could be raised to the novel chignon and its midnight scaffolding, when the interests of fashion are at stake.

JOHN THOMSON

John Thomson (1837–1921), a Scottish photojournalist, wrote these words after observing three middle-class women in Swatow Province, China (John Thomson quoted in Warner 1977: 72). Thomson traveled in China from 1868 to 1872, photographing the sites and the people, the first Westerner to do so. His publication, *Illustrations of China and Its People* (1873–74), provides an invaluable record of Chinese dress as embodied practice among all classes and across ethnic groups. His commentary shows attention to details of both male and female dress in the late Qing dynasty (1644–1911). He photographed and observed elaborate coiffures of middle-class women, distinctions in dress between the two dominant ethnic groups (Han and Manchu), and the rapid adoption of new materials. The complexity and variety of women's coiffures interested him greatly, and he noted in the above quote the lengths to which women went to preserve their hairdos for up to a week by sleeping with their necks supported on rigid headrests made from ceramic or other hard materials. Is this not fashion?

Two oft-quoted authors in the field of fashion studies, Fernand Braudel and Gilles Lipovetsky, would say no. Braudel, whose position on fashion as a phenomenon exclusive to the West was discussed earlier, quoted Sir George Staunton to support his claim that Chinese dress reflected a changeless society:

> "Dress is seldom altered in China from fancy of fashion," wrote a traveler in 1793. "Whatever is thought suitable to the condition of the wearer, or to the season of the year continues generally, under similar circumstances, to be the same. Even among the ladies, there is little variety in their dresses, except, perhaps, in the disposition of the flowers or other ornaments of the head." (Braudel 1981: 312)

For Braudel, fashion was about changing silhouettes and tailoring (e.g., cutting cloth and fitting it to the body). Thus, he viewed Chinese clothes as changeless. He also named Japan, India, Turkey, and Algeria as examples of countries where costume "scarcely changed over the centuries" (Braudel 1981: 312). Braudel's viewpoint has received critique for being Eurocentric (Finnane 2008: 7–9; Goody 2006: 180–211, 263–66; Lemire 2010: 11).

Lipovetsky (1994) also would say no to Chinese dress involving a fashion system for an additional reason beyond the fact that China is in the East, for he placed the origin of fashion squarely in the West's Industrial Revolution. He associated fashion with the increased pace of change in dress that occurred due to higher incomes and growth in product options. Asia and the rest of the world did not experience the same consumer-driven changes as the West and thus did not have fashion, according to Lipovetsky.

Jane Schneider described the operation of fashion in courtly societies (in contrast to capitalistic societies) in the *Handbook of Material Culture* (2006). She stated that "no cloth or clothing tradition was ever static," despite the propensity of museums and connoisseurs to collect and display exquisite textiles and dress as exemplars of a culture (Schneider 2006: 205). In courtly societies, artisan workshops attached to courts produced cloth from precious raw materials in techniques that required knowledge and skill. Artisans continually adapted to the world around them by incorporating new materials and techniques, as well as competing with other artisans. Thus, they kept up with changing tastes. Clothing constructed from artisan-made fabric was accorded high status and restricted to use by elites, culminating in regulations, which societies in Asia and South America enacted just as those in Europe and colonial America did. Schneider states that "the elitism of courtly societies generated the fundamental elements of fashion," citing the theories of Veblen, Simmel, and Bourdieu (207). Their theories, as described in chapters 3 and 4, attempt to explain the differentiation and emulation of social class evident in fashion systems. Schneider's implication is that this emulation of the elite occurs in courtly societies as well as capitalistic societies.

By the time John Thomson photographed China and its people, styles and behaviors that had originated in the courts among the elite, as well as those initiated by entertainers or officials, had trickled down to commoners. For example, the practice of foot binding, introduced by dancers at court during the Tang dynasty (618–907 CE), had spread to all Han Chinese women by the nineteenth century (Major 2005: 263).

In this chapter, we seek to illustrate fashion systems at work in various Asian societies. We lay out examples of behavior in dress and adornment that can be considered characteristic of a fashion system in Asian cultures where new styles emanated from rulers' courts and from outside influences. Examples are drawn from the dress histories of China, Korea, Japan, India, and Indonesia. We especially focus on China, where scholars have begun interpreting that country's dress history in light of fashion. In all these cultures, change occurred in fabrics, embellishments and trims, accessories, cosmetics, and hairdressing. Additionally, new garment styles first worn at court by royals and by stylish entertainers demonstrated fashion leadership.

Fashion in China's Tang and Qing dynasties

The Tang, one of the great dynasties in China's history, produced paintings and poetry that continue to receive acclaim today. Importantly, advances in woodblock printing allowed writing, notably religious texts and poetry, to reach wider audiences than previously had access. During its long stable periods, the empire benefited from the transcontinental commerce along the Silk Road. Some travelers from outside Asia, as noted by Braudel in the quote above, perceived Chinese dress as unchanging and therefore not engaged in a fashion process; however, Christine Tsui (2016) argued to the contrary. In her etymological study of fashion in Chinese culture, Tsui demonstrated that fashion is autochthonous to Chinese culture and that it was present in the first millennium in the Tang.

Tsui explained that the concept of fashion appeared in a work by Tang poet Bai Juyi that included the word "*Shishizhuang*" (2016: 52). Among other meanings, the character "zhuang" refers to "clothing" and "makeup" (53). Key to the argument is that the meanings of the ancient character "shi" include "fit for the time" (53). Use of the descriptive phrase "fit for the time" in regard to appearance shows cultural awareness in ancient China of fashionability; that is to say, that as time passes a style may move from "fit" to "unfit" for a particular time. Kyo Cho also discussed the poem, translating "*Shishi zhuang*" as "Contemporary

Makeup" (2012: 127). Although written in the ninth century, the poem includes a description of a woman's eighth-century makeup:

> Out from the city it spread in all four directions.
> Contemporary fashion has no sense of far or near:
> No rouge on the lips, no powder on the face,
> Black oil on the lips so lips resemble dirt,
> The two eyebrows slant to make the character for "eight".
> Fair or ugly, black or white, all lose original form,
> Once makeup is done, everyone looks as if with sad sobs.
>
> (Juyi in Cho 2012: 127)

Juyi describes the makeup of dark lips and painted eyebrows slanting upward from the outer forehead to the top center, like the Chinese character for eight: 八. He artfully portrays a makeup style named "weeping makeup" or "tears makeup" (Mei 2004: 37). The poet conveys the diffusion of the fashion from the city outward revealing awareness of fashion adoption moving from urban locales to more rural ones. Juyi's description of the occurrence of a diffusion process further confirms Tsui's argument that shishizhuang reveals that the Chinese have long recognized the concept of fashion in their culture.

Chinese makeup fashions are traced using archaeological evidence, surviving art works, prose, poetry, and written records. For information on materials used in makeup, Cho (2012) refers to the first comprehensive text of Chinese medicine, the *Compendium of Materia Medica* (aka *Bencao gangmu*) written by Li Shizen in the Ming dynasty. The text reports historical and contemporary practices of the sixteenth century. Despite Juyi's poem stating "no powder on the face," the record showed that a smooth white face served as the base of many ancient Chinese makeup styles. To whiten the face, Tang women used powder made of pulverized ceruse, a lead oxide, and the effect was called "lead flower" (Benn 2005: 107). Worth noting is that Europeans also used ceruse in later centuries for whitening cosmetics, and like the Chinese they were unknowing of lead's deleterious effects.

The practice of beauty held importance for Tang court women. Gods watched over cosmetics fashions. One watched over ointments and hair creams, another eyebrow paints, another facial powders, and one lip glosses (Benn 2005). Round mirrors of highly polished bronze and tools crafted from ivory, jade, or wood allowed perfect application of the various compounds, unguents, and paints. A wooden chest with drawers stored beauty supplies.

Tang women used facial masks to improve the complexion. The important ingredients might be as delightful sounding as peach tree blossoms or as pungent as raw chicken eggs mixed with ale and steeped for twenty-eight days, as one recipe specified. Benn (2005) reported a skin-smoothing salve recipe calling for ale scented with cloves and nutmeg, aged for one to three days and then boiled in a copper pot with sesame oil and lard.

In addition to often requiring a whitened face, a Tang woman's maquillage included additional enhancements. Lips, eyebrows, cheeks, temples, and foreheads received cosmetic additions or changes depending on the makeup fashion "fit for the time." Rouge of powdered vermillion, which the provinces of Hunan, Guizhou, and Sichuan provided, was brushed on cheeks adding red to the face. Beauty marks in red, black, or yellow were painted on, or adhered to, the forehead and cheeks. Stylized shapes of the beauty marks reflected nature, inspired by insects, flowers, leaves, and birds. Cho (2012) explained that although Chinese beauty marks originated in the second century, they became fashionable again in the early eighth century in the Tang court.

Natural eyebrows were plucked so that no hairs marred the fashion eyebrow. The fashion brows often were dramatically different from the natural brow in placement and angle, and were painted onto the forehead using a green-blue, indigo, or blue-black tincture. Mei lists eyebrow styles named "drooping pearl" and "dark fog" (2004: 35). A long and slender eyebrow style was described as a willow branch (Cho 2012: 134). Figure 7.1 illustrates an eighth-century lady of the palace wearing makeup with an eyebrow shape reminiscent of a leaf, set at about a forty-five-degree angle from the eyes, and that appears to be approximately one and a half centimeters at the widest point; her cosmetic brows are starkly different from natural brows. On her forehead between her eyebrows she wears a yellow dot beauty mark.

Women's mouths created for current makeup fashions showed similar dramatic differences from the natural mouth. The white powder base of the makeup worn by the lady of the palace (Figure 7.1) has suppressed the outline of her natural lips, thus allowing a new painted mouth shape to dominate. Brilliant vermillion lip color with animal fat as the base was painted on the lips in designs inspired by flowers; a single petal or an entire flower shape could be represented in the lips' new design. According to Benn, black lip gloss, noted by Juyi, achieved popularity among high-status women in the early ninth century (2005: 108). Lip fashions illustrated in the graphic in Figure 7.2 include three shapes popular in the Tang, and a range of styles from the third century BCE during the Han (206 BCE–220 CE) to the twentieth century at the end of the Qing (1844–1911 CE). The eighteenth-century Qing dynasty portrait of the First Imperial Concubine (Figure 7.3) shows a partially eclipsed upper lip and a full lower lip as illustrated at the bottom of Figure 7.2. Approximately 200 years later, the lips of the woman feeding silkworms (Figure 7.4) resemble the shape of a cypripedium orchid as illustrated in Figure 7.2 at the top of the three Qing lip designs (Lillethun et al. 2012). The woman was a laborer, not a figure at court, yet she followed fashion.

Figure 7.1 Detail from "Ladies of the Palace." Color woodcut on silk, ca. 1980. Copy of painting by Zhen Fang (ca. 720–800 CE). bpk, Berlin / Museum fuer Ostasiatische Kunst, Staatliche Museen zu Berlin, Germany. Peter Garbe / Art Resource, NY. This first millennium image of a lady with flowers and jewels in her hair shows a finely composed maquillage including a small lip style emphasizing a four-petal shape in the central lip area and an eyebrow style evocative of insect wings.

Tang court women, who were allotted funds specifically for their cosmetic products, set makeup trends for the larger culture. The dynamic variations in makeup styles clearly attest that fashion has been a long-established component of Chinese culture. Schneider pointed out that cloth and clothing were never static. Extending that statement to incorporate Eicher's definition of dress, which includes cosmetics, implies that makeup also was never static. Interesting to contemplate is the fact that makeup styles could be changed daily, while clothing

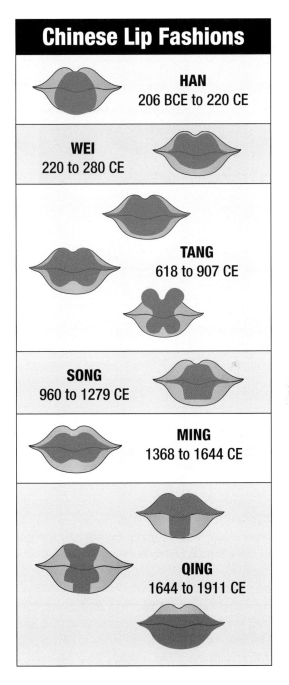

Figure 7.2 Chinese Lip Fashions. Illustration by Fafar Bayat. In China, makeup was used to mask the natural lip and emphasize a variety of fashionable shapes over time.

Figure 7.3 Detail from "Portrait of the First Imperial Concubine," China, reign of Qianlong (r. 1736–96). Qing dynasty. Gouache, 55.2 x 41.2 cm. Inv. MG26588. Musée des Arts Asiatique-Guimet, Paris, France. Réunion des Musées Nationaux / Art Resource, NY. The lip design in this portrait straightened and lowered the top of the upper lip from the natural lip line.

styles would not be so fleeting. Thus, cosmetics are an especially ripe vehicle for fashion.

While some aspects of Chinese dress and appearance changed over time, other features remained constant. One characteristic that had been a mainstay in China was the preference for silk. Silk has a long history in China dating back to the third millennium BCE (Major 2005). Sericulture and production of silk fabrics became a major industry supplying not only Chinese emperors and court officials with cloth, but also merchants with a valuable commodity to trade with cultures as far away as the Roman Empire (as discussed in Chapter 6). A second characteristic is an obsession with hair and headgear. Both men and women utilized hairstyles and headcoverings to express conformity (gender, class, ethnicity) and individuality (fashion, creativity). A third enduring feature of Chinese dress is the long-term use of loose robes made up of lengths of woven cloth. The cloth strips were assembled straight from the loom, which produced relatively narrow fabrics. Each robe consisted of two long panels seamed at center back, brought over the shoulders, and left open in the front. Rectangular sleeves were added at the shoulder. Borders placed at the front edges, sleeves and hems offered opportunity for embellishment. Loose robes had been worn

Figure 7.4 Detail from "Women feeding silkworms on mulberry leaves." Anonymous. Nineteenth century. Chinese tempura painting on rice paper. Ann Ronan Picture Library London, Great Britain. HIP / Art Resource, NY. The lower lip of this silk laborer is colored red only in the center.

by the Chinese since the Han Dynasty (206 BCE–220 CE). The elite donned silk robes while commoners wore shorter robes made of hemp. These robes with their loose sleeves signified sedentary "civilized" peoples who practised agriculture, not the nomadic horse riders of the Eurasian steppes who wore fitted garments evolved from skins that overlapped in the front (Vollmer 1977). China's sartorial history reveals tensions between the clothing practices of the Han and the nomadic groups that sometimes ruled China.

As noted above, the Tang dynasty was highly cultured. The capital city of Xi-an "supported a true fashion system, comparable to that of the modern West" with new modes seen at court and adopted through emulation, such as the so-called fairy dresses which had extended sleeves and wing-like appendages at the shoulders (Major 2005: 262). The Tang were receptive to cross-cultural influences such as the roundel patterns produced by weavers in Graeco-Roman Egypt, Persia and other Western locales, an innovation that reached China via the Silk Road. In the ninth century, advances in silk weaving, patterning, and dyeing as well as fluctuating tastes in width and length of sleeves and skirts inspired rapid changes in women's wardrobes (Chen 2016).

After the Tang, China passed through the Song Dynasty (960–1279 CE), during which the practice of foot binding increased among Han women. Next, Kublai

Khan, the grandson of the famous Mongolian leader Genghis Khan, overtook China and formed the Yuan Dynasty (1279–1368 CE). This brought "barbarian" influence to court including helmet-like caps, close-fitting riding jackets, trousers and boots appropriate to horsemen.

The pendulum swung back to ethnic Chinese rule with the Ming dynasty (1368–1644 CE). The Ming reinforced and extended the Great Wall on China's northern border to protect China against raids from the nomadic groups of the Eurasian steppes. Wishing to rid the court of the "barbarian" influence of the Yuan, the Ming reinstated Han culture including the loose robes made from lengths of patterned silk cloth. They expressed a distaste for wool because of its association with the felt-makers of the steppes who herded animals, unlike the sedentary people like themselves who lived in houses on the plains and practised agriculture. Hairstyles became very elaborate, necessitating a device to preserve the coiffures for a period of time; hence, the "pillows" (headrests) observed by John were already in wide use by the early Ming period.

The concept of applying fashion to Ming dress has been largely overlooked. Dorothy Ko, a professor of Chinese history, is one who has questioned the "only-Europe-has-fashion" discourse after finding many examples of the rapidity of changes in Chinese dress history. She cited comments by a resident of sixteenth-century Nanjing who noted that width and length of sleeves, height of collar, and hair ornaments changed so quickly that outfits just a few years old were so outdated that "everyone had to cover his mouth" (Ko 1997: 8). Antonia Finnane, citing recent work in Chinese by Wu Renshu, points to three manifestations of fashion during the Ming: fascination with the exotic, a return to styles of antiquity, and pursuit of novelty (2008: 45–47). The Ming experimented with new styles for men such as the Korean horsehair skirts introduced through trade, and various hat styles which served as "a convenient site of fashion experiment" (Finnane 2008: 47). The thirst for novelty even extended to adoption of "barbarian" tunics and hats as well as the flimsy gauze fabrics worn by prostitutes. Observers referred to this as shishizhuang. As noted by Tsui, this word means fashion.

In 1644, Manchu invaders from the north overthrew the Ming. Manchu rulers decreed that all men must adopt Manchu styles. This meant men of Han ethnicity had to shave the front part of their heads and braid the remaining hair in a long queue down the back. Men in government service had to wear Manchu styles (e.g., long robes with surcoats, jackets, or vests). Women, however, were to retain the dress of their native culture, either Han or Manchu, possibly because Han and Manchu were not allowed to intermarry. Han women wore loose calf-length robes over pleated skirts or trousers, and they displayed their "lotus" feet in tiny embroidered silk shoes. Manchu women wore long gowns with short outer jackets or vests, and they did not bind their feet. Differences could be noted in the sleeve and the front closure. The jackets of ethnic Han women had wide sleeves and center front openings while the gowns of the Manchu had sleeves with an elongated horseshoe shaped cuff and a side closure inherited from their nomadic ancestors. Another noticeable difference was hairstyles. While women of both cultures lavished attention on their hair, the Manchu developed elaborate coiffures that allowed for fashionable touches. The hair was wrapped around a horizontal device, like a fillet, allowing the tresses to extend to the back and sides of the head. This structure afforded sites to attach jewels, tassels, feather ornaments, even fresh flowers. Han women, meanwhile, pulled their hair back into buns.

The women in Figure 7.5 illustrate several of these features. The scene is a courtyard with a seated Han Chinese woman facing two Manchu women. The Han, whose "golden lily" bound feet are revealed, wears a loose-sleeved robe over gathered trousers. The Manchu women, positioned to show the front and back of their complicated hairstyles, wear coats and overvests with their long gowns. Yet the sleeves of their robes are wide and the coats and vests have center front closures, revealing the blurring of ethnic identity that was taking place in the late Qing period.

The Manchu decrees of 1644 instituted one of the most regulated dress systems in sartorial history with its system of badges and color symbolism to signify the rank of government officials. Yet the Chinese followed their fashion impulses in other ways, specifically through cosmetics, hairstyles, embellishments, and trims. Finnane (2008) tells of the rise of the salt merchants in the city of Yangzhou during the nineteenth century who displayed their wealth by wearing fur coats and carrying pocket watches. Yangzhou's courtesans and prostitutes introduced new styles emulated by respectable ladies. Likewise, the silk-producing city of Suzhou inspired trends in embroidered accessories, patterned ribbons, scented purses, and appliqués to trim collars and sleeves. It was not just the elite who pursued these trends, but commoners too (Silberstein 2016).

The rise of consumerism inspired interest in fashion. As China opened up to trade, foreign goods appeared in the market. New and different fabrics received approval, even European wools and Mongolian furs, which had once been anathema to ethnic Chinese. A craze for pocket watches and clocks commenced. One Westerner, upon entering empress dowager Cixi's palace to paint her portrait, counted "eighty-five clocks ticking and chiming" in the hall (Chang 2103: 318).

The photograph in Figure 7.6 shows a commoner in a velvet snood. Velvet had only recently become available in the Chinese market. In fact, affordable velvet was new in Western markets too as this soft pile textile was one of the last fabrics to be produced mechanically (Redaelli 1994). When John Thomson

Figure 7.5 "Manchu Ladies Peking," 1868–72. Photograph by John Thomson. Wellcome Library, London. Licensed by Creative Commons. License available online: https://creativecommons.org/licenses/by/4.0/. The seated woman, who is of Han ethnicity, shows her bound feet shod in embroidered silk shoes. The two standing ladies illustrate Manchu hairdressing. Thomson wrote, "I confess myself unable to explain the mysterious mode in which the tresses have been twisted, but careful study of the illustrations will, I doubt not, reward any lady who may desire to dress her hair 'à la Manchu.'"

photographed her in Shanghai, black velvet snoods were the rage, perceived as foreign, modern, and superior.

As the Qing dynasty approached its conclusion, empress dowager Cixi lifted the ban on Han-Manchu marriage and forbade foot binding for all women (Chang 2013: 371). Soon thereafter, the Nationalist Revolution brought China into the modern era. China's post-1911 dress history is a fascinating story of fashion and anti-fashion with its modern body-hugging *qi-pao* dress for women, gender-neutral Mao suit, and post-Cultural Revolution entry into the global fashion system.

Figure 7.6 "Amoy Woman," 1869, Shanghai. Photograph by John Thomson. Wellcome Library, London. Licensed by Creative Commons. License available online: https://creativecommons.org/licenses/by/4.0/. Black velvet snoods became fashionable in China shortly after machine-woven velvet fabric appeared in the marketplace.

Korean Hanbok reconsidered

Korean traditional dress demonstrates elements of a fashion system despite its recognition by scholars as "essentially unchanged" since the first century BCE (Lee 2010: 315). Korean traditional dress is termed *hanbok*, which translates as "Korean clothing." The basic garments consist of pants (*baji*) and jacket (*jeogori*) for men, and skirt (*chima*) and jacket (*jeogori*) for women. Women's dress and appearance was especially subject to changes in taste.

Korea is located on a peninsula separated from China, Russia, and Japan by rivers and/or seas. These cultures influenced Korea over the course of its history. The basic garments listed above are believed to have been introduced from the steppe nomadic cultures of northern Asia (Lee 2010). China had kept sericulture a secret for millennia, but finally knowledge of silk production reached Korea by 200 BCE, quickly becoming the fiber of choice for court wear.

During the United Silla period (668–935 CE), Korean culture was influenced by China's Tang dynasty. The court adopted Chinese dress, including love of elaborate ornamentation and decorative hairpieces (Magliaro 1988). Women braided their hair and decorated it with natural pearls. During the Goryeo dynasty, which lasted until 1392, crane and dragon motifs became popular along with contrasting bands on the edges of jackets. While the same basic garment forms continued to be used, it was the cut, trims, and decoration that changed, just as in China. In 1231, a Mongol princess married into the Korean monarchy, which introduced Mongol styles to court. Jacket sleeves, which formerly had been wide thanks to Tang influence, changed to the narrow sleeves preferred by the Mongols. But not all Mongol fashions were adopted: a male hairstyle that was cut short in front, characteristic of nomadic cultures, was rejected in favor of long hair knotted on the top of the head, a sartorial trait representative of sedentary cultures. This act of resistance illustrates the selective adaptation of foreign styles in fashion systems.

When the long-lasting Joseon dynasty (1392–1910 CE) was established, the monarchy looked to Ming China for cultural inspiration. Ming styles were worn by the upper classes and at court, but with a twist to make them distinctively Korean. This is when the women's hanbok style features formed, which have continued into the twenty-first century. The woman's jeogori had been a hip-length jacket that tied around the waist in the sixteenth century. From the seventeenth to the nineteenth century, it shortened considerably, moving up from the hips, and developed distinctive contrasting borders at the collar and cuffs, patches under the armpits, and ties at the breast. The skirt was made from rectangular fabric panels gathered or pleated to an elevated waistband; the waistband extended into ties that were artfully arranged in the front. The skirt, held up by shoulder straps, was worn over petticoats, and consequently was very full. Elaborate hairstyles completed women's dress.

During the Joseon period, state-sponsored workshops produced new and interesting fabrics for use by high-ranking officials at court. Korean dress scholar Kyung Ja Lee wrote that "accumulation of wealth produced extravagant trends in dress among the upper classes, which the lower classes tended to imitate" (Lee 2010: 315). By the eighteenth century, the jeogori had become very short, which showed the waistband of the chima. This was a style first seen on female entertainers at court; it soon became the fashion for women of all ranks.

The woman depicted in Figure 7.7 was not of high rank, but she had a talent for dancing, singing, and playing traditional Korean musical instruments. In the picture, she is wearing a full outer skirt (chima) and an underskirt. The wide waistband of the underskirt shows above the tie at the waist. The jeogori, described as organza, had become so short that it barely covered the breasts. Red ribbons, intended to secure the undergarment, hang from under her arm. The ties at the elevated waistline cover the mid-section in keeping with Confucian ideals of modesty. At this time, elaborate wigs for women signified wealth and power. The limited supply of human hair caused prices to spiral upwards as

Figure 7.7 "Mindo." Joseon Dynasty. Scroll painting on silk, probably mid-nineteenth century. Attributed to Young Yun. Gosan Yunseondo Artifact Museum, Haenam City, Jeolla Province, Korea. By permission of Hyungsik Yun. "Mindo" means "portrait of a beauty." She is donning an elaborate wig, a fashion that became popular in the eighteenth century.

demand increased (Lee 2010: 317). The figure here is placing a large wig on her head. Long decorative hairpins that secured the wigs along with colorful ribbons became a focus of fashion. All these features of Korean female dress resonate with the features of a courtly fashion system according to Schneider: artisan workshops, fashion trends, and fashion leadership.

Sumptuary laws attempted to prevent commoners from wearing the trappings of the elite. Commoners continued to wear the older styles on a daily basis, but were allowed to wear court styles for weddings. By the nineteenth century, however, restrictions eroded and ordinary women wore silk shoes and used decorative hairpins (Lee 2010).

When the Japanese invaded Korea in 1905, they attempted to exercise cultural dominance by insisting that men cut their hair. For Korean men, long hair was a badge of national identity. They resisted, thus retaining their Korean hairstyles knotted on top of their heads. In the modern era, Korea transitioned to Western dress. This happened in stages: first with the arrival of Christian missionaries after 1919, and then during the Korean War of 1950–53 (Magliaro 1988). Hanbok continues to be worn today for ceremonial occasions such as first birthdays, weddings, and New Year's celebrations. Hanbok responds to innovations in textiles and embellishments, as observed by Ruhlen (2003). She wrote about new styles of women's hanbok that emerged in the late 1990s designed to be worn on a daily basis.

The art of fashion in Japan

Japan is an archipelago of four islands in the Pacific Ocean. China and Korea lay to the West. From China Japan inherited the kernels of its distinctive culture, including a preference for dress styles consisting of loose robes. Japan, on the tail end of the Silk Road, probably learned the secret of sericulture from Chinese settlers in the fourth or fifth century (Slade 2009).

The form of dress that became the kimono arrived during the Heian Period (794–1185 CE). It developed into a single garment worn by young and old, male and female, for all occasions and during all seasons. Like the Chinese robes of the Tang era, the kimono consisted of lengths of cloth sewn together without cutting into the fabric to shape it. A kimono required one bolt of fabric, about 13 ½ yards long by 15 ¾ inches wide (van Assche 2010). It was made from any of the different fibers available to Japanese, namely silk and cotton, but also hemp, ramie, linen, and banana fiber. Fabrics could be plain, elaborately patterned through weaving, resist dyeing, embroidery, gold-leaf appliqué, even painting directly on the fabric surface (Gluckman and Takeda 1992). Highly trained textile artisans thus became the essential conduits for new fashions. Popular designs for women's kimono included cranes and other birds, flowers, butterflies, dragonflies, animals, calligraphy, scenes from well-known poems and stories, and landscapes celebrating nature's beauty ("Kimono" 2016). Men preferred kimono made of resist-dyed ikat or other textiles with small patterns.

Kimono was, and still is, worn wrapped left over right and closed with an *obi* sash. Its length was manipulated by folding excess fabric under the obi, which worked well in a culture where many activities took place seated on the floor. Kimono was suited to Japan's climate: cool in winter but very hot and humid in the summer. Lining and padding a kimono rendered it warm enough for winter. For summer, unlined breathable fabrics such as gauze were popular. A related garment is the *haori*, which is similarly shaped to, and worn over, the kimono.

Since its introduction, the kimono's form changed little. The only alteration was in the sleeve opening: a *kosode* (literally "small sleeve") had a narrow opening while *osode* had a large opening (Gluckman and Takeda 1992). The potential for fashion was in the fabrics, the length of the sleeves, the width of the obi, and the manner in which the kimono was worn. Artful selections and combinations received admiration. Layering, collars, color combinations, and the design and tying of the obi offered sites for fashionable display. For example, during the

Heian Period, the 5000-member aristocracy took to expressing luxury through fine clothing, including the so-called twelve-layer garment, which in actuality might have anywhere from ten to twenty-five layers reflecting variations on the seasons, nature, and earth's colors (Slade 2009).

During the Edo period (1603–1868) Japan closed itself off to outside influence, resulting in a long period of stability and prosperity. The old capital of Kyoto retained its reputation for culture and luxury production, while the new city of Edo (Tokyo) grew rapidly. The newly wealthy merchant class gave rise to a sophisticated urban culture. In contrast to the Heian Period, fashionable behavior did not restrict itself to aristocrats. Luxury consumption spread far beyond the court to all who could afford it (Dalby 1993). Writing in 1688, Ihara Siakaku noted, "Fashions have changed from the simplicity of the past to great ostentation. People today crave finery above their station and their purse in everything they say and do" (quoted in Dalby 1993: 271).

Entertainment districts were instituted in walled-off sections of large cities where visitors could enjoy teahouses and restaurants, view kabuki theater, and patronize courtesans and geisha (Gluckman and Takeda 1992). Both "pleasure women" and actors were eyed for their clothing. They functioned as style leaders, subtly altering their appearance and creating new fashions. The *oiran* (courtesan) depicted in Figure 7.8 wears a low-cut summer kimono with long sleeves, holds a fan and sports an elaborate hairstyle. Behind her is a rack on which to display kimono when not worn. The kabuki actors, men who played both male and female parts, endorsed fashion products as seen in popular woodblocks of the period (Slade 2009).

A regulated class system developed in the Edo period, which consisted of samurai warriors at the top, followed by farmers, artisans, and merchants. Sumptuary laws, which were enacted after commoners embraced fashion (much to the chagrin of the ruling class), restricted what artisans and merchants could wear, with samurai being the primary consumers of fashion. But those merchants and artisans who had grown wealthy followed fashion as best they could while trying to dress to their station. As Toby Slade notes, the "pleasure of consumption" and "styling oneself" led to a blossoming fashion system (2009: 34). Flagrant violations sometimes led to arrest, as with the beautifully dressed wife of a merchant whom the visiting Tokugawa shogun thought was the wife of a samurai (Slade 2009). Incorporating the notion of "hidden beauty," rich merchants got around the laws by commissioning paintings from artists as one-of-a-kind linings for their haori jackets. The jackets' exterior was a subdued black, but the linings revealed brush paintings in black ink (van Assche 2010).

Commodore Matthew Perry arrived in Japan in 1853, opening its ports to trade with the West. During the Meiji period (1868–1912), sumptuary laws disappeared allowing all Japanese to wear the fashions that pleased them. Toby Slade (2009) and Penelope Francks (2015) have studied the fashions of the Meiji period, concluding that this is when Japan became integrated into a global fashion system. Urban men began wearing Western business suits while women continued to

Figure 7.8 "Oiran in Summer Kimono." Attributed to Hosoda Eishi, Japan. Eighteenth /
early nineteenth century. Scroll painting on silk. Los Angeles County Museum of Art.
54.37.3 *Oiran* were courtesans of the highest rank in Japan's pleasure quarters. They
were widely watched for their fashion. Here the courtesan wears a summer kimono with
wide sleeves that is partially open in the front.

wear the kimono in the home. Women did not begin adopting Western styles
until the 1910s. Words developed to distinguish Western-style dress (*yôfuku*) from
Japanese dress (*wafuku*). Interestingly, kimono was not a word prior to the mid-
nineteenth century; each type of kimono had its own name (van Assche 2010).

Indian dress as fashion

Indian dress evokes visions of the *sari*, *dhoti*, and *salwar-kamiz*. The sari, a four-
to-nine-yard length of cloth draped on the body, is essentially the national dress

of India. The dhoti, a man's lower-body garment, is also an example of draped clothing. In fact, draping has been part of India's way of dressing since 3000 BCE. The salwar-kamiz (pants and tunic), a product of sewn clothing, arrived much later with the advent of Islam (Dhamija 2010).

India has a multiethnic cultural heritage from Central Asia. The Indian sub-continent is large with varied geography and climate, both of which contribute to a patchwork-like sartorial history. In terms of fashion, India reflects some of the same features that characterize other Asian countries: court systems with artisan workshops, sumptuary laws, and gradual adoption of the fashion process by commoners.

India inherited Central Asia's custom in ancient times of draping and wrapping lengths of woven cloth on the body. Already in the fourth century BCE, the Greek ambassador to the Mauryan court commented on the "flowing garments worn by both men and women, and printed and woven with gold, dyed in multiple colors, and draped a number of ways" (Dhamija 2010: 62).

When stitched garments displaced drapery in the West, men in India adopted the tunic to wear over the dhoti. During the Gupta period (400–750 CE), stitched garments for women also entered the repertoire. These include the *ghagra* (skirt) and *choli* (blouse), worn with a veil. After 997 CE, Afghans, Turks, and Arabs introduced the Islamic religion along with Muslim dress habits. The practice of installing artisan ateliers in royal courts, customary for Islamic courts in Spain and Syria, was firmly in place in India by the fourteenth century. The historian Ibn Fadl Allah al-'Umari wrote about the splendors of court dress, mentioning workshops for silks and brocades, linen imported from Russia and Egypt, and gold-embroidered robes in Persian style (Dhamija 2010).

At the onset of Mughal rule in 1526, dress divided the country. Muslims wore tailored garments while Hindus wore unstitched clothing. Mughal rulers actively sought to fuse the two traditions in an attempt to harmonize cultural relations. Akbar the Great (1483–1530) imported master craftsmen from many countries, resulting in a panoply of styles. Mughal miniature paintings chart a variety of changing fashions that moved from court to upper- and middle-class commoners. Men's fashion alternated between turbans and hats, beards and clean-shaven faces, knee-length and ankle-length tunics.

Miniatures from the prolific Guler school illustrate classic Indian stories, and they show a wide variety of fashions. In the miniature illustrated in Figure 7.9, a man and woman are eyeing an approaching storm. The man wears a superfine white muslin *jama* (coat or tunic) over yellow *payjama* pants. It fastens to the right as per Mughal instructions for men of Muslim faith. A colorful sash with gold borders secures the jama. On his head, he wears a turban secured with a separate patterned textile. The woman wears a red choli and multicolored ghaghra seemingly constructed of horizontally sewn strips of cloth. A sheer *dupatta* (scarf) is draped across her chest, over the back of her head and down

Figure 7.9 "Premonition of a Storm." 1750–60. Indian miniature, Guler School. British Museum. Scala / Art Resource, NY. The male in this Indian miniature wears a superfine muslin *jama* (tunic) over yellow *payjama* pants. The woman wears a red *choli* (blouse) and multicolored *ghaghra* (skirt) with a sheer *dupatta* (scarf), plus numerous jewelry items.

her left shoulder. She is barefoot, but her toes are stained red from henna or lac. Her arms are festooned with bangles, and she wears an armlet, earrings, rings, brooch, and a gold necklace. Bangles have been a feature of Indian women's dress for millennia, as evidenced by female statues from 3000 BCE (Dhamija 2010).

During the Mughal period, India experienced economic growth resulting in the rise of merchants and clerks who could afford modest luxury items. The fashion process was very much in evidence as clothes worn at court became the frame of reference. As Carlo Marco Belfanti notes: "Cycles of change in clothing taste did exist and that here was mature awareness of such a phenomenon" (2008: 425).

The Age of Exploration brought Europeans to India as trading partners. Eventually the English colonized India, taking pains to distinguish themselves from the colonized by following Western styles of dress. Regional differences in Indian dress evolved with North India adhering to the Muslim tradition of salwar-kamiz for both men and women. Hindu women, on the other hand, wore a sari over the choli and petticoat. Since Independence (1947), fashion has existed in both these sartorial strands. Color, fabric, and embellishment introduce fashionability to the salwar-kamiz. The sari has a style history of its own with changes in type of fabric, pattern and color as well as length and method of draping. There are reportedly over 100 different ways to drape a sari. In the new millennium India has developed a full-blown fashion scene with strong fashion leadership coming from prominent politicians such as Indira Gandhi and Bollywood film stars (Banerjee and Miller 2003).

Recent research by Arti Sandhu (2016) posits that India had fashion prior to the presence of the British during colonial rule. Before the nineteenth century, trade networks introduced variations on Chinese and Persian caps, trousers, tunics, and coats. Sophisticated networks of manufacturers and artisans spurred style innovations and changing patterns of consumption. When the British arrived, fashion change accelerated, but with unique responses fusing local with global. The tension between adopting modern Western styles of dress and retaining Indian garments for the sake of identity resulted in hybridity, a process that is still affecting fashion in India today.

Fashion and Javanese batik design

Design and production of batik cloths in Java illustrates a fashion process that emanated from the island's Muslim courts. The nominally "forbidden" batik motifs of the courts flowed outward to the populace, and the heterogeneous coastal enclaves incorporated and innovated beyond the courtly traditions. Repetition and diagonal lines evoked a unified cosmology through water, earth, and sky motifs that permeate the designs. Despite these underlying precepts, the "main color and pattern styles" of batik from the North Coast and from Central Java "have never been static" (Heringa 2010: 128). The change that occurred from the court to the towns is a demonstration of fashion.

Muslim sultanates established in Java in the early second millennium were either agrarian-based in the inland sectors, or sea trade-based on the coastline. The sultanate courts enfolded the already embedded Hindu-Buddhist beliefs concerning cosmology and the life cycle, and these concepts continue to influence Javanese arts. That scope of influence included textiles, wherein motifs and symbolic-spiritual beliefs attributed to cloth endured.

When the VOC, aka the Dutch East India Company, took control of the archipelago in 1602, the Muslim sultanate courts—the reigning sultan, his wives and extended family, and courtiers—and the populace, became vassals in the service to the company's usurpation of the natural resources, labor, and trade location (Taylor 2007). The VOC and later the Dutch government allowed the courts to continue since they served initially to stabilize the general population.

In the late nineteenth century, Hamengku Buwono VII (1839–1931), sultan of Yogyakarta in Central Java from 1877 to 1920, sat for a portrait by Javanese photographer Kassian Céphas (Figure 7.10). The sultan's garments included a silk patchwork jacket, batik trousers, and a batik wrapped skirt (*kain panjang*). His jacket was reportedly a copy of one Muhammad had bestowed on his ancestor, thus providing the dynasty's sultans the right to reign ("Staatsiejas van de Sultan . . ." 2015). While the jacket provided Islamic authority, the batiks that the sultan wore provided connection to the long Hindu-Javanese heritage. The Muslim courts honored the batiks made in their own workshops above imported court cloths such as *patolas* (double ikat cloth), and single ikat. (In double ikat, both warp and weft yarns are resist dyed, resulting in complex patterning.) Thus, batiks were preferred to adorn court figures for formal ceremonies. The dotted grid design of the sultan's batik trousers reflects order (Heringa 2010). Dot pattern batik is the region's oldest batik tradition that used a pointed object such as a stick or metal tool to deposit hot wax dots on cloth to resist dye (Heringa 2010). The sultan's kain panjang shows a batik method called *batik tulis* that is historically associated with the palace batik workshops. These workshops, run by the sultan's head wife, created the highest quality batiks exclusively for the court (Gittinger 2005).

Batik tulis uses a *canting*, a tool that draws designs in hot wax, which provides for flowing lines and elements, rather than designs comprised of dots (Gittinger 2005). The flowing serpentine design on the sultan's kain panjang is *parang rusak*; parang refers to broken swords and suggests power. The *parang rusak* worn by Hamengku Buwono VII is the large size parang that was reserved for sultans. The batik cloths that he wears may be presumed to reflect the color

Figure 7.10 Studio portrait of Hamengku Buwono VII, sultan of Yogyakarta. Kassian Céphas, albumin print. 1880–91. By permission of the Collection Nationaal Museum van Wereldculturen. Coll. no. TM-60001455. Reproduced by permission. The sultan's wrapper called *kain panjang* shows the *parang rusak* batik motif. This parang motif once was restricted to the royal court and the large-sized version was the sultan's alone. By the late nineteenth century, women's fashion sarongs incorporated the parang, even the parang rusak.

palette found in extant court batiks that used locally available natural dyes. The light tone is the beige cotton ground that was soaked in oil and washed to facilitate the smooth flow of hot wax on the cloth. The natural dye colors of soga (browns from soga tree bark), saturated indigo, and plum red (from the *morinda citrifolia* tree) were also used in homemade batiks. Thus, the sultan's garments dressed him as the pinnacle of Java-ness, enrobed in textiles that symbolized power and lasting heritage. In her historical study of batiks, Heringa notes that

Central Java court batik designs have become increasingly abstracted (2010: 130), yet they also use the ancient motifs.

Specific batik motifs used by the Central Javanese courts, such as the parang and *kawung* (a stylized cross section of an oval palm fruit representing fertility), were forbidden for commoners' use (Pemberton 1994; Taylor 2007). However, in emulation of court elites, forbidden designs were in use more broadly by the nineteenth century. An example that parallels Hamengku Buwono VII's portrait is found in a woman's fashionable sarong dated 1890. The sarong from the North Coast of Java is made using the batik tulis technique and it includes six wide diagonal parang bands (Heringa and Veldhuisen 1996: 124–25). The design reveals the chasing of elite motifs by a person of lesser status; the sarong was made in a commercial batik factory, not in a court workshop. The 1890 sarong further portrays engagement in fashion through motifs of lilies and chrysanthemums, flowers that grow in a temperate European climate. The floral designs, part of a popular trend, present innovation as well as local group identity. The final edicts restricting use of court batik patterns occurred in 1927, well after the public had adopted them for their own use (Heringa 2010: 180). The desire of the non-regal public to wear batik, which was expensive, and presumably incorporated the restricted motifs, was facilitated by the innovation of the *cap*, a copper stamp. After its arrival, male workers stamped hot wax onto the cloth and thus the batik patterning process was accelerated at lower labor costs; batiks became more widely worn (Taylor 2007). Another factor coalesced to democratize the wearing of batik in addition to the technique of stamping the pattern onto the cloth in a factory-like setting instead of hand drawing it in an artisan workshop: the arrival of machine-made cotton cloth from Europe, whose fineness and regularity greatly eased the achievement of sharp, evenly printed designs (Gittinger 2005: 45). As a result of these factors, batik quickly became the everyday wear for people of all classes (Taylor 2007: 105).

Batik sarongs, including the 1890 sarong discussed previously, that emerged in the nineteenth century from the ethnic mélange on the North Coast of Java, incorporate naturalistic motifs that represent water, earth, and sky, such as crabs, flowering plants, and butterflies (Heringa 2010). Such naturalistic motifs might appear as the foreground to a grid or an all-over pattern of forbidden kawung motifs. While keeping those concepts, entrepreneurs who produced batiks departed from the local natural dye color palette and showcased greens, yellows, oranges, pinks, and lavenders from newly introduced synthetic dyes from the mid-nineteenth century forward (Heringa and Veldhuisen 1996; Veldhuisen 1993).

Also called the *Pasisir* (coastline), the north coast included communities of Javanese, Chinese, Indo-Arabians, Indo-Europeans, and the Paranakan (mixed ethnicities). Batik made in that thriving batik tulis industry is referred to as *batik Pasisir*. Designed for the various ethnic identities and faiths living there, batik

Pasisir were often signed by the women entrepreneurs, lending cachet based on branding; a local sarong fashion system took root in the Pasisir and lasted into the 1930s. The subset of Indo-European batik manufacturers incorporated European motifs, as mentioned previously, and these batiks are called *batik Belanda*. Surviving examples show lace patterns, human figures, and a panoply of Europe's flora and fauna (Heringa and Veldhuisen 1996; Veldhuisen 1993). One may imagine the dynamic and competitive environment for makers and consumers alike, as the attributes of batiks were evaluated and purchased in pursuit of fashionability.

These examples illuminate fashion in a range of Asian contexts. Despite the reports of observers whose ethnocentric and/or naive perception led them to see Asian dress as unchanging, that was not the case. Fashion resided in these cultures on terms shaped by each culture; leadership from Europe was unneeded.

8
ALTERNATIVE FASHION HISTORIES IN EURO-AMERICA

At that time much wickedness began to prevail . . . . The men attached
to the military service first set the example of departing from the habits
of their fathers in their dress and manner of wearing the hair, which
was soon followed by the burghers and country folk, and almost all the
common people.

ORDERIC VITALIS

The Benedictine monk Orderic Vitalis wrote these words about the rapid adoption of a new fashion in 1089, just a few decades after the Battle of Hastings (Vitalis [1075–1143] 1854: 9). His *Ecclesiastical History of England and Normandy*, compiled from contemporary historical sources, is considered to be a reliable source of Anglo-Norman society in medieval Europe.

The quotation speaks to the mechanics of a fashion system in which an admired stratum of society, in this case knights, changed their style of dress from that worn by the previous generation. Others rapidly imitated the new style until everyone had copied it. What was so novel about this youthful new look? Contemporaries complained about long trailing sleeves, shoes with pointed toes, and straggly hair.

The date of this incident of fashionable behavior trickling down from the elite to the common people highlights the need to rethink the origins of fashion in the West. As discussed below, many standard fashion histories have fingered the middle of the fourteenth century as the period in which fashion began in Europe. The quotation above proves that assumption wrong. Dating fashion's birth to ca. 1350 is just one of the fallacies refuted in this chapter.

Another mistaken assumption is that peasants, or country folk, did not participate in a fashion system. In this fallacy, fashion practice occurred only among the elite in urban settings. It links the history of fashion to the history of capitalism and the rise of a market economy in medieval Europe. This narrow version of dress history ignores what most Europeans wore.

In this chapter, we explore how the notion that fashion began in mid-fourteenth-century Europe became embedded in the scholarly literature. We then offer selected examples of fashionable behavior prior to the mid-1300s in Europe, and among cultures in Europe and America long thought to wear unchanging "traditional" dress or to have limited options to act on their fashion impulses.

The problem of "The Birth of Fashion"

Costume history literature, particularly textbooks, make the claim that fashion began in the fourteenth century. Further, as noted in Chapter 1, the literature firmly equates the wearing of fashion with Western Europe's urban culture. Chapter 4, in Part 1, expands on some of the reasons why this happened by presenting a historiography of fashion history from the European perspective. In this chapter, we explore how this claim came to be and provide examples to refute the claim.

That fashion began in Western Europe sometime in the Middle Ages permeates the literature published from the late 1960s until the present. How did this widely accepted premise get started? Pre-1960s authors do not observe or comment on the beginnings of fashion. For those authors, the goal was to chronicle the changes in "costume" over time in one geographical area, Europe. For example, titles such as Joan Evans's *Dress in Mediaeval France* describe increasingly rapid changes in French dress after 1100, noting that the appearance of new styles accelerated in the period 1320–80 (Evans 1952). To explain the quickening pace of change, Evans cited the emergence of fitted garments such as the *pourpoint*, an example of which survives in the Musée des Tissues et des Arts Décoratifs in Lyon, France. It belonged to Charles de Blois, who died in 1364, shortly after the pourpoint had been made. Evans also noted the appearance of extremisms in dress such as shoes with long pointed toes known as *poulaines*, which became very popular in the second half of the fourteenth century. Parti-colored hose, assembled from two or more different-colored fabrics, also served as an example; young men in the French court wore these. But nowhere did Evans state that this period in time was the "birth of fashion." In fact, she employs the word "fashion" to mean a change in style, and she applies it to dress before 1340. To wit: "A little before 1100 a change of fashion becomes evident in civil dress" (4).

Likewise, costume history textbooks did not specifically state when fashion began until the late twentieth century. Blanche Payne's widely used textbook *History of Costume* (1965) did not mark a beginning of fashion although the author started using the term "fashion" after the chapter on fourteenth-century dress. When Geitel Winakor and Jane Farrell-Beck revised Payne's textbook in 1992, they stated that "the middle fourteenth century marked a major turning point in costume history" in that novelty and competition between classes spurred faster change. "This was an atmosphere in which fashion could flourish" (Payne, Winakor, and Farrell-Beck 1992: 187). Phyllis Tortora and Sara Marcketti stated that "some historians and social scientists believe that the phenomenon of fashion in dress in western society began in, or at least accelerated during, the Middle Ages" (Tortora and Marcketti 2015: 103).

In trying to determine how the "birth of fashion" claim got started, we zero in on the later 1960s, when two well-respected dress historians—François Boucher and James Laver—began linking dress in the 1300s with the word "fashion." Boucher and Laver published books at about the same time, which helped to establish the claim. Boucher stated in the introduction to *20,000 Years of Fashion* that "it was in the fourteenth century that clothing acquired personal and national characteristics; it began to undergo frequent variation in which we must recognize the appearance of fashion in the modern sense of the term" (Boucher 1966: 13). Then in the chapter on dress in Europe from the fourteenth to the early sixteenth century, the subheading "The Birth of Fashion" appeared; under that subheading Boucher wrote: "The development of fashion is a capital change, and of far greater significance than a mere passing change of style" (Boucher 1966: 192). He gave the example of the short tunic as the first manifestation of fashion and noted its spread across Europe in national variations. He emphasized the influences that each nation's courts and growing towns had on the development of fashion. Sarah-Grace Heller pointed out that Boucher and others relied on Paul Post, whose 1910 dissertation proposed that modern male dress first appeared in France around 1350 (Heller 2007: 48–49). But Boucher's costume history book was the one that changed the discourse by announcing the birth of fashion in the fourteenth century.

British fashion historian James Laver, in his 1969 book *A Concise History of Fashion*, made the specific statement that "it was in the second half of the fourteenth century that clothes for men and for women took on new forms, and something emerges which we can already call 'fashion'" (Laver 1969b: 26).

Figure 8.1 illustrates what these authors are referring to. This miniature by Jacques de Longuyon is dated 1345–50, and it was produced in French Belgium. It shows four young men in short tunics. Recall that Boucher identified the tunic as the clothing item that started fashion. On their heads are hoods, which display dagging (i.e., edges cut in decorative strips). The seated woman wears a surcote with deep open armholes over her fitted gown. The standing woman on the right, who is receiving romantic advances from the man behind her, has long tippets hanging from her sleeves. All three women have their hair arranged over their ears. Both men's and women's garments are fitted, a feature that both Boucher and Laver link to the beginning of fashion.

Figure 8.1 *Les voeux du paon*, fol. 25v. Jacques, de Longuyan. Belgium, probably Tournai, ca. 1350. The Pierpont Morgan Library, New York. MS G.24. Gift of the Trustees of the William S. Glazier Collection, 1984. This miniature shows young men wearing the latest fashion—short tunics and hoods with dagged edges—about the time some dress scholars claim that fashion started in Europe.

Fernand Braudel's *Civilization and Capitalism, 15th–18th Century* also influenced scholarship on the birth of fashion. Published in French, then translated to English in 1981, this work reached a wide academic audience interested in the emerging field of cultural studies. It connected cultural studies to the history discipline. He devoted twenty-three pages to "costume and fashion," a subject that had previously been ignored by historians in academia. He distinguished between "costume" and "fashion" based on the pace of change in dress. He stated that this change occurred around 1350 when men's tunics suddenly became shorter. He went on: "One could say that fashion began here. For after this, ways of dressing became subject to change in Europe" (Braudel 1981: 317). Interestingly, Braudel appears to have obtained his information from Boucher, as he quoted Boucher in the section where he identified 1350 as the starting date for fashion.

Braudel made the clear claim that fashion began in Europe as a way for the elite to distinguish themselves from those lower on the social scale. His argument centered on tailoring, or "fashioning" clothes to the body, which ignored body modifications and hairstyling, as well as changing tastes in textiles. In Braudel's eyes, fashion applied only to Europe's elite, not to the clothing of Europe's peasants. He described costume as a manifestation of stable societies. Yet, in apparent contradiction, he stated that costume the world over was "subject to incessant change" (Braudel 1981: 311).

British scholar Stella Mary Newton made a deep impression on the field with the publication of her study on fashion during the age of Edward, the Black Prince (1330–76). She examined surviving evidence for the years 1340–1365, specifically British royal wardrobe accounts; chronicles and poetry; and representations in painting, sculpture, and illuminated manuscripts. She published her findings in 1980 as *Fashion in the Age of the Black Prince: A Study of the Years 1340–1365*, in which she traced the increasing rapidity of change in clothing that began around 1340. She cited sumptuary laws, women's hairdos, dagging on the edges of clothing, and the appearance of set-in sleeves as examples of changing fashions. Newton's scholarship was impeccable, and it influenced subsequent authors. She did not say that fashion began during that period, but other authors used her work to support their own explorations. For instance, in their oft-cited study *Dress in the Middle Ages*, Françoise Piponnier and Perrine Mane noted that many costume historians consider the middle of the fourteenth century to be the beginning of fashion (1997: 65). They expanded this observation with the explanation that the details of dress were in a constant state of change and that the silhouette was modified every fifty years. They include Newton as well as Braudel in their bibliography.

Paula Mae Carns chose 1340 as the benchmark year for a study of costume depictions on French Gothic ivories (Carns 2009). She stated that until the 1340s, men and women wore the same basic outfit consisting of undertunics, overtunics, and a head covering, but that "in the late 1330s, a fashion revolution swept France as well as other parts of Europe" (56). By way of explanation, she said that clothes started to be cut to fit with set-in sleeves, often with extensions hanging from the elbows. She cited Stella Mary Newton as the reason why she used 1340 as her start date.

In 2011, the Morgan Library in New York City displayed over fifty illuminated manuscripts and early books in an exhibition on the theme of fashion. The exhibition and accompanying catalog were entitled "Illuminating Fashion: Dress in the Art of Medieval France and the Netherlands, 1325–1575." Both exhibition and catalog were divided into four parts, beginning with the "fashion revolution" that swept northern Europe around 1330. The image in Figure 8.1 was included in that exhibition as exemplifying the beginning of fashion. The text pointed to the set-in sleeve, again, as evidence for this fashion revolution. The catalog's author, art historian Anne van Buren, modulated the "fashion revolution" claim by stating that "fashion—a style subject to imitation and change—had existed in every society since the Romans and before, but it had been slow-moving and restricted to a small and mostly invisible segment of society" (van Buren 2011: 3). She interpreted fashion as a style subject to imitation and change, thus an important signifier in an increasingly stratified society. Van Buren had studied the dress illustrated in illuminated manuscripts for thirty years, beginning her work in the early 1980s, when the Newton and Braudel publications were new, and when scholars embraced semiotics to interpret fashion. Her bibliography includes both Roland Barthes and Boucher.

Yet even in comparatively recent scholarship, the "birth of fashion" concept is accepted. Laurel Ann Wilson completed a PhD in history at Fordham University with a dissertation titled "'De Novo Modo': The Birth of Fashion in the Middle Ages" (2011). Focusing on menswear, her main goal was "an attempt to establish and historicize the birth of fashion at a specific time in the history of the West" (Wilson 2011: 1). She defined fashion as the commodification of change and display of gender difference, linking it to the expansion of the woolen trade in northern Europe (90).

Thus, we have seen how the conclusions of a few authors were repeated and quoted by subsequent scholars. The assertion that fashion emerged in Western Europe in the middle of the fourteenth century is alive and well in books, textbooks, journals, exhibitions, museum catalogs, and PhD dissertations. Even the authors of this book were guilty of unquestioningly repeating the claim in the first edition of *The Fashion Reader* (2007). The student of fashion has been indoctrinated to believe that fashion did not truly exist before the fourteenth century.

Note that the scholars cited above do not identify the same feature of dress and appearance as the one that sparked the birth of fashion. Some say it was fitted clothing in general; others say it was the practice of tailoring specifically exemplified by the set-in sleeve; still others point to extremisms in dress; while most claim it was the increasingly rapid pace of change. To boot, authors do not even settle on the same time period. The late Anne Hollander, an art historian, identified the thirteenth century as the period when the modern notion of fashion appeared in Western Europe. Her argument is familiar, except that her date is 100 years earlier than Boucher's mid-fourteenth-century date: "Sometime during the thirteenth century, the aesthetic impulse toward significant distortion and creative tailoring (as opposed to creative draping and trimming) arose in European dress and established what has become the modern notion of fashion" (Hollander 1978: 17). Thus, we urge readers not to pinpoint a specific start date for fashion, for the reasons given in the next section.

Excluding pre-1340 from the fashion discourse

Excluding the centuries preceding the 1340s misses what can be considered fashionable behavior in earlier cultures in Europe. We argue our point by drawing on examples from two broad time periods: the early medieval period in Western Europe and the ancient world.

Fashion in early medieval sources

Two authors—Christine Waugh and Sarah-Grace Heller—have pushed back the date of fashion's arrival in Europe after studying contemporary written sources. Previous scholarship relied on visual evidence, which is mainly limited to church sculptures and miniatures. Christine Waugh, citing monastic writers (e.g., monks and abbots) and the emerging genre of French romance literature, noted a new ideal of beauty that appeared around 1100. Young noblemen began manipulating their appearance after inheritance laws changed, which forced them to rely on fashion and unusual behavior to gain attention and secure a good match. They grew their hair long and started wearing tight-fitting tunics and pointed shoes. Their long trailing sleeves provoked commentary, as did their mannerisms. At Canterbury, Eadmer wrote in 1094 that "almost all the youth of the court let their hair grow long . . . and, with their hair combed, it was usual for them to walk around glancing about them and nodding in ungodly fashion, with delicate steps and a mincing gait" (quoted in Waugh 1999: 6). Orderic Vitalis, writing here about the late eleventh century in Normandy, criticized the young men who "delighted in wearing long and excessively tight undershirts and tunics" as well as attaching things at their toes that resembled "serpent's tails . . . which appear just like scorpion's tails before their eyes" (quoted in Waugh 1999: 16). Vitalis even complained that "these days old ways are almost all changed for new." This sounds as much like fashionable behavior as the short tunics of the fourteenth century cited by Boucher, except centuries earlier.

Women were not to be left out, as evidenced by the romance literature of the Middle Ages. These were tales of courtly love and adventure with moral overtones. They taught the aristocracy how to behave. The stories relay scenes where young women wear dresses "well-cut through the body." Again and again the sources mention well-cut clothing that fits snugly. The use of curved seams, tight lacing at the side seams, and inset gores helped to achieve the close fit. Sometimes the fine linen inner chemise peaked through at the lacings, or in warm weather, the skin itself was revealed as indicated in these lines:

> Because of the great heat, she had taken
> Her cloak from her shoulders,
> And her body was revealed, long and beautiful;
> The white skin of her sides and of her arms
> Appeared between the laces.

(quoted in Waugh 1999: 7)

These dresses were seductive and sent noblemen into fits of desire. In another romance, a fair lady was wearing a *bliaut* (fitted tunic) of figured silk, "tightened with laces over her torso, which is well-shaped." When Guillaume, a young nobleman, sees her, "his whole body trembles" (quoted in Waugh 1999: 7).

Sarah-Grace Heller also used French romance literature to study fashion in medieval France. She concluded that fashionable behavior was occurring in France as early as the twelfth century, as evidenced by detailed descriptions in Old French literature. She cited the emphasis on individuality and the demonstration of taste and refinement in this literature as evidence. Yet she rejected the temptation to say that fashion was born in France during the twelfth century because "fashion seems to stage its own birth again and again." She continued: "A fundamental characteristic of fashion is declaring the past invalid in favor of a new, improved present" (Heller 2007: 59). In fact, after reciting the litany of authors who have announced the birth of fashion at different times and places, she suggested that "fashion is born whenever you study it" (Heller 2007: 47). Heller, however, proposed that there was a period in the early Middle Ages when a fashion system did not exist in France.

Sumptuary laws are another indicator of authorities attempting to control what they perceived to be extremes in dress. These began to appear in the eleventh century to curb vanity and sartorial excess among the clergy in Italy. Soon they extended to the laity, particularly women. A 1279 edict from Cardinal Latino Malabranca harped on women who did not wear veils, who had garments that trailed on the ground, and who wore clothes "sewn together artificially from [different] types of cloth" (Izbiki 2009: 46). This was the fashion for parti-colored garments reportedly brought back from the Crusades.

Fashion in the ancient world

Garments of the ancient Greek and Roman worlds that were draped from lengths of woven textiles have been widely regarded as unchanging and therefore not as fashion. However, the evidence now shows that there was fashion in antiquity; change was present and may be documented in draped garments and other aspects of Greek and Roman dress. This discussion focuses on Hellenistic Greece (323 BCE–31 BCE), the era before the Roman Empire was established, and on imperial Rome (27 BCE–396 CE) to portray fashion's diverse occurrences and dimensions.

The problems in establishing the existence of fashion in ancient times lie in the limited archaeological record and in the definition of fashion. The archaeological evidence and texts form an incomplete record, and therefore, an assessment of dress as worn styles versus idealized forms of dress in statues, bas relief, and other representations is critical. Several factors assist in confronting the problems of interpreting limited archaeological remains. First, new remains are routinely discovered providing additional information for previously excavated artifacts. Second, constantly advancing technologies are applied and the resulting data may reveal additional information, even in regard to well-known artifacts. Third, interdisciplinary research that may propose new interpretations has gained ground, particularly in the study of dress and textiles (Harlow, Michel, and Nosch, 2014). The increasing evidence allows observation of fashionability in operation. Another problem in establishing fashion in the ancient world is the definition of fashion as originating in the Middle Ages, as discussed previously in this chapter, or to an origin in the Industrial Revolution (Lipovetsky 1994). Such perspectives link fashion to capitalistic structures. However, the previous discussion has shown that the notion of the birth of fashion in Europe in the Middle Ages is flawed and indeed that Heller, for example, understands the occurrences of fashion more broadly. The discussion below presents examples of fashion in antiquity, long before the Middle Ages and capitalism.

Ancient Greek (800 BCE–146 BCE) dress forms, based upon textiles woven to size for the individual, were draped and wrapped on the body. Pins, buttons, belts, and some sewing kept garments in place. Over time the rectangular forms of the garments were rather stable, and this lack of fast-moving change contributed to the interpretation that ancient Greek dress was not fashion. However, change occurred in textile width and length, textile decoration, forms of overfolds and blousing, and belting, such as high on the ribs, low on the hips, and so on. The *chiton*, the ubiquitous gown-like garment, varied in width. In the sixth and fifth centuries BCE, the Doric version was woven on a narrower loom and slim on the body, while the later Ionic style of lighter weight textiles was constructed on wider looms and consequently more voluminous on the body. While much more research is needed to better understand the variations of fashion in antiquity, it is already clear that fashion change occurred in ancient Greece.

Mary Harlow and Marie-Louise Nosch (2014) discuss the apparent stasis in Greek clothing shapes, but assert that among scholars studying Greek dress and textiles, "many (including ourselves) take it for granted that ideas of fashion existed" (22) in antiquity. Drawing on Sheila Dillon's (2010) analysis of Hellenistic portrait statues, Harlow and Nosch point out that changes in ways of draping and a range of choices of material and colors were the means of expressing fashion. Dillon characterized the trend for new transparent mantles, or long rectangular wraps, in the Hellenistic era. Representation of goddesses of the time maintained unchanging, or "conservative," dress (64), but many Hellenistic portrait statues of elite women diverged from the goddesses' classical styles. Portrait statues show the elite subjects with a transparent, thin mantle draped snuggly about the arms and shoulders, and falling at the ends over the chiton's heavier textile. On observing one of these portrait statues, one may see through the outer mantle's sheer weave to the fabric underneath it. Dillon suggests that the thin mantles were made "of fine Coan silk or Egyptian linen" (100). The style "was more common in the Greek East (e.g., Magnesia, Kos, Pergamon, Rhodes), which Dillon interprets to indicate a taste that diverged from the conservative dress worn in Athens to the more liberal west" (100). The new sheer mantle broadcast one's wealth and ability to access luxurious finely woven textiles of soft fibers. Research on scant remains of pigment on statues, which were once painted, suggests that pastel tones graced the elite women's mantles (Østergaard 2010). Employing Heller's observation that "fashion is born whenever you study it" (2007: 47), and in agreement with Harlow and Nosch, we suggest that in Hellenistic Greece, women expressed fashion through the textile weight, fiber, weave, and color of their mantles.

Imperial Roman culture identified itself as superior to the cultures that it encountered and/or dominated. This primacy concept included valuing Roman appearance maintained through social constructs and expectations of conformity. Standards included the culture's garments and accessories, the mode of wearing them, cleanliness, and hairstyles. Citizenship, a critical element of status, was made obvious through hairstyles that distinguished between Roman citizens and those from other cultures. Roman men were differentiated from the "barbarians" (foreigners), who often wore long hair, by wearing short-length hairstyles. Roman women engaged in wearing elaborate coiffures.

Scholarly literature on dress and appearance in imperial Rome notes the expression of fashion by women (van Driel Murray 1987; Olson 2002), including pursuit of up-to-date hairstyles (Bartman 2001; Furnée-van Zwet 1956). In

Figure 8.2 Head of Vibia Matidia (85–165 CE). Flavian dynasty, Imperial age. Marble. Musei Capitolini, Rome, Italy. G. Dagli Orti. ©DeA Picture Library / Art Resource. In the Flavian hairstyle, the hair is separated into front and back sections. The front curls required a vertical support.

imperial Rome, which was a conservative time, a Roman woman's hairstyle displayed her wealth and status through its intricacy (Bartman 2001: 1–5). It also denoted her conformity to prevailing status markers and taste (Bartman 2001: 1, 8–9). Imperial Roman women's hairstyles survive in statuary, portrait busts, and hairstyling scenes in funerary stelae, allowing for a close analysis of styles and thus to their actual existence rather than being interpreted as merely imaginary (Bartman 2001: 8l). Archaeological funerary remains also inform understanding of the styles. Such artifacts include bodkins, or thick needles— plain and decorated—crafted in glass, ivory, or bone that are now interpreted to have been used to secure a hairstyle using sewing with yarns (Stephens 2008). Nets, including ones of gold such as those found at Vetralla, Via Tiburtina, and Vallerano, Tombs 2–4, covered a bun or part of a style.

A Roman woman's engagement in her toilette signified appropriate feminine behavior. Attaining the intricate hairstyle would require an *ornatrix*, a slave trained to do hairstyling. This would have been the case for Vibia Matidia (85–165 CE), who wore the Flavian hairstyle (Figure 8.2). The Flavian style separated the hair

Figure 8.3 Bust of Julia Domna (d. 217 CE), called "Plutilla," second wife of Emperor Septimus Severus. Severan dynasty, Roman imperial age. Marble. MA 1103. Jean Schormans. Musée de Louvre, Paris. ©Réunion des Musées Nationaux / Art Resource, NY. In the Severan dynasty, Empress Julia Domna wore a thick waved wig. A strand of her own hair shows by her ear.

into front and back sections. The front hair, styled in a crescent of tight curls about the wearer's face from ear to ear, extended five inches high or more in the center front. An armature or support may have been used to hold it up. The hair combed to the back was formed into a bun, probably using a bodkin and wool yarn to secure it. Possibly, hairpieces added to the front and the back sections helped to execute the Flavian style (Bartman 2001: 10). The very wealthy were not the only fashion followers; freed woman Vibia Drosis's self-commissioned funerary stele shows her wearing the Flavian style, although the style was executed with less finesse than that of Vibia Matidia (Metropolitan Museum of Art, NY, AE 1992.202-204).

The elaborate hairstyles of the Flavian and Antonine dynasties (96–192 CE) used dyes and false hair. In the first quarter of the second century, false hair in colors that were not a match to the wearer's color gave focus to a style's complexity (Bartman 2001: 7). Braids made of hair or wool and approximately a half inch wide cover the hairline in many bust portraits of Antonine women and are assumed to show a real style detail. Women used dyes such as henna for reddish tones and saffron for golden ones to alter their own hair color.

In the Severan Dynasty (193–212 CE), Empress Julia Domna (170–217 CE) wore a wig, called a *capillamentum*. One of her bust portraits shows a wisp of hair at the hairline that is not apparently from the wig (Figure 8.3). Such bust portraits highlight the social importance of following hair fashions with precision, even while Roman garments changed little.

These examples of fashion in antiquity range from the extremely subtle to the boldly obvious. Wearing a delicate pastel mantle in Hellenistic Greece showed that the wearer was aware of the new trend in mantles and with it she could display her fashionability. Likewise, traced over 200 years, the intricate Imperial Roman hairstyles reveal changing fashion. Fashion's temporal framework extends well before the Middle Ages and to non-capitalistic societies.

Excluding the non-elite from fashion

Fashion history has an extensive record of focusing on the dress of the elite. Prior to 1800, surviving examples of dress are rare, and these most often represent the attire of the nobility and landed families. Evidence favors the wealthy who could afford to have their portraits painted, who could store out-of-date clothing in their ancestral houses, and who—as educated, literate people—penned observations about dress practices in letters and journals. Peripheral to the fashion discourse have been the dress practices of the common people in England, the so-called folk of Europe, and slaves from Africa in antebellum America and the Caribbean. This section presents selected examples from those cultures that exemplify participation in a fashion system, whether localized or transnational.

Everyday fashion in seventeenth- and eighteenth-century England

Economic historian Beverly Lemire has argued persuasively about the fashion change that occurred in England when printed cottons arrived from India in the seventeenth century (Lemire 2011). After the Dutch, French, and British East India companies began transporting Indian calicoes to Europe, a consumer revolution occurred. In England, women from "many social milieus engaged in creative self-fashioning" by buying and displaying gowns, petticoats, jackets, handkerchiefs, stockings, beribboned caps, and hats (Lemire 2011: 50). The new calicoes from India offered advantages over the alternatives—wool and silk—in that they were washable and inexpensive. Unlike domestic printed linens and fustians (cotton/linen fabrics), the colors were bright and colorfast. The importation of Indian calicoes threatened domestic textile production of wool fabrics upon which England depended. The silk weavers of Spitalfields, who supplied the wealthy with dress and furnishing fabrics, also felt the squeeze. Anti-calico sentiment soon developed and created a mass hysteria during which angry weavers tore printed cotton gowns off the backs of women walking in the street. In 1721, Parliament passed a law banning Indian textiles. Similar laws had been enacted in France in 1686, where not only the import of Indian textiles but also the domestic printing of cotton was banned. The French also banned importation of Chinese silk textiles to protect their silk-weaving industry. The bans eventually were lifted in both countries—1759 in France, 1774 in England—which allowed the development of French and English textile printing industries. In England, a partial lifting of the ban in 1736 allowed English printers to print on mixed cotton/linen fabrics. The increased availability of printed cottons lowered the price, allowing people from all social levels to acquire this new fashionable material.

We relate this history of Indian cottons because it provides an example counter to the usual dissemination of fashion at the time, which was from the monarchs and courtiers to the lesser nobility and then to merchants, artisans, and yeoman, finally ending at the low end of the social scale in a watered-down form. The rapid acceptability of printed cottons for women's gowns and neckerchiefs and men's banyans happened across social strata. Both mistress and maid wore gowns of similar fabrics. What distinguished status were the small niceties and accessories. Even a small border of calico on a plain petticoat allowed common women to participate in fashion.

John Styles's multiyear study showed how, beginning in 1660, ordinary English people enjoyed access to new fabrics and fashion. These included the aforementioned calico gowns and neckerchiefs for women and watches and wigs for men (Styles 2007). Styles used a wide variety of documentary records to support his points: travelers' accounts, court records of clothing thefts, fugitive ads, and an array of account books. His study focused on the lower half of society. Travelers to various parts of England observed the high quality of everyday clothing. Articles in the press complained that people were dressing above their station. Even for the working poor, propriety and fashion were important. Nowhere is this more evident than in the billet books of London's Foundling Hospital, which survive from 1741 to 1760. Clerks snipped small swatches from the clothing of infants dropped off at the hospital by impoverished mothers to provide identification if someone came back for a child; the swatches were attached to records along with written descriptions of the fabrics. The textiles, which may have been recycled from adult clothing, included calicoes, flowered silks, embroidered flannels, and silk ribbons.

Studies like those of Lemire and Styles enrich our understanding of the history of fashion among England's majority, not just the elite.

Folk dress

Folk dress, also described as peasant dress, rural dress, national dress, ethnic dress, or traditional dress, is associated with rural Europe and has long been considered separate from fashion. Scholars of Western dress and fashion pointedly exclude European folk dress from their research. Mary Ellen Roach and Kathleen Musa, who headed up a project funded by the US National Endowment for the Humanities, explained European folk dress as slow-changing garb that is bound in custom rather than the continual change that characterizes Western fashionable dress. They noted that rural dwellers used dress to "identify with their own small groups rather than respond to changes in Western fashionable dress" (Roach and Musa 1980: 2). Therefore, the authors chose to "omit European peasant dress from the definition of Western dress" along with all dress styles originating outside of Europe (Roach and Musa 1980: 3).

The notion of fashion being only Western and urban has also influenced the study of fashion history in textbooks. Indeed, Phyllis Tortora and Sara Marcketti's *Survey of Historic Costume* reiterates the separation of folk dress from fashionable dress. The authors state: "Although folk dress has sometimes influenced fashionable dress and fashionable elements may appear in folk styles, folk dress in western Europe diverges from the mainstream of fashionable dress and is not covered in this book; it is too complex and varied a subject to be included in a general survey of western dress" (Tortora and Marcketti 2015: 10). Course titles at American colleges and universities reflect this division: "history of costume" (or "fashion" or "Western dress") versus "ethnic dress." Only in recent years have scholars begun to question these maxims.

One of the authors of this book, Welters, has conducted research on folk dress in two geographically separate parts of Europe, Greece and Latvia. Their sociopolitical history is quite different, but fashion played a part in the rural cultures of both countries.

In Greece, Welters visited villages in Attica, a region that surrounds and includes Athens. In the 1800s, northern Europeans and Americans visited the Attica villages on the Grand Tour because of their proximity to Athens. Some of these visitors observed and collected local dress of village women, providing us with temporal evidence. The outfits worn by the women in these villages consisted of long sleeveless dresses lavishly embroidered at the hems, sleeved over-bodices, and sleeveless wool jackets. The embroideries are immediately identifiable as coming from the Attica villages, yet the variations show individuality. After studying museum examples and talking to villagers, Welters concluded that one of the main factors explaining the variety was that some embroidery designs were older than others (Welters 1988: 70). In other words, the preferred colors and designs changed over time. The embroideries could be roughly broken down into four time periods based on their design characteristics: late eighteenth century to the 1830s, 1840–1875, 1875–1910, and 1910–1935. When shown photographs of museum pieces, the interviewees themselves pointed out that some designs were older than others. They often described the changes in embroidery design as generational. As one woman in the village of Menidi explained, "The dark colored embroideries were the ones worn by our great grandmothers" (interview, July 7, 1983).

The notion of generational change bears further consideration. In subsequent research in Greece, Welters heard women explain their clothing choices as dependent on their generational cohort. They would say things like: "These were the clothes of our grandmothers," or "This was worn by my mother's generation." They would claim: "My sister who was older than me wore that style," but "We didn't wear such things." The custom of assembling a lifelong wardrobe around the time a woman married guaranteed generational change. Girls approaching marriageable age began assembling their dowries, which included clothing, even before they were engaged. Great effort and expense went into young women's bridal attire, and the latest materials and styles were employed (Figure 8.4). The couple in the photograph were high-status individuals within their village as can be seen in the amount of jewelry adorning the bride as well as the elegant ensemble worn by the groom. After marriage, women wore what they had in their dowries, replacing worn pieces when necessary. Women with children wore age-appropriate clothing with subdued colors and embellishment. To summarize, it was the young women approaching marriageable age who were the change agents for their generation.

Style leadership, a feature of fashion systems, also impacted clothing choices in Greek villages. Young women wanted to look like the other young women in their village and nearby villages, and thus they conformed to the current ideals. The interviewees consistently explained differences as driven by what other girls were wearing. They noted fashion leaders in their villages who influenced other women's fashion choices. For example, a woman in Koropi who had worked as a tailor said: "One show-off came out and said she wasn't going to wear the *griza* [sleeveless wool overcoat] and the others followed" (interview, June 22, 1983). Prior to its demise, the *griza* had gone through its own generational changes. It began as a garment made from homespun wool with dark homespun wool embroidery, eventually becoming a showy jacket made from imported red and white English broadcloth embellished in gold thread. The propensity to add gold thread to the *griza* intensified in the early decades of the twentieth century; some *grizes* were covered in gold.

Figure 8.4 Photograph of a bridal couple, Attica, Greece, 1878. Photograph: Private Collection. Copied with permission during field research. This couple, both from prominent local families in the village of Spata, wear the bridal attire popular in the Messoghia villages of Attica in the last quarter of the nineteenth century. Men had adopted the skirted attire of Albanian fighters who aided the Greeks in their quest for freedom from the Ottoman Turks.

Change could also come from outside the community. Urban styles were modified and adapted in folk dress for short periods of time. One of these was the hoop petticoat popular in Western fashion in the 1860s. Village women in Attica began wearing hoops under their bridal and festival dresses toward the end of the nineteenth century. Some of the interviewees criticized one of the museum post cards, complaining that the dresser had forgotten to put the hoop on the mannequin. The rounded shapes created by hooped petticoats eventually disappeared from folk dress as they did from fashion. Another urban style that was incorporated into the Attica folk dress was the long frilly white apron. This style, popular in the early 1900s, might have been adapted from the white cotton lingerie dresses worn by urban women at the time. Numerous photographs dating from the early twentieth century show long white aprons covering the embroidered hems of engaged girls' chemises.

Another characteristic of fashionable dress is that individuals believe that they are expressing uniqueness through their appearance. This occurred in Greek villages even though the styles worn by an individual resembled those worn by the majority. Welters asked women how they decided which design to embroider. Repeatedly the women said that they embroidered whatever design they wanted. If they saw a design they liked, they copied it. Thus, the embroideries and woven patterns of the fabrics continually evolved rather than remaining static.

Critics of fashion have long complained that people spend too much money following the latest trends. This was also a complaint in the Messoghia villages of Attica, where the amount of gold incorporated into the wedding ensemble became a concern for local authorities. One interviewee from Markopoulo explained: "People were going to extremes and spent whole fortunes, all the money they had, on the costumes and jewelry" (Interview, July 9, 1983). The brides who had the richest-looking ensembles, covered in gold, provoked jealousy among poorer brides. One interviewee, sixty years later, still cried at the memory of the secondhand outfit she had to wear as a bride, while the better-off girls got to wear new gold-embroidered ensembles. Eventually, local authorities passed sumptuary laws preventing people from paying to have a professional embroider their wedding garments.

Men's clothing in Greece was not immune to fashion. During the Turkish occupation, men were depicted in Turkish-style *vraka* (baggy breeches). After the Greeks won their independence from the Ottoman Turks, they adopted the full white skirt known as the *foustanella.* This was the dress of the fierce Albanian soldiers who helped the Greeks during the war. Grooms who married in the mid- to late nineteenth century wore the *foustanella*, which had become standard formal wear (see Figure 8.4) By the turn of the century, men started wearing Western-style trousers with abbreviated *foustanella* shirts. As the twentieth century progressed, grooms gave up the *foustanella* and wore Western-style suits.

The situation in Latvia was different than in Greece. Latvia, like Greece, had a long history of foreign domination. But unlike the Greek villagers studied by Welters, Latvian peasants were part of a feudal economy: German overlords controlled Latvian serfs, who worked their land. Prior to the arrival of Christian conquerors in the thirteenth century, Latvian tribes, who traded in amber, practised a pre-Christian religion. The women wore linen tunics, wool skirts, and mantles while men wore linen shirts, trousers, and woolen coats or wraps. This attire was similar to that of other northern European societies as revealed by archaeological finds in locations such as Danish peat bogs.

During the medieval era, peoples of many nations traveled to or lived in Latvia, bringing European fashions. Latvian serfs lived in proximity to urban centers and the manor houses of the Germans. They saw new fashions and incorporated them into their own dress when possible. The landed rulers did not want their serfs to dress like they did, and discouraged wholesale adoption of Western styles through sumptuary legislation. Nevertheless, changes in cut and decoration ensued. Latvian folk dress gradually developed into regional variations by selectively incorporating urban styles. For instance, in the province of Kurzeme, Baroque-style silk caps entered women's wardrobes in the eighteenth century (Latvian History Museum 1997: 341). In Vidzeme, the old bronze clasps that held the mantles in place were exchanged for brooches from the town jewelers (Latvian History Museum 1995: 281). Church attendance offered the opportunity for sartorial display. For instance, in 1841 German traveler J. Kohl noticed that the everyday footwear made from bast fibers or animal hides was laid aside on Sundays: "To imitate Germans out of pride some peasants wear boots or shoes on Sundays" (Latvian History Museum 1995: 282).

Fashion manifested itself not only in fashionable German styles adapted for folk dress, but also in their own unique material culture. Latvians had a deep affinity for mittens and gloves, which they made themselves and gave away as gifts and at events such as weddings. J. Kohl, again, wrote: "These mittens they make themselves of soft wool, knitting red starlets, flowers or hooks from thousands of samples that they never tire of inventing" (Latvian History Museum 1995: 283). The repertoire of design motifs included pre-Christian symbols that had lost their original meanings by the nineteenth century, becoming decorative units to be utilized creatively by knitters.

Nineteenth-century industrialization along with land reforms resulted in Latvians gradually switching to town dress. This occurred about the same time as romantic nationalism with its focus on languages, folklore, customs and traditions for determination of national identity. This prompted Latvian intellectuals to start recording folk songs and collecting material culture for newly formed national museums. Latvians returned to their regional costumes during the period of national independence between the First and Second World Wars. They wore them to festivals, parades, and weddings to demonstrate national pride. When the Soviets controlled the country after 1945, a bastardized version of cheap acetate was permitted for parades and other demonstrations of political allegiance. When the Soviet Union dissolved in the summer of 1991, the national costumes reemerged in a new form, in materials as close to the museum versions as could be produced. Welters observed these costumes at a song festival in the capital of Riga in 1991 just as independence was occurring (Figure 8.5).

Similar use of folk dress as an expression of national pride has played out in Lithuania (Saliklis 1999) and Iceland (Aspelund 2011). In each country, folk dress

Figure 8.5 Women at a song festival in Riga, Latvia, 1991. Photograph by Linda Welters. These women are wearing Latvian folk costumes, which undergo their own style changes to conform to what is considered most authentic. The outfits function as costumes to be worn on festival days to demonstrate national pride.

has gone through sequential iterations that reflect political and cultural beliefs, and are often contested by competing cultural creators over what is perceived to be most authentic. One could say that these iterations represent a fashion system of their own.

Fashion in the dress of enslaved people

Enslaved people were brought to North America and the Caribbean in large numbers for more than three centuries. They came from thriving cloth cultures in Africa, memories of which they brought to America. They arrived from the Middle Passage naked, with only body modifications to individualize them. Slave owners were obliged to clothe their slaves, which they did by giving them new ready-made outfits once or twice a year, often at Christmas, or by giving them fabric to make their own clothes. Enslaved people also spun yarns and wove fabric for themselves and their masters. Sometimes the masters gifted them their own clothes, especially to house slaves who were expected to show a better appearance than field slaves. Typical slave attire for men was a shirt, breeches or trousers, and a vest or coat. For women, it was a shift, petticoat, short gown, or just before the Civil War, a dress. Children often went naked; boys were allotted long shirts called "shirt-tails," and girls were given dresses termed "slips" (Knowles 2012: 32). Cheap uncomfortable shoes called brogans constituted the main footwear; however, slaves often went barefoot rather than suffer the consequences of blistered feet. Cloth, clothing, and footwear were produced on the plantation itself, bought from local suppliers, or sourced from northern mills. Being provided with clothing did not leave much room for individual expression, but African-American and African Jamaican slaves found a way to participate in fashion just as the lower half of British society did.

Helen Bradley Foster's work helps us to flesh out the picture of American slave dress. Her work is grounded in the Works Progress Administration slave narratives assembled in 1937. She compiled those interviews with former slaves who discussed clothing and concluded that "the clothing worn during the period of slavery was not stylistically static; it changed as fashions always do" (Foster 1997: 12). Slaves sought to individualize themselves through fashion. Female slaves bought calicoes for dresses, bonnets, and ribbons, while male slaves bought cloth that they took to tailors to have fashioned into suits. They did this with money they earned on the side or by bartering with crops that they raised. During the period when hoopskirts were fashionable, slave women made their own hoops out of grapevines. They wore their fashionable attire on Sundays and to dances. One accessory that differentiated black women was the head tie, believed by some to have its roots in West African attire. Foster researched its connection to West Africa and found that it did not appear there until the eighteenth century. Thus, only slaves arriving in the eighteenth and nineteenth centuries would have remembered it from their homelands. Enslaved African women in the Caribbean and in the antebellum South wore such headwraps, but they also wore caps, bonnets, and hats.

Africans on the island of Jamaica learned how to make lace bark cloth, which they used for their clothing. It has been interpreted as a manifestation of resistance against enslavement (Buckridge 2016). Bark cloth had been manufactured by some cultures in West Africa, notably the Ashanti, although it had low status there because it was considered a mark of poverty. Jamaican slaves from West Africa learned from the indigenous Taino people that the inner bark of the *lagetto* tree made a lacy-looking cloth. The tree grew only in specific areas of the island, one of which was settled by a group of escaped slaves known as the Maroons. They developed its production, which consisted of collecting the bark, separating the inner bark, and stretching out the fibers to make the cloth (Brennan, Harris, and Nesbitt 2013). African Jamaican slaves and the Maroons used bark cloth to fashion cravats, collars, cuffs, shawls, veils, bonnets, and slippers.

For many decades, the study of fashion history has been limited to Western dress worn primarily in urban environments beginning with the middle of the fourteenth century. The study of ancient dress, folk dress, and non-elite dress was framed within disciplines such as anthropology and ethnography, rather than as fashion. In this chapter, we have shown that dress in the ancient world and in Europe in the late eleventh century demonstrated features of a fashion system. Further, we have discussed research that shows how the dress practices of the common people in England, villagers in Greece and Latvia, and African slaves in America and Jamaica were not immune to fashion.

9
GLOBAL FASHION

Perhaps the most successful cultural bequest from the West to the rest of the world has in fact been precisely Western dress. Mankind is getting rapidly homogenised by the sheer acquisition of the Western shirt and the Western trousers. The Japanese businessman, the Arab Minister, the Indian lawyer, the African civil servant have all found a common denominator in the Western suit.

ALI A. MAZRUI

African scholar Ali Mazrui made this observation in an essay ruminating on nakedness in the history of thought (Mazrui 1970: 22). He was responding to a new policy statement issued by the Tanzanian government in 1968, which attempted to modernize the Maasai by forcing them to dress in Western clothes instead of their own abbreviated skin garments, loose blankets, and "soiled pigtailed hair" (Mazrui 1970: 19). Called Operation Dress-Up, the policy equated Western dress with modernity and progress (Schneider 2006). As we observed in Chapter 5, European colonizers affected similar influence in attempting to Christianize indigenous groups in the Americas.

In previous chapters, we have seen how new styles were initiated at times and in places that ordinarily are not included in fashion history. Also, we viewed how fashion innovations made their appearance in multiple ways including emulation of elites, cross-cultural exchange, trade, and subcultural rejection of mainstream styles. This chapter extends the discussion into modern times by examining the spread of European styles, the so-called Western dress, to societies around the world through globalization. The chapter also considers the inverse to the spread of Western dress: the adoption of non-Western styles by Westerners.

Globalization and interdisciplinary Histories of dress

Globalization encompasses the interaction of nations, states, or societies that creates and maintains interdependencies and that provides a process for the spreading of ideas. The globalization process expanded during the Silk Road era and continues today in multiple trajectories. The effects of globalization, about which numerous individuals and groups have written, intersect with fashion because the diffusion of technologies and ideas affecting dress travels along those same trajectories. A growing number of interdisciplinary scholars have examined fashion's globalization by investigating the spread of Western dress from the onset of the Age of Exploration to the present.

Among the first of those scholars was Wilbur Zelinsky, a cultural geographer, who undertook an impressive review of the literature to trace the global diffusion of what he termed "Modern Western Male Attire," specifically the man's "Standard Suit" of jacket, trousers, shirt, and tie (Zelinsky 2004: 84). He explained the phenomenon as a classic example of spatial and social diffusion that began around 1500 when fashion news spread from European style centers—notably London and Paris—to rural areas across Europe and beyond to colonies established by the English, Dutch, Spanish, German, Portuguese, and French. This spatial expansion of European style resulted from trade and then colonization of the Americas, parts of Africa, Australia, New Zealand, and the Philippines followed by more recent inroads into places where Euro-Americans fanned out, such as Hawai'i, India, and Vietnam. Many indigenous peoples in the employ of the colonizers wore some version of Western styles. Men wore the "Standard Suit" when at work in colonial government offices or in private service, such as for the European trade companies, although they might not wear it at home. Catholic and Protestant Christian missionaries were also agents of change by encouraging converts to don Western dress. Finally, government decrees to adopt Western dress to visibly modernize a country, as occurred under Peter the Great's rule in Russia in 1701, with Kemal Atatürk's clothing reforms in Turkey in 1925, and the aforementioned Maasai of Tanzania in 1968, evinced change from local styles to international styles. Typically, locals only partially accepted Western ideas about dress and appearance, resulting in creolized or hybrid styles. Zelinsky also noted that men were more likely to adopt Western dress than women, who remained longer in their local attire.

Robert Ross, an Africanist and historian, investigated the global homogenization of clothing from the sixteenth century to the twenty-first century. He preferred the term "clothing" for his analysis of the globalization of Western dress, as opposed to "fashion," which he saw as "ephemeral" (Ross 2008: 5–6). He concentrated on the spread of Western dress in early modern times rather than on the recent global expansion of Western styles. He touched on some of the same themes as Zelinsky, although his embrace of clothing went far beyond the man's suit to include cosmetics and body modification, despite the "clothing" moniker. Like Zelinsky, he relied on published scholarship to substantiate his investigation, excepting his own area of Africa. He reported, for example, that African diamond mine workers in the 1870s spent most of their wages on clothing, acquiring trousers and tailcoats to signal worldliness. Ross includes the effects of the Industrial Revolution on the spread of Western-style clothing, but he also acknowledges the roles played by nationalism and resistance to colonialism. Further, he cited examples of colonists adopting the clothing of the colonized. He concluded with commentary on clothing production and distribution in the world economy, stating that "homogenization of clothing may be a symptom of globalization, but at the same time the profits deriving from the clothing industry have made that globalization possible" (Ross 2008: 172).

In 2016, Robert DuPlessis, a historian, picked up on the economic thread of Western dress's globalization. He examined trade records and other primary documents to trace the spread of globally produced and traded cloth and what he termed "dress regimes" in the geographical areas bordering the Atlantic Ocean. These areas included the eastern coasts of North America, Central and South America as well as the Caribbean, and coastal Africa down to Cape Town. Silks from China, cottons from India, and wools and linens from England and Holland circulated through the Atlantic world courtesy of Arab, African, and European merchants. DuPlessis stressed the role European colonialism and commerce played in the absorption of European commodities in the seventeenth and eighteenth centuries. He also noted that despite the similarity of the goods on offer, selective adoption resulted in hybrid fashions. Throughout the period studied, tastes changed after the introduction of new goods to markets.

DuPlessis's close attention to Caribbean fashion is refreshing. European settlement on the Caribbean islands brought Old World dress regimes despite their unsuitability for the climate. The French donned silk while the British and Dutch wore wool and linen. The slaves, meanwhile, displayed "self-fashioning" from available materials (DuPlessis 2016: 152–53). As the 1700s came to a close, the use of cotton materials rose while that of linen declined, which aligned with developments in European textile production. DuPlessis repeatedly pointed out that fashion overrode comfort.

Other historians who have been instrumental in drawing attention to textiles and fashion in globalization studies are Beverly Lemire and Giorgio Riello, both of whom have researched cotton and its expansion into the world's wardrobes over the course of its long history (Lemire 1992, 2011; Riello 2013). Lemire dubbed cotton "fashion's favourite" as she traced its path from East to West, linking it to the development of popular fashions in England prior to industrialization (Lemire 2011: 33). Riello explores cotton's history over the past 1,000 years, from a widely traded commodity produced in India to its central role in Europe's Industrial Revolution after which factory-produced European cottons found their way back into wardrobes in China, India, and the Ottoman Empire. He argues that the story of cotton exemplifies the history of globalization.

Museums are also turning attention to the "Interwoven Globe," which was the title of an exhibition and catalog on the worldwide textile trade from 1500 to 1800 (Peck 2013). Numerous studies on the spread of specific styles and commodities, some of which are cited elsewhere in this book, have also aided our understanding of the relationship of fashion and globalization since the late 1500s.

Here we describe selected interactions of non-Western and Western cultures that reveal the complexities and fluidities of fashion systems in the era of globalization. After the turn of the millennium, it is no longer accurate to separate the West from the rest. Local fashion contexts almost inevitably connect to the external or global world through complex trade networks, travel and tourism, and satellite and internet access to visual media, to mention a few of the ways that humans interact with cultures beyond their own. Benefits include understanding the economic variability of world markets and appreciating the sheer inventiveness of the human mind, particularly those from outside the expressions of a person's own society.

Fashion in Polynesia: Hawai'i

As observed by the authors cited above—Zelinsky, Ross, and DuPlessis— Christian missionaries introduced Euro-American styles to converts in China, India, Japan, and other places where they were sent to Christianize native peoples. The Polynesian Hawaiian archipelago presents an example par excellence.

Captain James Cook, a British explorer, and his crew landed in Hawai'i in 1778, the first Westerners to do so. He and his men commented on the dress of the natives, which included feather capes, helmet-like headdresses, ornaments, tattoos, and wrapped garments made from tree bark (Samwell [1788] 1967). Many Polynesian cultures make bark cloth, which resembles flexible parchment. Hawaiian women made the cloth by stripping the bark from the paper mulberry tree, beating it into felted sheets and decorating it by applying geometric patterns. The designs resembled those used for their tattoos (Arthur 2010). Native Hawaiians wore this cloth—called *kapa*—by wrapping it around the lower body. Men wore it as a loincloth while women layered it like a skirt, wearing from "one to ten layers" at a time (Arthur 1997: 131).

No written evidence prior to Cook's arrival exists, but documents penned by Westerners who visited the islands after 1788 indicate that a local fashion system existed. Dress operated as a status marker that signified the difference between royalty and commoners, and the kings and queens initiated all new styles. The sandalwood trade that commenced in 1810 brought many Western goods to the islanders, including cloth (Arthur 1997). From the late eighteenth century to the mid-nineteenth century, kapa went through several stylistic changes before it was completely replaced for use as clothing by woven cloth. Kapa artisans made the sheets thinner and the designs smaller than before as evidenced by comparing nineteenth-century examples to those collected in the late eighteenth century (Kaeppler 1980). Figure 9.1 is an illustration of Queen Ka'ahumanu in 1816 prior to the arrival of American missionaries. She wears a wrapped skirt of bark cloth decorated with rows of moderately sized geometric designs. Her ample body displays a Polynesian preference for corpulence, viewed as beautiful within Hawaiian culture (Teilhet-Fisk 1999).

When American missionaries arrived in 1820, they expressed shock at the half-naked dress of the Hawaiian natives; meanwhile, the local elite admired the empire-waisted dresses then in fashion among the missionary women. The empire style's bodice reached to just below the bust, and the skirt of the dress extended from the elevated waistline to the ankle. The dresses worn by the

Figure 9.1 Queen Ka'ahumanu, 1816. Original artwork by Louis Choris. Reproduced photographically by J. J. Williams with charcoal work by J. Ewing. Courtesy of Hawai'i State Archives, Digital Collection, PP-96-6-004. The Hawaiian queen is wearing a wrapped skirt of bark cloth.

missionaries had long sleeves. The dowager queen Kalakua requested such a dress for herself, but because of her large size, the dress style was modified to fall straight from the shoulders to the ankle instead of from under the bust. That dress style, which replaced bark cloth skirts by the mid-1800s, became known as the *holokū* (Arthur 1997: 131).

Holokū remained fashionable for decades, with changes to fabrics and details. Black silk gained popularity after one queen favored it for her dresses. In the 1850s, some royal Hawaiians began wearing Western fashions when out in public, but holokū while at home. In the 1870s, trains were added, and in the 1890s leg-of-mutton sleeves (Arthur 1997: 134). Holokū styles reflected varied aspects of European fashions observed in the nineteenth century, and in the twentieth century, adaptation to the tubular silhouette showed continued response to changes in European fashion.

A photograph of Lucy Muolu Moehonua dated ca. 1853 shows how the holokū was blended with local and imported styles to create a distinctive look (see Figure 9.2). Lucy wore a shawl, a black lace mantilla, a velvet choker, earrings, brooch, and a ring on her left hand, all of Euro-American origin. But she has added her own uniquely Hawaiian elements by wearing fresh flowers in her hair and a *lei* (flower garland) around her neck.

These examples illustrate that the fashion impulse was alive and well in the Hawaiian Islands, both in native-made kapa and in the Western-introduced holokū. Both the quality and the quantity of kapa signified status among Hawaiians prior to the arrival of Westerners. Immediately afterward, kapa underwent changes to make it thinner with smaller-scale designs perhaps in response to printed cottons. The modifications made to missionary women's dresses for use by Hawaiian women created the holokū, which demonstrated stylistic changes of its own in response to shifts in Western silhouettes. Further, the photograph of Lucy Muolu Moehonua displays self-fashioning in a local-global context.

Local-global style in sub-Saharan Africa

Sub-Saharan Africa has a complex textile heritage that includes both locally made textiles in many varieties and imported textiles. Dress styles include both wrapping cloth on the body and tailored or sewn garments. Across many centuries, trans-Saharan trade brought commodities, including textiles, from North Africa and the Arabian Peninsula, which as described in Chapter 6 enjoyed trade with regions to the East by land and sea. Textiles came to West Africa along transcontinental trade routes that linked to the East Coast's sea trade with the Asian kingdoms on the Indian Ocean. In the fifteenth century, Portuguese ships arrived on the coast of West Africa sometimes referred to as the Slave Coast. The captains traded with local chiefs, exchanging colorful

Figure 9.2 "Portrait of Lucy Muolu Moehonua," ca. 1853. Daguerreotype by Hugo Stangenwald. Hawaiian Mission Children's Society Library. This young Hawaiian woman is wearing a missionary-designed *holokū* dress, shawl, black lace mantilla, velvet choker, earrings, brooch, and other jewelry. She has fresh flowers in her hair and around her neck.

cloths for slaves (Hopkins 1973). Inventories included "Indian chintz, silk socks from Nepal, Bengali fabrics, Arabic linen, and Schlesinger cloth" (Sylvanus 2016: 53). The observations of native women's dress practices made by Willem Bosman, chief merchant of the Dutch West India Company, in 1705, reveal their commitment to elaborate dressing, replete with voluminous wrapped garments, lace embellishments, fine silks, and armbands of silver, gold, and ivory. He wrote: "These Female Negroes, I can assure you, are so well-skilled in their Fashions, that they know how to dress themselves up sufficiently tempting to lure several Europeans" (Bosman 1705: 121). Sylvanus concluded that "Africans tapped into imperial spheres of circulation, extracted their visual signifiers, and assembled them with local references to form a distinctive image culture" (Sylvanus 2016: 55). In a similar way, in regions influenced by Islam, inhabitants adapted locally made textiles to Muslim clothing consisting of loose robes with sleeves and turbans. Some African societies structured these robes by sewing narrow strip-woven cloth lengths together, for example, the *tobe* illustrated in Figure 4.5.

Somali dress is another example that can be viewed as emblematic of globalization (Akou 2011). After European trade commenced around 1800, Somali nomads rapidly adopted white factory-woven cotton imported from India, England, and America in place of their locally produced goat-leather garments. Termed *merikani*, the cloth was sometimes colored with natural dyes to resemble leather. European caravans traded glass beads, but learned that preferred colors and styles changed frequently.

One of the commodities brought to West Africa by European ships was hand-loomed Indian madras, a tightly woven cotton cloth in checks or plaids. The Kalabari women of Nigeria, rather than wearing the cloth "as is," refashioned it by cutting away threads in intricate designs to create a lightweight, lacy fabric. The cloth is known as *pelete bite*, or cut-thread cloth. The process of manipulating this imported cloth generated a theory termed *cultural authentication*. The theory identifies four stages through which a material product from one culture emerges as meaningful in another culture. The stages of cultural authentication include selection, characterization, incorporation, and transformation (Erekosima and Eicher 1981). Extant cloth and biographies of female Kalabari artisans, however, indicate that the fashion process was also at work (Eicher and Erekosima 1982).

The oldest known pelete bite cloth was cut in the 1830s in the city of Buguma in the Niger Delta (Eicher 2014). More recent cloths show the development of a range of designs that have names drawn from nature (tiger's paws, tortoise bones), but also English vocabulary (wineglass, cross). Women learn to cut pelete bite by apprenticing with established artisans or by observing them at work. Some originate new designs. Amonia Akoko, for example, developed the "comb" design after learning how to cut from her grandmother (Eicher and Erekosima 1982). In Figure 9.3, she holds one of her creations while wearing a pelete bite wrapper that she designed herself (Eicher 2014).

Both men and women wear pelete bite as wrappers. Because of the time that goes into cutting the threads of the cloth and the resultant cost, pelete bite accompanies special occasions, such as funerals, and is given as gifts. Interestingly, foreign traders observed the value attached to this cloth and began

Figure 9.3 Nigerian *pelete bite* (cut-thread cloth). Buguma, Nigeria. Photograph by Joanne B. Eicher. Amonia Akoko, a Kalabari woman, is holding a length of pelete bite. She is also wearing a wrapper of pelete bite of her own design.

making machine-cut cloth to sell to the Kalabari, an example of an imported cloth transformed into a local cloth that is copied by foreign manufacturers for sale to the local market (Eicher and Erekosima 1982 :10).

Indonesian textiles experienced a similar process in Africa as an in-demand textile that European manufacturers imitated and replaced in the market. Batik cloths probably arrived on the African west coast via Portuguese or Dutch ships: the Dutch trading companies traded along the Slave Coast for 300 years and Indonesia for nearly as long (Sylvanus 2016). Batik cloth from Indonesia engaged the taste of coastal Africans, and trade in handmade batiks ensued, but by the late nineteenth century, replacements took hold. Batik cloths, described in Chapter 7, contain patterns created by using wax to resist dye. Wax, applied by a drawing tool or a stamp, prevents the cloth covered by the wax from receiving color. The wax is then removed and the process is repeated for additional colors. The use of wax to resist dye absorption also produces veins of color in the cloth; the dye reaches the cloth through cracks in the wax resist. This "aesthetics of imperfection" and the hand or feel of the cloth that results from the use of wax indicate authenticity (Sylvanus 2016: 57).

In the mid-nineteenth century, European cloth printing innovations prompted the development of machine-printed, or faux, batik. European traders eagerly offered these to the African and Asian markets. The first European machine-printed batik cloth was actually only partially mass manufactured. Machine-woven cotton cloth was first roller printed with a wax resist, then dyed, then the wax was removed, and lastly the cloth was block printed to add additional patterns and colors (Steiner 1985). The most successful imitation batik company is Vlisco Ltd., which had traded Indonesian handmade batiks in prior centuries. Vlisco's factory in Holland began producing machine batik cloth in 1914 and continues to serve the African market in the twenty-first century (Sylvanus 2016: 62). The company initiated and maintained constant consultation with its African consumers. Now called "wax-print" cloth, the design development responds to the changing tastes of West and Central African consumers. Thus, the faux batik trade to West Africa is another example of globalization where a foreign-manufactured product must keep generating new designs to meet the desire for changing fashions on a local level.

Another wrinkle in the fabric of African fashion history is the rapid increase in secondhand clothes from Western countries since the early 1990s. Karen Tranberg Hansen's review of the history of the used clothing market suggests that the trade is not new. Europeans transported new and used clothing to West African ports intended both for trade and to clothe slaves, probably since the sixteenth century (Hansen 2000: 8–12). For centuries, the used clothing trade had been a viable way of acquiring a wardrobe inexpensively in the West; if not up-to-the-moment fashion-wise, at least the clothes were presentable. Secondhand clothing served local markets in major metropolitan areas in the West, and it reached rural areas through peddlers. But with the decreasing prices of clothing in the late twentieth century, consumers in Europe and the United States sped up their fashion consumption, casting off clothes that were barely worn. Many companies specializing in the secondhand clothing trade sprang up, and began shipping 500-pound bales of used clothing to developing countries, notably countries in sub-Saharan Africa and Central America. Entrepreneurs in places like Zambia purchased bales, and then sorted and sold this clothing in open markets and boutiques. Hansen (2000) researched this trade and its effect on African dress practices in Zambia. In parts of Zambia, secondhand clothing from Western countries is called *salaula*, which means "to select from a bale in the manner of rummaging" (Hansen 2000: 69). Hansen pointed out that "past and present, people in Zambia want to wear clothes that make them look good" (Hansen 2000: 250). Secondhand fashion allows participation in global fashion.

Resistance to globalization materialized in Africa around the practice of fashion, notably the desire to wear Western styles. After independence in the 1960s and 1970s, some African countries banned the importation of used clothing as well as new clothing from Western countries because it hurt local textile and clothing production (Gott 2010). Especially in West Africa, with its rich history of innovative textile production, local tailors and dressmakers transitioned from copying Western styles to creating unique designs. Leslie W. Rabine examined fashion and "tradition" in late-twentieth-century Senegal, a nation that was known at that time for fashionability (and remains so today). She observed that the fashion system involved negotiating tradition, modernity, and faith (Christian or Muslim) in the hybrid fashions that incorporated textiles from local dyers, imported wax prints, and locally executed needlework (Rabine 2002).

Currently, fashion designers in many African countries market their creations through local fashion weeks. Victoria L. Rovine, chronicler and interpreter of contemporary and historic African textiles and fashion artistry, endorses Kwame Anthony Appiah's concept of "contamination" (Rovine 2015: 26). Appiah (2005) uses fashion as an emblem of contamination, pointing out that cross-cultural transfer results in innovations that enrich and transform people's lives. Using Appiah's terminology, contamination has long been present in Africa as a result of the globalization of fashion.

The street fashion phenomenon made its mark in twenty-first-century Africa. Finnish photographer Joona Pettersson (2016) captured looks of men and women in Benin and Dakar. In 2006, in South Africa, Nontsikelelo "Lolo" Veleko snapped original looks in Johannesburg (Enwezor 2006). Her subjects included a group of four young men—Kepi, Sibu, Floyd, and Sabo—from Soweto who received fashion school training. A fashion design collaborative, they call themselves *Smarteez*. In 2012, they appeared in Scott Schuman's blog *The Sartorialist*. They continue to produce their fashion designs. Such recent African street fashions and those of emerging designers reflect the differentiation commonly observed in youth fashions. Innovative combinations of long-established garment forms with contemporary ones, or new looks with fresh proportions and silhouettes, abound in the African fashion design scene (Rovine 2015).

Elsewhere in the Congo, a unique fashion culture emerged among male youth. A subculture arose based upon dressing well—despite dire economic circumstances—in European designer clothes and accessories. The group is called *la Sape*. Members of the group, or club, are *sapeurs*. The name derives from the French verb *saper* meaning "to dress elegantly" (Friedman 1990: 128) and is an acronym for the longer descriptive name *Société des Ambianceurs et des Personnes Élégantes* (the Society of Tastemakers and Elegant People). The practice of local men dressing in stylish European business clothes is not new; it stretches back at least to the 1910s in colonial Brazzaville where African house servants, office clerks, and popular musicians all wore European menswear styles. Men's social clubs soon emerged in Brazzaville for dancing, enjoying beverages, and displaying Western men's fashion (Martin 1994).

How did the fascination with Western fashion happen? France had colonized the region on the north and west side of the Congo River, now comprising the Republic of Congo, where Brazzaville is the capital and the clubs first appeared. The colony of French Congo dates from 1888 to 1960. Belgium colonized the region on the south and east side of the river, now the Democratic Republic of Congo. Belgian Congo dates from 1876 to 1960. Directly across the river from Brazzaville in Kinshasa, the neighboring capital, subsequent branches of the club appeared.

Following independence, dictatorships in both nations led to economic decline. The clubs experienced a new phase when in the late 1960s and early 1970s, disenfranchised Brazzaville youths began devoting considerable effort and resources to dressing in European designer garb, worn at selected times and events, in contrast to their work clothes. This sartorial engagement occurs as defiance of their overt poverty and of the legacies of French and Belgian colonialism (Gondola 1999; Martin 1994). A month's wages as a laborer might be spent on shoes or other parts of an ensemble (Gondola 1999; Martin 1994). Even unemployed sapeurs, salient in the group, make the pilgrimage to Paris or Brussels to acquire the requisite designer items—suits, pocket squares, silk socks, crocodile shoes, watches, sunglasses, and scents with luxury designer labels: they gain prestige upon their return home (Gondola 1999). La Sape clubs have now spread beyond the Congo to Senegal and Côte d'Ivoire. Eventually women sapeurs were recognized, although men maintain the starring roles in *la Sape*.

Rather than wholesale adoption of Zelinsky's "Standard Suit," sapeurs create their own looks. Rules or codes of dress and behavior guide members to perfect their fashion practice, or *sapology*: individuals create dandified elegance within the complicated system despite economic sacrifice and risk. Le Sape boasts its own legacy as the club claims its third generation of practitioners. The gentlemen in Figure 9.4 are from Bacongo, a working-class sector of Brazzaville, where the sartorial code limits to three the number of colors used in an ensemble (excepting white). The man on the left wears a pale yellow suit, blue shirt, and rust-orange tie and pocket square. The man on the right wears a black jacket, blue shirt, and peach-colored tie, gauzy pocket square, and cuffed trousers. Each holds a cigar and its metal storage case. In praise of sapology and characterizing its unique aesthetics, the musician Papa Wemba claimed, "White people invented the clothes, but we made an art of it" (Evans 2013).

Figure 9.4 Gentlemen of Bacongo, ca. 2006. Photograph by Daniele Tamagni. Reproduced with permission. The two men are *Sapeurs*, a group of men in the Congo who practice the art of dressing as a cultural statement.

Colonialism and fashion in Cambodia

The spread of Euro-American styles from the colonizer to the colonized occurred in multiple countries in the twentieth century. Such was the case in Cambodia, which had been a colony of France for 100 years (1863–1953). Male Cambodians in government service adopted versions of Zelinsky's Standard Suit. After independence, a period of instability followed in Southeast Asia due to communist expansionism. Cambodia suffered during the Khmer Rouge period (1975–79), during which more than 2 million people died.

The man on the bicycle in Figure 9.5 grew up in Cambodia, serving as a police officer in the 1980s after the fall of the Khmer Rouge (Penh 2015). He related to his son that no fashion was available to buy during the Khmer Rouge period. In the 1980s and early 1990s, imported and secondhand clothing returned to the marketplace. It took until the late 1990s for Cambodian-made clothing to return. He married in 1989 wearing a Western-style suit rather than traditional Cambodian clothes. In Figure 9.5, he wears a white V-neck T-shirt, black pants, and sandals while off duty as a policeman. Zelinsky would call his outfit the Vernacular Version of the Standard Suit (e.g., pants and shorts). In increasing numbers, men in Southeast Asia wore Western-style pants—instead of a

Figure 9.5 Man on bicycle, 1980s. Cambodia. Family Collection. Young Cambodian men wore Western styles like T-shirts, black pants, and sandals for daily wear after the fall of the Khmer Rouge government in 1979.

wrapped and draped rectangle of cloth on the lower body—with Western-style shirts as the world globalized.

Asian influences on Western dress

Fashion history is replete with examples of non-Western influences on Western dress. For example, printed and painted textiles from India, the fashionable *indiennes*, entered the European marketplace via the seventeenth-century trade with India. *Chinoiserie*, or Chinese-inspired design, was especially fashionable in Europe during the eighteenth century in products ranging from fabrics to furniture. Turkish styles also appeared in the West, as discussed in Chapter 6. Such influences are often described as manifestations of Orientalism, a now contentious term that describes Western representations of Asia. Edward Said (1978) identified Orientalism as problematic because Western interpretations of eastern cultures, including all of Asia and North Africa, viewed the people and their societies as inferior to the West.

Terminology/nomenclature aside, influences from the "Orient" continued into the nineteenth and twentieth centuries. Transfer of an indigenous Asian style to a Western culture, however, was never simply a straightforward fashion adoption.

As with the Nigerian pelete bite and faux batik, Westerners modified material objects to meet local taste.

In the nineteenth century, shawls originating in Kashmir, India, became wildly popular in Western fashion. The first shawls, displaying floral designs and pine cone (*butah* or paisley) motifs, had appeared in the London market in 1767 (Peck 2013). By 1800, fashionable women in Paris wore long Kashmir shawls with their Greek-inspired chemise dresses, originally made of white Indian muslin, as evidenced in David's painting of Christine Boyer. Napoleon's wife, Josephine, is reputed to have owned more than fifty Kashmir shawls (Peck 2013: 270). Made of cashmere fiber in a twill tapestry technique, they were extremely time consuming to weave and expensive to buy. Their growing popularity encouraged European manufacturers to imitate them using jacquard looms. At the same time, European importers were sending design ideas to India so that Indian weavers could better accommodate changing Western tastes. During the 1830s, women's fashion in the West entered a phase in which skirts widened and large shawls provided the perfect substitute for coats and cloaks. Production of shawls inspired by the Kashmir originals boomed. Firms in France and in the towns of Norwich, England, and Paisley, Scotland, wove machine-made versions out of wool and silk, many of which survive in museum collections. The mills in Paisley produced so many shawls that they, and the butah designs, assumed the name of the town. Some paisley shawls were even printed, making the fashion affordable for all but the most indigent.

Paisley shawls gradually fell out of favor when the bustle silhouette entered fashion at the end of the 1860s because the shawls covered the drapery of the bustle. To keep the mills working, manufacturers devised other products to make out of paisley-embellished cloth such as men's narrow scarves and women's dress fabrics. Paisley designs were tailored into bustle skirts and matching jackets as well as house dresses known as wrappers. Figure 9.6 illustrates a French bustle-style visiting dress made from paisley fabric. The University of Rhode Island's Historic Textile and Costume Collection owns a partially assembled skirt of a paisley-printed wool fabric similar to the one illustrated in Figure 9.6 (accession number 1962.31.662). This demonstrates the extended duration of the fashionability of the Indian motifs in the West.

Japonism, the influence of Japanese art and design on Western culture, influenced the West in the second half of the nineteenth century after Commodore Perry negotiated the opening of trade with Japan. European and American artists became enamored of Japanese woodblock prints, many of which featured the fashionable beauties of Tokyo (*William Merritt Chase* 2016–2017). The main outer garment became known as the kimono in the West. Kimono-clad women became a favorite subject of European and American artists (Geczy 2013: 122). August Renoir, Claude Monet, James Tissot, James McNeill Whistler, and

Figure 9.6 "Toilette de Ville," *La Mode Artistique,* 1874. Gustave Janet, Paris, France. Lithograph. Historic Textile and Costume Collection, University of Rhode Island. This bustle-style dress is shown in a paisley fabric. Paisley shawls, extremely popular in the mid-nineteenth century in Western fashion, evolved from Kashmiri shawls with *butah* (paisley) motifs.

William Merritt Chase often dressed their sitters in kimono. William Merritt Chase (1849–1916), an American, used Japanese objects such as fans and screens for props in his full-length and bust-length paintings of Western women in kimono (*William Merritt Chase* 2016–2017). He had several kimonos in his studio as his paintings depict women wearing them in different colors. In Figure 9.7, the woman wears a white kimono while contemplating a Japanese woodblock print.

Kimono soon became fashionable for at-home wear in Western countries. Japanese department stores, such as Takashimaya in Kyoto, began exporting their own lines for the Western market (Geczy 2013). Initially their wares appeared in the Japanese pavilions at world's fairs, but eventually the company opened offices in Paris and London. Takashimaya employed artists to develop kimono designs that would appeal to the international market. This is another variation of globalization; this time Japan capitalized on the West's desire for fashionable Japanese kimono.

Figure 9.7 "The Japanese Woodblock Print," ca. 1888. William Merritt Chase (1849–1916). bpk Bildagentur, Berlin / Neue Pinakothek, Bayerische Staatsgemaeldesammlungen, Munich, Germany. European and American artists became enamored of Japanese woodblock prints in the second half of the nineteenth century. Artists such as William Merritt Chase sometimes draped their sitters in *kosode*, a type of kimono.

Japan, along with other Asian cultures, inspired Paris fashion in the early 1900s. The couture designer who best incorporated "Oriental" details was Paul Poiret. He used kimono sleeves on tunic dresses, turbans for headdresses, and Chinese-inspired robes as prototypes for coats. Other designers, dressmakers, and manufacturers quickly followed his lead.

Postmodern global fashion

On the heels of the Beat counterculture in the 1960s, youth rejected social norms that they found materialistic and motivated by conformity. Known as hippies, they became the dominant counterculture in the United States after the movement's appearance on the national stage in 1967, during the "summer of love" in San Francisco and other cities. The name "hippie" came from the slang word "hip" that referred to being "in the know" in the Beat and jazz circles of the 1940s and 1950s. The hippie movement promoted human equality, opposed the Vietnam War (1955–75), and had liberal ideas regarding sex and recreational drug use. They emerged when postmodern philosophy (see Chapter 4) was taking hold in the academy; thus, college-age students comprised the prime members of the hippie movement. The movement's actualization of the postmodern concepts of deconstruction and multiple truths resulted in breaking boundaries or social rules, giving voice to marginalized groups and engaging bricolage in their dress. This meant creating solutions from available elements such as mixing ethnic styles with mass-manufactured products to signify their anti-establishment and anti-fashion sentiments. Likewise, they incorporated secondhand clothes and military surplus into their wardrobes. Young people in other Westernized countries followed suit, notably university students in France and England.

The hippie generation traveled with ease to international destinations, especially India, North Africa, and Central and South America. Their fashion incorporated their global trekking, and a global aesthetic extended to non-traveling hippies through textiles and garments imported from international sources, in particular India, North Africa, and Mexico. The woman in Figure 9.8 wore a cotton kaftan

Figure 9.8 A woman in a colorful kaftan with her young child at the Sunbury Music Festival, Australia. 1973. Photo: The AGE / FairfaxMedia, Getty Images. Young people in Westernized countries adopted ethnic styles in the late 1960s and early 1970s to signify their anti-establishment and anti-fashion sentiments.

representative of the hippie preference for physical comfort and for colorful garb. Psychedelic design and the 1960s peacock revolution in men's dress, which spread from London, also influenced hippie fashion.

Hippies identified with the working class whom the movement's philosophy considered to be oppressed by the commercial-industrial establishment, and they adopted elements of workers' clothing, in particular denim blue jeans from US manufacturers. The cultural meaning of blue jeans as symbolic of American identity links to prior historical moments, as well as to the hippie revolution. Miners, farmers, ranchers, railway men, and factory workers alike donned denim styles, such as overalls, jackets, and jeans in the United States since the later nineteenth century.

Male and female hippies combined jeans with a range of tops. They might wear an Indian block-printed cotton top, or a natural cotton Mexican wedding shirt, or a T-shirt with a protest slogan printed on it. Outer garments included ponchos, Army fatigue jackets, and long coats inspired by Edwardian fashions. Among a panoply of choices from the global marketplace, leather accessories such as bags, wallets, wristbands, headbands, and shoes (including sandals and boots) added to the hippie look. These might be made by Native Americans, or made and embroidered in Morocco or India, or by a local hippie entrepreneur. Hippie fashions drew upon the available elements, which in the increasingly global market were materially and ethnically diverse, to create self-fashioned bricolage ensembles; hippies created fashions using unexpected combinations broadcasting their identity and aesthetic that contrasted with the dominant culture.

Musicians Jimi Hendrix and Janis Joplin exemplified the iconoclasm of hippie fashion. Hippie style spread globally in part through the music scene of concerts and festivals. From the urban avant-garde centers of Haight-Ashbury in San Francisco, Greenwich Village in New York City, Carnaby Street in London, and the Latin Quarter in Paris, hippie fashion flowed globally.

The story of jeans becoming a mass market fashion phenomenon beginning in the 1960s starts with the initial selection of jeans by hippies as a core wardrobe item with multivalence. Jeans were long lasting and made of cotton, thus thought to be good for the environment. They could be personalized with embroidery and patchwork (Reich 1970). Jeans provided comfortable wear, freeing the body from the prevailing man's Standard Suit and woman's dress or skirt. Simultaneous to these signals, jeans projected an American identity within the cultural memory that grew from roots in the Gold Rush era sense of exploration and discovery. Wearing jeans moved into the mass market as manufacturers offered bell bottoms to a wide public. It was during the 1970s that jeans became a hot commodity on the international market, growing increasingly globalized as the years wore on. In the late 1970s, American designers offered their versions of jeans, which departed from functionality and responded to trends (Miller and Woodward 2011). This is a classic example of the trickle-up theory at work.

Japanese subcultural fashion

Kawaii, or "cute," is a dimension of Japanese cultural aesthetics. It has been apparent in the well-known Hello Kitty product line, in the proliferation of cartoon character logos in Japan (e.g., for municipalities and government agencies), and in the globally popular Japanese *manga* (a style of comics and graphic novels). Artist Takashi Murakami, who deploys kawaii in his works—including in his multi-year leather accessory product collaborations with Marc Jacobs at Louis Vuitton—declared that a "heritage of eccentricity" underlies Japanese creative culture (Matsui 2005: 226).

Starting in the late twentieth century, a new type of Tokyo youth subculture emerged that incorporated the Japanese kawaii aesthetic and eccentric creativity in the expression of fashion. They were, and still are, centered in Tokyo's Harajuku and Shibuya districts. The two districts flowered as sites where fashion-obsessed youth gathered to buy and show their idiosyncratic creations. Specific fashion subgroups took shape with such varied types as *Ganguro* with tanned skin and long bleached hair, and *Yamamba* with style references to a mountain witch (Kawamura 2011). Up-to-the-minute knowledge marked participation in a specific subgroup, and the age range for group membership was about fourteen to eighteen years when adult life took precedence (Kawamura 2011). In the early twentieth century, photographer Shoichi Aoki recorded passing looks for posterity (Aoki 2001, 2005).

A style called *Lolita* was among the more widely adopted by females. It drew upon Western elite women's fashions of the eighteenth century and of the Victorian era. The silhouettes required full-gathered skirts with net and ruffled petticoats, or bustle styles with ruffles. Trimmings and ruffles were essential. Colors such as pink and white dominated the style. An offshoot of Lolita style called *Gousurori*, or Gothic Lolita, developed, taking aspects from Western Goth subculture; looks were typically black from head to foot, but may incorporate white elements or red plaid elements. By 2005, the Gothic Lolita style gained global membership due to the ability to connect across space by the internet (Monden 2013). The American teenager in Figure 9.9 styled her all-black look with a ruffled choker, ruffled and lace petticoats, and an up-do hairstyle, all of which invoke past elite female fashions, in combination with knee-high stockings and platform lace-up shoes, which echo little girls' dress as well as Goth style.

Some scholars characterize the feminine styles of Lolita and its subgroups such as Gothic Lolita as childlike and infantilizing, as well as sexualizing and eroticizing (Monden 2013). However, the participants experience it differently. In an analysis of the global Euro-American Gothic Lolita community via blog conversations, Masafumi Monden found that Gothic Lolitas expressed emphases on "femininity,

Figure 9.9 American teen girl wearing authentic Japanese-style Gousurori or Gothic Lolita fashion. Duplass/Shutterstock.com. Subcultural styles that originated with teenage girls in Japan spread to Euro-American cultures in the early twenty-first century.

cuteness, elegance and elaborate details" and "opulently flounced dress styles" and resistance to casual dress (2013: 173). Clearly, they have engaged the materiality of their fashion. Monden (2013) proposed that the globalization of a culture, such as a fashion-centered subculture like the Gothic Lolita subculture, results in hybridity rather than homogeneity as the global and local intermix.

10
CONCLUSION

Fashion: global but Western. A complex, ambiguous, and not just a little bit murky relationship exists between Western fashion and other clothing systems, especially non-Western, found throughout the world.
SANDRA NIESSEN

Sandra Niessen penned these words in *Re-Orienting Fashion* addressing "troublesome boundaries" set by fashion theory in relationship to its subject (2003: 243). Much has happened in the period since *Re-Orienting Fashion* was published. Fashion studies has fully embraced the global, yet Niessen finds that the field still tends "to be Eurocentric, evolutionary, Orientalist, and in urgent need of review and revision" (Niessen 2016: 209). She asks, "Why is the Western bias so deeply entrenched in fashion studies?" pointing to the unchanging course of the field even in the face of "well-formulated and exceptionally serious charges." The same is true of fashion history; the fashion systems that operated historically in geographical regions beyond Euro-America remain neglected. The same drive for novelty and change related to appearance within societies is little recognized and therefore not integrated into our fundamental understanding of fashion.

In this book, we have laid out an argument for a global fashion history. The argument is presented in two parts. In Part 1, we first reviewed scholarship in the field of fashion history. After discussing the various interpretations surrounding fashion's lexicon, we examined key theories that attempt to explain how fashion systems operate. Following that foundation, we surveyed the historiography of fashion history literature, beginning with the earliest sixteenth-century costume history books that indicated curiosity about dress practices in lands beyond Europe. We summarized developments in subsequent centuries that led to the belief that fashion is exclusive to the West and that it appeared there first in the mid-fourteenth century. We offered reasons explaining how the field of fashion history arrived at the current juncture through a review of major developments in scholarship, including the rise of cultural studies. We explained the reasons behind our argument that fashion existed in Europe prior to the medieval period and in cultures outside the West.

In Part 2, we presented a range of examples across time and space to support our argument. Through these examples, we elucidated the importance of changing tastes in fabrics, hairstyles, and cosmetics—elements sometimes forgotten in fashion history. The notions of hybridity, creolization, and bricolage raise questions about the dominant theories of fashion adoption such as those that consider a capitalist society necessary to have fashion. We have synthesized research in which the behavior we call fashion was present. We presented the work of interdisciplinary scholars who study dress of non-Western cultures as fashion, for example, Jennifer Ball, who researched Byzantine fashion, (2005) and Barbara Voss, who extrapolated data about fashion from archaeological finds in Spanish Colonial America (2008). The work of scholars like these indicates that the field is at a turning point and that the time is right to reconceptualize fashion as a phenomenon that occurred historically around the world. For, as Jennifer Craik states, the fashion impulse is a human impulse. Craik's observation echoes psychologist J. C. Flügel, who identified decoration as the primary reason that people wear clothes in *The Psychology of Clothes* (1930).

We presented examples of rare evidence that humans utilized beads as body embellishments in prehistoric times. These examples featured the earliest artifacts in the form of shell beads from North Africa dated to approximately 110,000 years ago and a more recent site in France from the late Mesolithic Era. Such beads are interpreted to indicate symbolic behavior. We included mastodon tusk beads numbering over 13,000 found at Sungir, Russia, dated to approximately 32,050–28,550 BCE that apparently decorated garments. We presented prehistoric body markings in a general discussion of early known tattoos.

Several examples of fashion systems in ancient times involved trade routes that resulted in innovations in garments and new materials. When cultures intersected in the exchange of goods, the transfer of ideas also occurred. The discussion of coats, for example, drew on the Silk Road routes that traversed the Asian continent. The style of coats first seen on the Asian steppes developed across time in the oases on the Taklamakan Desert. We interpret these transformations as signs of fashion and as indications that change in style involved a shift in collective taste. Changes in jewelry worn in Bronze Age Greece also demonstrate style change; trade in stones such as beads of lapis lazuli and ostrich shell allowed the fashionable woman in Thebes to be up-to-date in her jewelry. More recent trade patterns that intersected with the Age of Exploration and colonization revealed the fashion preferences of New England's native peoples, textile fashions in West Africa, and the fashion systems in Latin America from Contact Period to the eighteenth century.

Examples of fashion change in places normally excluded from the fashion discourse such as China, Korea, Japan, and Indonesia in the East and in the Americas before European colonization demonstrate why their dress should be interpreted as fashion. Likewise, India, Persia, and the Ottoman Empire illustrate cases where the fashion was in the fabric rather than the cut of the garment. Additionally, Europeans in rural areas and enslaved people within Euro-America possess the changing taste along with the desire to embellish the body that characterizes fashion.

A dominant theory in Western fashion history, the trickle-down theory, explains fashion change as emulation of elites. The elite classes formulated sumptuary restrictions to preserve their position in society. The case studies in this book demonstrate that emulation of elites is not restricted to the West; in fact, it is a common theme across fashion history.

Some may argue that the examples discussed in this book are not fashion because of the long spans of time needed for change to occur in places such as colonial Peru, where indigenous peoples were subjected to sumptuary laws, or ancient Rome, which has always been considered a prefashion era. The measurement of time is a flexible concept, however, and the desire for novelty existed across time and space. Yet a slower arc of change than in Western capitalistic societies should not be a hindrance for conceptualizing change in styles in both premedieval and non-Western dress as fashion. Given that humans inherently possess the desire to decorate themselves and that evidence of fashion change has been demonstrated in the case studies and examples in this book, as well as by scholars elsewhere, it is time to stop limiting ourselves to the West after the mid-fourteenth century in the telling of fashion's history.

The increase in published research relevant to the globalization of fashion history is heartening. We think that many more examples are out there waiting for scholars to discover them through pictorial, material, and documentary evidence. The challenges in pursuing those examples include language barriers and access to publications and museum catalogs in distant places.

We finish with a call to scholars around the globe to assess new evidence and reinterpret already available evidence, including artifacts in museums, toward writing new fashion histories in light of the reconceptualization of concepts presented here. Scholars must overcome disciplinary boundaries by collaborating with colleagues. To amplify the fashion history knowledge base with exemplars beyond the West, dress history scholars should learn the language of their targeted society and work with others to reach the depth needed. Each study, no matter how small, will contribute to a truly global history of fashion.

BIBLIOGRAPHY

Agins, T. (1999), *The End of Fashion*, New York: William Morrow.

Akou, H. M. (2011), *The Politics of Dress in Somali Culture*, Bloomington: University of Indiana Press.

Al-Maqdissi, M. (2008), "The Development of Trade Routes in the Second Millennium B. C.," in J. Aruz, K. Benzel and J. M. Evans (eds.), *Beyond Babylon: Art, Trade and Diplomacy in the Second Millennium B.C.*, 42–43, New York: The Metropolitan Museum of Art.

Allinson, M. (1916), *Dressmaking as a Trade for Women in Massachusetts*, Bulletin of the U. S. Bureau of Labor Statistics, Boston: Women's Education and Industrial Union.

Anawalt, P. R. (1981), *Indian Clothing Before Cortés: Mesoamerican Costumes from the Codices*, Norman: University of Oklahoma Press.

Anawalt, P. R. (2007), *The Worldwide History of Dress*, New York: Thames and Hudson.

Aoki, S. (2001), *FRUITS*, London: Phaidon Press.

Aoki, S. (2005), *FreshFRUITS*, London: Phaidon Press.

Appiah, K. A. (2005), *Cosmopolitanism: The Ethics of Identity*, Princeton: Princeton University Press.

Aravantinos, V. (2008), "176a,b: Beads," in J. Aruz, K. Benzel and J. M. Evans (eds.), *Beyond Babylon: Art, Trade and Diplomacy in the Second Millennium B.C.*, 280–81, New York: The Metropolitan Museum of Art.

Arnold, J. (1964), *Patterns of Fashion 1: Englishwomen's Dresses & Their Construction c. 1660–1860*, London: Wace.

Arnold, J. (1966), *Patterns of Fashion 2: Englishwomen's Dresses & Their Construction c. 1860–1940,* London: Wace.

Arnold, J. (1985), *Patterns of Fashion: The Cut and Construction of Clothes for Men and Women c. 1560–1620*, London: Macmillan.

Arthur, L. B. (1997), "Cultural Authentication Refined: The Case of the Hawaiian Holokū," *Clothing and Textile Research Journal* 15 (3): 129–38.

Arthur, L. B. (2010), "Hawaiian Dress Prior to 1898," in M. Maynard (ed.), *Australia, New Zealand, and the Pacific Islands*, Vol. 7, *Encyclopedia of World Dress and Fashion*, 389–93, Oxford and New York: Berg Publishers and Oxford University Press.

Aspelund, K. (2011), "Who Controls Culture? Power, Craft and Gender in the Creation of Icelandic Women's National Dress," PhD diss., Boston University, Boston.

Bagneris, M. L. (2013), "Reimagining Race, Class, and Identity in the New World," in R. Aste (ed.), *Behind Closed Doors: Art in the Spanish American Home, 1492–1898*, 161–208, New York: Brooklyn Museum of Art & The Monacelli Press.

Baizerman, S., J. B. Eicher, and C. Cerny (1993), "Eurocentrism in the Study of Ethnic Dress," *Dress* 20: 19–32.

Ball, J. L. (2005), *Byzantine Dress: Representations of Secular Dress in Eighth-to-Twelfth-Century Painting*, New York: Palgrave Macmillan.

Banerjee, M., and D. Miller (2003), *The Sari*, Oxford and New York: Berg.

Barber, E. J. W. (1991), *Prehistoric Textiles: The Development of Cloth in the Neolithic and Bronze Ages with Special Reference to the Aegean*, Princeton: Princeton University Press.

Barber, E. W. (1994), *Women's Work: The First 20,000 Years. Women, Cloth, and Society in Early Times*, New York: Norton.

Barber, E. W. (2010), "Early Textiles," in V. Mair (ed.), *Secrets of the Silk Road: An Exhibition of Discoveries from the Xinjiang Uyghur Autonomous Region, China*, 70–79, Santa Ana, CA: Bowers Museum.

Barnard, M., ed. (2007), *Fashion Theory: A Reader*, Abingdon and New York: Routledge.

Barnard, M. (2014), *Fashion Theory: An Introduction*, Abingdon and New York: Routledge.

Barthes, R. ([1967] 1983), *The Fashion System*, New York: Hill and Wang.

Bartman, E. (2001), "Hair and the Artifice of Roman Female Adornment," *American Journal of Archaeology* 105 (1): 1–25.

Barton, L. (1935), *Historic Costume for the Stage*, Boston: W. H. Baker Co.

Barton, R. N. E., A. Bouzouggar, S. N. Collcutt, J-L. Schwenninger, and L. Clark-Balzan (2009), "OSL Dating of the Aterian Levels at Dar es-Soltan I (Rabat, Morocco) and Implications for the Dispersal of Modern Homo Sapiens," *Quaternary Science Reviews* 28 (19–20): 1914–31.

Baudelaire, C. ([1863] 1964), *The Painter in Modern Life and Other Essays*, New York and London: Phaidon Press.

Baudrillard, K. ([1981] 1994), *Simulacra and Simulation*, translated by S. Glaser, Ann Arbor: University of Michigan Press.

Baumgarten, L., and J. Watson (2002), *What Clothes Reveal: The Language of Clothing in Colonial and Federal America*, Williamsburg, VA: Colonial Williamsburg.

Becker, M. J. (2005), "Matchcoats: Cultural Conservatism and Change in One Aspect of Native American Clothing," *Ethnohistory* 52 (4): 727–87.

Belfanti, C. M. (2008), "Was Fashion a European Invention?," *Journal of Global History* 3 (3): 419–43.

Benjamin, W. (1999), *The Arcades Project* (written 1927–40, first published in 1982), translated by H. Eiland and K. McLaughlin, Cambridge, MA: Harvard University Press.

Benn, C. D. (2005), *China's Golden Age: Everyday Life in the Tang Dynasty*, Oxford: Oxford University Press.

Black S., A. de la Haye, J. Entwistle, A. Rocamora, R. Root, and H. Thomas (eds.), (2013), *The Handbook of Fashion Studies*, London and New York: Bloomsbury Academic.

Blanchard, P. (2008), *Human Zoos: Science and Spectacle in the Age of Colonial Empire*, Liverpool: Liverpool University Press.

Blumer, H. (1969), "Fashion: From Class Differentiation to Collective Selection," *Sociological Quarterly* 10: 275–91.

Bogatyrev, P. (1976), "Costume as a Sign," in L. Matejka and I. R. Titunik (eds.), *Semiotics of Art*, 13–19, Cambridge, MA: MIT Press.

Bonnard, C. (2008), *Renaissance and Medieval Costume*, Mineola and New York: Dover.

Bosman, W. (1705), *A New and Accurate Description of the Coast of Guinea, Divided into the Gold, the Slave, and the Ivory Coasts*, London: J. Knapton, A. Fell, R. Smith, D. Midwinter, W. Haws, W. Davis, G. Strahan, B. Lintott, J. Round, and J. Wale.

Boucher, F. (1966), *20,000 Years of Fashion: The History of Costume and Personal Adornment*, New York: Harry N. Abrams.

Bourdieu, P. (1977), *Outline of a Theory of Practice*, Cambridge: Cambridge University Press.

Bourdieu, P. (1984), *Distinction: A Social Critique of the Judgment of Taste*, New York: Routledge.

Bourdieu, P. (1990), *The Logic of Practice*, Stanford, CA: Stanford University Press.

Brandt, L. Ø. (2014), "Unravelling Textile Mysteries with DNA Analysis," in M. L. Nosch, Z. Feng, and L. Varadarajan (eds.), *Global Textile Encounters*, Ancient Textile Series Vol. 20, 81–85, Oxford and Philadelphia: Oxbow Books.

Brannon, E. L. (2005), *Fashion Forecasting*, New York: Fairchild Books.

Brasser, T. J. (1978), "Early Indian-European Contacts," in B. G. Trigger (ed.), *Handbook of North American Indians, Vol. 15: Northeast*, 78–88, Washington, DC: Smithsonian.

Braudel, F. (1981), *Civilization and Capitalism, 15th–18th Century, Vol. 1. The Structures of Everyday Life*, New York: Harper and Row.

Brennan, E., L. Harris, and M. Nesbitt (2013), "Jamaican Lace-Bark: Its History and Uncertain Future," *Textile History* 44 (2): 235–53.

Brenninkmeyer, I. (1973), "The Diffusion of Fashion,"' in G. Willis and D. Midgley (eds.), *Fashion Marketing*, 259–302, London: Allen and Unwin.

Brereton, J. ([1602], 1966), *Discoverie of the North Part of Virginia*, Ann Arbor: University Microfilms, Inc.

Breward, C. (1995), *The Culture of Fashion: A New History of Fashionable Dress*, Manchester: Manchester University Press.

Breward, C., and D. Gilbert, eds (2006), *Fashion's World Cities*, Oxford and New York: Berg.

Brydon, A., and S. Niessen, eds (1998), *Consuming Fashion: Adorning the Transnational Body*, Oxford: Berg.

Buck-Morss, S. (1991), *The Dialectics of Seeing: Walter Benjamin and the Arcades Project*, Cambridge, MA and London: MIT Press.

Buckridge, S. O. (2016), *African Lace Bark in the Caribbean: The Construction of Race, Class and Gender*, London and New York: Bloomsbury.

Butler, J. (1988), "Performative Acts and Gender Construction: An Essay in Phenomenology and Feminist Theory," *Theatre Journal* 40 (4): 519–31.

Butler, J. (1990), *Gender Trouble: Feminism and the Subversion of Identity*, New York: Routledge.

Canby, S. R., D. Beyazit, M. Rugiadi, and A. C. S. Peacock (2016), *Court and Cosmos: The Great Age of the Seljuqs*, New York: Metropolitan Museum of Art.

Cannon, A. (1998), "Cultural and Historical Contexts of Fashion," in A. Brydon and S. Niessen (eds.), *Consuming Fashion: Adorning the Transnational Body*, 23–38, Oxford: Berg.

Cantacuzène, Princess (J. D. Grant), (1921), *My Life Here and There*, New York: Charles Scribner's Sons.

Carns, P. M. (2009), "Cutting a Fine Figure: Costume on French Gothic Ivories," in R. Netherton and G. R. Owen-Crocker (eds.), *Medieval Clothing and Textiles* 5, 55–87, Woodbridge, Suffolk: Boydell.

Carter, M. (2003), *Fashion Classics from Carlyle to Barthes*, Oxford and New York: Berg.

Casanova, M. (2008), "Lapis Lazulis," in J. Aruz, K. Benzel and J. M. Evans (eds.), *Beyond Babylon: Art, Trade and Diplomacy in the Second Millennium B.C.*, 68, New York: The Metropolitan Museum of Art.

Chagnon, M. (2013), "'Clothed in Several Modes': Oil-on-Canvas Painting and the Iconography of Human Variety in Early Modern Iran," in A. Langer (ed.), *The Fascinations of Persia: The Persian-European Dialogue in Seventeenth-Century Art & Contemporary Art from Iran*, 238–63, Zürich: Museum Rietberg and Verlag Scheidegger & Spiess AG.

Challamel, M. A. (1882), *The History of Fashion in France*, New York: Scribner and Welford.

Champlain, S. ([1604–1618] 1907), *Voyages of Samuel de Champlain*, edited by W. L. Grant, New York: Charles Scribner's Sons.

Chanel, Chanel (1986), [Videocassette (VHS)] Dir. E. Hershon and R. Guerra, Berlin: RM Arts.

Chang, J. (2013), *Empress Dowager Cixi: The Concubine Who Launched Modern China*, New York: Anchor Books.

Chavalit, M., and M. Phromsuthirak (2000), *Costumes in ASEAN*, Bangkok: ASEAN Committee on Culture and Information.

Chen, B. (2016), "Material Girls: Silk and Self-Fashioning in Tang China (618–907)," *Fashion Theory*. Available online: http://doi: 10.1080/1362704X.2016.1138679 (accessed October 20, 2016).

Chico, B. (2010), "Mexican Headwear," in M. B. Schevill (ed.), *Latin America and the Caribbean*, Vol. 2, *Encyclopedia of World Dress and Fashion*, 57–65, Oxford and New York: Berg Publishers and Oxford University Press.

Cho, K. (2012), *The Search for the Beautiful Woman: A Cultural History of Japanese and Chinese Beauty*, translated by K. Selden, Lanham, MD: Rowan & Littlefield.

Christie, J. W. (1998), "Javanese Markets and the Asian Sea Trade Boom of the Tenth to Thirteenth Centuries," *Journal of the Economic and Social History of the Orient* 41, 3: 344–81.

Church, B. ([1675–76] 1975), *Diary of King Philip's War*, Chester, CT: Pequot Press.

Clark, I. (2013), "Chinese Hairpins: Rhapsody in Blue," in *Rethinking Pitt Rivers: Analyzing the Activities of a Nineteenth-century Collector*, The Oxford: Pitt Rivers Museum, University of Oxford. Available online: http://web.prm.ox.ac.uk/rpr/index. php/object-biography-index/1-prmcollection/290-chinese-hairpins/k (accessed October 30, 2016).

Condra, M. E. (2013), *Encyclopedia of National Dress: Traditional Clothing Around the World*, Santa Barbara, CA: ABC-CLIO.

Connor, C. L. (2004), *Women of Byzantium*, New Haven: Yale University Press.

Cordwell, J. M., and R. A. Schwarz, eds (1979), *The Fabrics of Culture: The Anthropology of Clothing and Adornment*, The Hague: Mouton Publishers.

Craik, J. (1994), *The Face of Fashion*, New York: Routledge.

Craik, J. (2009), *Fashion: The Key Concepts*, Oxford and New York: Berg.

Crawley, G., and D. Barbieri (2013), "Dress, Time, and Space: Expanding the Field through Exhibition Making," in S. Black, A. de la Haye, J. Entwistle, A. Rocamora, R. A. Root, and H. Thomas (eds.), *The Handbook of Fashion Studies*, 44–60, London and New York, Bloomsbury Academic.

Dakouri-Hild, A. (2012), "Making La Difference: Production and Consumption of Ornaments in Late Bronze Age Boeotia," in R. Laffineur and M.-L. Nosch (eds.), *KOSMOS: Jewellery, Adornment and Textiles in the Aegean Bronze Age, Proceedings of the 13th International Aegean Conference, University of Copenhagen (21–26 April 2010)*, Aegaeum 32: Annales d'archéologie égéenne de l'Université de Liège et Centre for Textile Research, University of Copenhagen. Belgium: Kliemo: 471–81 & Plates CXVII–CXXIIc.

Dalby, L. C. (1993), *Kimono: Fashioning Culture*, New Haven and London: Yale University Press.

Darwin, C. ([1859] 1999), *The Origin of Species: By Means of Natural Selection*, New York: Bantam Books.

Davenport, M. (1948), *The Book of Costume*, New York: Crown Publishers.

Davies, M. (1982), "Corsets and Conception: Fashion and Demographic Trends in the Nineteenth Century," *Comparative Studies in Society and History* 24 (4): 611–41.

Davis, F. (1992), *Fashion, Culture, and Identity*, Chicago: University of Chicago Press.

Dawson, T. (2006), "Propriety, Practicality and Pleasure: The Parameters of Women's Dress in Byzantium A.D. 1000–1200," in L. Garland (ed.), *Byzantine Women: Varieties of Experience 800–1200*, 41–76, Aldershot and Hampshire: Ashgate.

Denny, W. B., and S. B. Krody (2012), *The Sultan's Garden: The Blossoming of Ottoman Art*, Washington DC: The Textile Museum.

Derrida, J. ([1967] 1978), *Of Grammatology*, translated by G. C. Spicak, Baltimore and London: Johns Hopkins University Press.

Dhamija, J. (2010), "India," in J. Dhamija (ed.), *South Asia and Southeast Asia*, Vol. 4, *Encyclopedia of World Dress and Fashion*, 61–71, Oxford and New York: Berg Publishers and Oxford University Press.

Dillon, P. (1980), "Trade Fabrics," in S. B. Gibson (ed.), *Burr's Hill: A 17th Century Wampanoag Burial Ground in Warren*, *Rhode Island*, 100–07, Bristol, RI: Haffenreffer Museum of Anthropology.

Dillon, S. (2010), *The Female Portrait Statue in the Greek World*, New York: Cambridge University Press.

Donkin, R. A. (2003), *Between East and West: The Moluccas and the Traffic in Spices Up to the Arrival of Europeans*, Philadelphia, PA: American Philosophical Society.

Douka, K., C. A. Bergman, R. E. M. Hedges, F. P. Wesselingh, and T. F. G. Higham (2013), "Chronology of Ksar Akil (Lebanon) and Implications for the Colonization of Europe by Anatomically Modern Humans," *PLoS ONE* 8 (9): e72931. Available online: http://dx.doi.org/10.1371/journal.pone.0072931 (accessed July 31, 2016).

Duan, X. (2016), "Fashion, State, Social Changes: Chinese Silk in the Seventeenth Century Global Trade," paper presented at *Dressing Global Bodies* Conference, Edmonton, Canada (July 7).

DuPlessis, R. S. (2016), *The Material Atlantic: Clothing, Commerce, and Colonization in the Atlantic World, 1650–1800*, Cambridge: Cambridge University Press.

Earle, R. (2001), "'Two Pairs of Pink Satin Shoes!!' Race, Clothing and Identity in the Americas (17th –19th Centuries)," *History Workshop Journal* 52: 175–95.

Eicher, J. B. (2000), "The Anthropology of Dress," *Dress* 27: 59–70.

Eicher, J. B. (2001), "The Fashion of Dress," in C. Newman, *Fashion*, 17–23, Washington DC: National Geographic Society.

Eicher, J. B., ed. (2010), *Encyclopedia of World Dress and Fashion*, 10 vols. Oxford and New York: Berg Publishers and Oxford University Press.

Eicher, J. B. (2014), "India to Africa: Indian Madras and Kalabari Creativity," in M. L. Nosch, Z. Feng, and L. Varadarajan (eds.), *Global Textile Encounters*, Ancient Textile Series Vol. 20, 295–302, Oxford and Philadelphia: Oxbow Books.

Eicher, J. B. (2016), "Editing Fashion Studies: Reflections on Methodology and Interdisciplinarity in *The Encyclopedia of World Dress and Fashion*," in H. Jenss (ed.), *Fashion Studies: Research Methods, Sites, and Practices*, 198–214, London and New York: Bloomsbury.

Eicher, J. B., and T. V. Erekosima (1982), *Pelete Bite: Kalabari Cut-Thread Cloth*, St. Paul, MN: Goldstein Gallery, University of Minnesota.

Eicher, J. B., and B. Sumberg (1995), "World Fashion, Ethnic, and National Dress," in J. B. Eicher (ed.), *Dress and Ethnicity*, 295–306, Oxford and Washington DC: Berg.

Eicher J. B., S. L. Evenson, and H. A. Lutz (2008), *The Visible Self: Global Perspectives on Dress, Culture and Society*, 3rd edn, New York: Fairchild.

Entwistle, J. (2000), *The Fashioned Body*, Cambridge: Polity Press.

Enwezor, O. (2006), *Snap Judgments: New Positions in Contemporary African Photography*, New York: International Center for Photography and Göttingen: Steidl.

Erekosima, T. V., and J. B. Eicher (1981), "Kalabari Cut Thread Cloth: An Example of Cultural Authentication," *African Arts* 14 (2): 48–51.

Evancie, A. (2013), "The Surprising Sartorial Culture of the Congolese 'Sapeurs'," *The Picture Show*, NPR (National Public Radio), May 7. Available online: http://www.npr.org/sections/pictureshow/2013/05/07/181704510/the-surprising-sartorial-culture-of-congolese-sapeurs (accessed November 15, 2016).

Evans, C. (2003), *Fashion at the Edge: Spectacle, Modernity, and Deathliness*, New Haven, CT: Yale University Press.

Evans, C. (2013), *The Mechanical Smile: Modernism and the First Fashion Shows in France and America, 1900–1929*, New Haven, CT: Yale University Press.

Evans, H. C., and B. Ratliff, eds (2012), *Byzantium and Islam: Age of Transition, 7th–9th Century*, New York: Metropolitan Museum of Art.

Evans, J. (1952), *Dress in Medieval France*, Oxford: Clarendon Press.

Fales, J. (1911), "The Value of a Course in Historic Costume," *The Journal of Home Economics* (June): 243–45.

Faroqhi, S. (2004), "Introduction, or Why and How One Might Want to Study Ottoman Clothes," in S. Faroqhi and C. K. Neumann (eds.), *Ottoman Costumes: From Textile to Identity*, 15–48, Istanbul: EREN Press.

Fashion Theory (1998), Methodology Special Issue, 4 (2).

Field, G. A. (1970), "The Status Float Phenomenon: The Upward Diffusion of Innovation," *Business Horizons*, 13 (4): 45–52.

Finlay, R. (2008). "The Voyages of Zheng He: Ideology, State Power, and Maritime Trade in Ming China," *Journal of the Historical Society* 8 (3): 327–47.

Finnane, A. (2008), *Changing Clothes in China: Fashion, Modernity, Nation*, New York: Columbia University Press.

Fluck, C. (2012), "Dress Styles from Syria to Libya," in H. C. Evans and B. Ratliff (eds.), *Byzantium and Islam: Age of Transition, 7th–9th Century*, 160, New York: Metropolitan Museum of Art.

Flügel, J. C. (1930), *The Psychology of Clothes*, New York: International Universities Press.

Foster, H. B. (1997), *"New Raiments of Self": African American Clothing in the Antebellum South*, Oxford and New York: Berg.

Francks, P. (2015), "Was Fashion a European Invention?: The Kimono and Economic Development in Japan," *Fashion Theory* 19 (3): 331–61.

Freidman, J. (1990), "The Political Economy of Elegance: An African Cult of Beauty," in J. Friedman, (ed.), *Consumption and Identity*, 120–34, Newark: Harwood Academic Publishers.

Furnée-van Zwet, L. (1956), "Fashion in Women's Hair-Dress in the First Century of the Roman Empire," *Bulletin van de Vereenigingtot Bevordering van de Kennis* 31: 1–22.

Garland, L. (1999), *Byzantine Empresses: Women and Power in Byzantium, AD 527–1204*, London and New York: Routledge.

Geertz, C. (1973), *The Interpretation of Cultures*, New York: Basic Books.

Gilbert, K. S., J. K. Holt, and S. Hudson (1976), *Treasures of Tutankhamun*, New York: The Metropolitan Museum of Art.

Gilbert, S. (2000), *Tattoo History: A Source Book*, New York: Juno Books.

Gittinger, M. (1979), *Splendid Symbols: Textiles and Traditions in Indonesia*, Washington, DC: The Textile Museum.

Gittinger, M. (2005), *Textiles for this World and Beyond*, London: Scala Publishers.

Gluckman, D. C., and S. Takeda, eds. (1992), *When Art Became Fashion: Kosode in Edo-Period Japan*, Los Angeles: Los Angeles Museum of Art.

Gondola, Ch. D. (1999), "Dream and Drama: The Search for Elegance Among Congolese Youth," *African Studies Review* 42 (1): 23–48. Available online: http://doi: 10/2307/525527 (accessed March 2, 2017).

Good, I. (2001), "Archaeological Textiles: A Review of Current Research," *Annual Review of Anthropology* 30: 209–26.

Goody, J. (2006), *The Theft of History*, Cambridge: Cambridge University Press.

Gookin, D. ([1792] 1970), *Historical Collections of the Indians in New England*, New York: Towtaid.

Gott, S. (2010), "Independence to Present," in J. B. Eicher and D. H. Ross (eds.), *Africa*, Vol. 1, *Encyclopedia of World Dress and Fashion*, 51–9, Oxford and New York: Berg Publishers and Oxford University Press.

Greenhalgh, P. (1988), *Ephemeral Vistas: The Expositions Universelles, Great Exhibitions, and World's Fairs, 1851–1939, Studies in Industrialism,* Manchester and New York: Manchester University Press.

Grumbach, D. (2014), *History of International Fashion*, Northampton, MA: Interlink.

Guengerich, S.V. (2013), "Unfitting Shoes: Footwear Fashions and Social Mobility in Colonial Peru," *Journal of Spanish Cultural Studies* 14 (2): 159–85.

Hansen, K. T. (2000), *Salaula: The World of Secondhand Clothing and Zambia*, Chicago: University of Chicago Press.

Hansen, K. T. (2004), "The World in Dress: Anthropological Perspectives on Clothing, Fashion, and Culture," *Annual Review of Anthropology* 33: 369–92.

Hansen, K. T., and D. S. Madison, eds (2013), *African Dress: Fashion, Agency, Performance*, London and New York: Bloomsbury.

Harlow, M., and M-L Nosch, (2014), "Weaving the Threads: Methodologies in Textiles and Dress Research for the Greek and Roman World," in M. Harlow, C. Michel and M-L. Nosch (eds.), *Greek and Roman Textiles and Dress: An Interdisciplinary Anthology.* Ancient Textiles Series, vol. 19, 1–32, Oxford and Philadelphia: Oxbow Books.

Harlow, M., C. Michel, and M-L Nosch, eds (2014), *Greek and Roman Textiles and Dress: An Interdisciplinary Anthology.* Ancient Textiles Series, vol. 19, Oxford and Philadelphia: Oxbow Books.

Hawley, G. ([1815] 1968), *A Description of Mashpee, in the County of Barnstable, Sept. 16th 1802*, Collections of the Massachusetts Historical Society, ser. 2, no. 3, New York: Johnson Reprint Corp.

Hebdige, D. (1979), *Subculture: The Meaning of Style*, New York: Methuen.

Heller, S. G. (2007), *Fashion in Medieval France*, Cambridge: D. S. Brewer.

Heringa, R, (1997), "Batik Pasisir: A Mestizo Costume," in R. Heringa and H. C. Veldhuisen (eds.), *Fabric of Enchantment: Batik from the North Coast of Java*, 46–69, Los Angeles: Los Angeles County Museum of Art.

Heringa, R. (2010), "Upland Tribal, Coastal Village, and Inland Court: Revised Parameters for Batik Research," in R. Barnes and M. H. Kahlenberg (eds.), *Five Centuries of Indonesian Textiles*, 121–85, Munich: Delmonico Books.

Heringa, R., and H. C. Veldhuisen. (1997), *Fabric of Enchantment: Batik from the North Coast of Java*, Los Angeles: Los Angeles County Museum of Art.

Hill, D. D. (2011), *History of World Costume and Fashion*, Upper Saddle River, NJ: Prentice Hall.

Hobsbawm, E., and T. Ranger, eds (1983), *The Invention of Tradition*, Cambridge and New York: Cambridge University Press.

Hollander, A. (1978), *Seeing Through Clothes*, New York: Viking Press.

Holt, A. (1887), *Fancy Dresses Described; or What to Wear at Fancy Balls*, London: Debenham and Freebody.

Hopkins, A. G. (1973), *An Economic History of West Africa*, New York: Columbia University Press.

Houston, S. D. (2000), "'Into the Minds of Ancients': Advances in Maya Glyph Studies," *Journal of World Prehistory* 14 (2): 121–201.

International Journal of Fashion Studies (2015), Special Issue, 2 (1).

Izbicki, T. (2009), "Failed Censures: Ecclesiastical Regulation of Women's Clothing in Late Medieval Italy," in R. Netherton and G. R. Owen-Crocker (eds.), *Medieval Clothing and Textiles* 5, 37–53, Woodbridge, Suffolk: Boydell.

Jager, U., and V. Mair. (2010), "The Yingpin Man," in V. Mair (ed.), *Secrets of the Silk Road: An Exhibition of Discoveries from the Xinjiang Uyghur Autonomous Region, China*, 55–57, Santa Ana, CA: Bowers Museum.

Jameson, F. (1998), *The Cultural Turn: Selected Writings on the Postmodern, 1983–1998*, London and New York: Verso.

Jansen, M. A., and J. Craik (2016), *Modern Fashion Traditions: Negotiating Tradition and Modernity Through Fashion*, London: Bloomsbury Academic.

Jasper, C., and M. E. Roach-Higgins (1987), "History of Costume: Theory and Instruction," *Clothing and Textile Research Journal* 5 (4): 1–6.

Jirousek, C. (2004), "Ottoman Influences in Western Dress," in S. Faroqhi and C. K. Neumann (eds.), *Ottoman Costumes: From Textile to Identity*, 231–51, Istanbul: EREN Press.

Johnson, K. P., S. J. Torntore, and J. B. Eicher, eds (2003), *Fashion Foundations: Early Writings on Fashion and Dress*, Oxford: Berg.

Jones, J. M. (2013), "Gender and Eighteenth-Century Fashion," in S. Black, A. de la Haye, J. Entwistle, A. Rocamora, R. Root, and H. Thomas (eds.), *The Handbook of Fashion Studies*, 121–36, London and New York: Bloomsbury Academic.

Josselyn, J. ([1674] 1988), *John Josselyn, Colonial Traveler: A Critical Edition of Two Voyages to New-England*, edited by P. J. Lindholt, Hanover, NH and London: University Press of New England.

Kaeppler, A. L. (1980), *Kapa: Hawaiian Bark Cloth*, Hilo Bay and Hawai'i: Boom Books and the Bishop Museum.

Kaiser, S. B. (2012), *Fashion and Cultural Studies*, London and New York: Bloomsbury Academic.

Kant, I. ([1790] 2007) *Critique of Judgement*, translated by J. C. Meredith, Oxford: Oxford University Press.

Kawamura, Y. (2005), *Fashion-ology: An Introduction to Fashion Studies*, Oxford and New York: Berg.

Kawamura, Y. (2011), "Japanese Street Fashion: The Urge to be Seen and to be Heard," in L. Welters and A. Lillethun (eds.), *The Fashion Reader*, 2nd ed., 467–69, Oxford and New York: Berg.

"Kimono" (2016), London: Victoria and Albert Museum. Available online: http://www.vam.ac.uk/page/k/kimono/ (accessed October 23, 2016).

Kindseth, T. (9 September 2009), "Angkor Thom," *Time*, Time, Inc. Available online: https://content.time.com/time/ travel/article/0,31542,1921229,00.html (accessed October 30, 2016).

King, C. W. (1963), "Fashion Adoption: A Rebuttal to the 'Trickle-Down Theory'", in S. A. Greyser (ed.), *Toward Scientific Marketing*, 108–25, Chicago: American Marketing Association.

Knowles, K. (2012), "Fashioning Slavery: Slaves and Clothing in the United States South, 1830–1865," *Dress* 38: 24–36.

Ko, D. (1997), "Bondage in Time: Footbinding and Fashion Theory," *Fashion Theory* 1 (1): 3–27.

Köhler, K. (1963), *A History of Costume*, New York: Dover.

Kriger, C. E. (2006), *Cloth in West African History*, Lanham, MD: AltaMira Press.

Kuhn, T. S. (1962), *The Structure of Scientific Revolutions*, Chicago: University of Chicago Press.

Kurath, H. ed. (1952), *Middle English Dictionary*, Part E, Ann Arbor: University of Michigan Press.

Laiou, A. E., and C. Morrisson (2007), *The Byzantine Economy*, Cambridge: Cambridge University Press.

Lascaratos, J., C., Tsiamis, G. Lascaratos, and N. G. Stavrianeas (2004), "The Roots of Cosmetic Medicine," *International Journal of Dermatology* 43: 397–401.

Latvian History Museum (1995), *Latvian National Costumes I. Vidzeme*, Riga: Jana seta.

Latvian History Museum (1997), *Latvian National Costumes II. Kurzeme: Latvian and Liv Costumes*, Riga: Jana seta.

Laver, J. ([1937] 1945), *Taste and Fashion: From the French Revolution to the Present Day*, rev. edn., London: George G. Harrap and Co. Ltd.

Laver, J. (1969a), *Modesty in Dress*, Boston: Houghton Mifflin.

Laver, J. (1969b), *The Concise History of Costume and Fashion*, New York: Harry N. Abrams.

Lee, K. J. (2010), "Overview of Korea: Traditional," in J. E. Vollmer (ed.), *East Asia*, Vol. 6, *Encyclopedia of World Dress and Fashion*, 315–19, Oxford and New York: Berg Publishers and Oxford University Press.

Lehmann, U. (2000), *Tigersprung: Fashion in Modernity*, Cambridge, MA: MIT Press.

Leibsohn, D., and B. Mundy (2005), "Vistas: Visual Culture in Spanish America, 1520–1820," Washington, DC: The Smithsonian Institution. Available online: https://www.smith.edu/vistas (accessed September 20, 2016).

Lemire, B. (1992), *Fashion's Favorite: The Cotton Industry and the Consumer in Britain, 1660–1800*, Oxford: Oxford University Press.

Lemire, B. ed. (2010), *The Force of Fashion in Politics and Society*, Farnham: Ashgate.

Lemire, B. (2011), *Cotton*, Oxford and New York: Berg.

Levine, D. ed. (1971), *Simmel: On Individuality and Social Forms*, Chicago: University of Chicago Press.

Lillethun, A., L. Welters, and J. B. Eicher (2012), "(Re)Defining Fashion, *Dress* 38: 77–99.

Lineberry, C. (2007), "Tattoos: The Ancient and Mysterious History," Smithsonian, Available online: http://www.smithsonianmag.com/history/tattoos-144038580/ (accessed August 21, 2016).

Lipovetsky, G. (1994), *The Empire of Fashion: Dressing Modern Democracy*, translated by C. Porter, Princeton, NJ: Princeton University Press.

Liu, R. K. (2010), "Beads: Prehistory to Early Twenty-first Century," in J. B. Eicher and P. G. Tortora (eds.), *Global Perspectives*, Vol. 10, *Encyclopedia of World Dress and Fashion*, 33–46, Oxford and New York: Berg Publishers and Oxford University Press.

Loren, D. D. (2010), *The Archaeology of Clothing and Bodily Adornment in Colonial America*, Gainesville: University of Florida Press.

Loren, D. D. (2012), "Fear, Desire, and Material Strategies in Colonial Louisiana," in B. L. Voss and E. C. Casella (eds.), *The Archaeology of Colonialism: Intimate Encounters and Sexual Effects*, 105–21, New York: Cambridge University Press.

Loschek, I. (2009), *When Clothes Become Fashion: Design and Innovation Systems*, Oxford and New York: Berg.

Lurie, A. (1981), *The Language of Clothes*, New York: Random House.

Lynch, A., and M. D. Strauss, eds (2015), *Ethnic Dress in the United States: A Cultural Encyclopedia*, Lanham, MD: Rowman & Littlefield.

Lyotard, J-F. (1979), *The Postmodern Condition: A Report on Knowledge*, Minneapolis: University of Minnesota Press.

McCarthy, B., and E. S. Chase. (2003), "Feathers of Blue on a Field of Gold: Chinese Ornament with Kingfisher Feather Cloisonné," in J. Alt (ed.), *Scientific Research in the Field of Asian Art: Proceedings of the First Forbes Symposium at the Freer Gallery of Art Held Fall, 2001*, 15–23, Washington, DC and London: Freer Gallery of Art. Smithsonian Institution and Archetype Publications Ltd.

McCracken, G. (1986), "Culture and Consumption: A Theoretical Account of the Structure and Movement of the Cultural Meaning of Consumer Goods," *Journal of Consumer Research* 13 (1): 71–84, Bloomington: Indiana University Press.

McLuhan, M. (1967), *The Medium is the Massage: An Inventory of Effects*, New York: Random House.

McNeil, P., and V. Karaminas, eds (2009), *The Men's Fashion History Reader*, Oxford and New York: Berg.

McRobbie, A. (1991), *Feminism and Youth Culture: From "Jackie" to "Just Seventeen,"* Houndmills, UK: Macmillan.

Ma, H. ([1433] 1970), *Ying-Yai Sheng-Lan: The Overall Survey of the Ocean's Shores*, translated by F. Ch'eng-Chün and J. V. G Mills, Cambridge: Hakluyt Society and Cambridge University Press.

Magliaro, I. (1988), [Videocassette (VHS)] *Korean Costume: Changes in View of Her History* and *Culture Contact*, UA–Columbia Cablevision of Massachusetts.

Mair, V., ed. (2010), *Secrets of the Silk Road: An Exhibition of Discoveries from the Xinjiang Uyghur Autonomous Region, China*, Santa Ana, CA: Bowers Museum.

Major, J. S. (2005), "China: History of Dress," in V. Steele (ed.), *Encyclopedia of Clothing and Fashion*, Vol. 1, 260–66, New York: Charles Scribner's Sons.

Marten, C. (1970), "The Wampanoags in the Seventeenth Century," *Occasional Papers in Old Colony Studies* 2, Plymouth, MA: Plimoth Plantation Inc.

Martin, P. M. (1994), "Contesting Clothes in Colonial Brazzaville," *The Journal of African History* 35 (3): 401–26.

Matsui, M. (2005), "Beyond the Pleasure Room to the Chaotic Street: The Transformation of Cute Subculture in the Art of the Japanese Nineties," in T. Murakami, ed., *Little Boy: The Art of Japan's Exploding Subculture*, 208–39, New York and New Haven: Japan Society and Yale University Press.

Maynard, M. (2004), *Dress and Globalisation*, Manchester: Manchester University Press.

Mazrui, A. A. (1970), "The Robes of Rebellion: Sex, Dress and Politics in Africa," *Encounter* 34 (2): 19–30.

Mei, H. (2004), *Chinese Clothing*, translated by Y. Hong and Z. Lei, Cultural China Series, Beijing: China Intercontinental Press.

Meisch, L. (2010), "Overview of South America," in M. B. Schevill (ed.), *Latin America and the Caribbean*, Vol. 2, *Encyclopedia of World Dress and Fashion*, 301–15, Oxford and New York: Berg Publishers and Oxford University Press.

Merleau-Ponty, M. (1976), *The Visible and the Invisible*, trans. A. Lingus, Chicago: Chicago University Press.

Middleton, J. (2014), "'Their Dress is Very Different'—The Development of the Peruvian Pollera and the Genesis of the Andean Chola," *Abstracts of the Costume Society of America 40th Annual Meeting and Symposium*, Baltimore, MD, 29.

Miller, D. I., and S. Woodward, eds (2011), *Global Denim*, Oxford and New York: Berg.

'Miss Julia Grant's Wedding' (October 7, 1899), *Harper's Bazar*, 853.

Monden, M. (2013), "The 'Nationality' of Lolita Fashion," in F. Nakamura, M. Perkins and O. Krischer (eds.), *Asia Through Art and Anthropology: Cultural Translation Across Borders*, 165–78, London and New York: Bloomsbury Academic.

Montgomery, F. M. (1984), *Textiles in America 1650–1870*, New York: W. W. Norton.

Morgado, M. A. (1993a), "Animal Trademark Emblems on Fashion Apparel: Λ Scmiotic Interpretation: Part I. Interpretive Strategy," *Clothing and Textiles Research Journal* 11 (2): 16–20.

Morgado, M. A. (1993b), "Animal Trademark Emblems on Fashion Apparel: A Semiotic Interpretation: Part II. Applied Semiotics," *Clothing and Textiles Research Journal* 11 (3): 31–8.

Morriss-Kay, G. M. (2010), "The Evolution of Human Artistic Creativity," *Journal of Anatomy* 216 (2): 158–76. Available online: http://doi: 10.1111/j.1469-7580.2009.01160.x (accessed March 26, 2017).

Morton, T. ([1637] 1969), *New English Canaan*, Amsterdam; New York: Theatrum Orbis Terrarum Ltd; Da Capo Press.

Newton, S. M. (1974), *Health, Art and Reason*, London: J. Murray.

Newton, S. M. (1975), *Renaissance Theatre Costume, and the Sense of the Historic Past*, New York: Theatre Art Books.

Newton, S. M. (1980), *Fashion in the Age of the Black Prince: A Study of the Years 1340–1365*, Woodbridge and Suffolk: Boydell.

Newton, S. M. (1988), *The Dress of the Venetians, 1495–1525*, Aldershot, UK: Scolar Press.

Nicklas, C., and A. Pollen, eds (2015), *Dress History: New Directions in Theory and Practice*, London and New York: Bloomsbury Academic.

Niemeyer, H. M., and C. Agüero (2015), "Dyes Used in Pre-Hispanic Textiles from the Middle and Late Intermediate Periods of San Pedro de Atacama (Northern Chile): New Insights into Patterns of Exchange and Mobility," *Journal of Archaeological Science* 57: 14–23.

Niessen, S. (2003), "Re-Orienting Fashion Theory," in S. Niessen, A. M. Leshkowich, and C. Jones (eds.), *Re-Orienting Fashion: The Globalization of Asian Dress*, 243–66, Oxford: Berg.

Niessen, S. (2016), "Afterword: Fashion's Fallacy," in M. A. Jansen and J. Craik (eds.), *Modern Fashion Traditions: Negotiating Tradition and Modernity through Fashion*, 209–17, London and New York: Bloomsbury Academic.

Niessen, S., A. M. Leshkowich, and C. Jones, eds (2003), *Re-Orienting Fashion: The Globalization of Asian Dress*, Oxford: Berg.

Olian, J. A. (1977), "Sixteenth-Century Costume Books," *Dress* 3: 20–48.

Olson, K. (2002), "Matrona and Whore: Clothing of Women in Roman Antiquity," *Fashion Theory* 6 (4): 399–400.

O'Neal, G. S. (1998), "African-American Aesthetic of Dress: Current Manifestations," *Clothing and Textile Research Journal* 16 (4): 167–75.

Orr, H., and M. Looper, eds (2014), *Wearing Culture: Dress and Regalia in Early Mesoamerica and Central America*, Boulder: University Press of Colorado.

Østergaard, J. S. (2010), "The Polychromy of Antique Sculpture: A Challenge to Western Ideals," in V. Brinkmann, O. Primevessi and M. Hollein (eds.), *Circumlitio: The Polychromy of Antique and Mediaeval Sculpture*, 78–107, Munich: Hirmer Publishers.

Owen-Crocker, G. R. (2004), *Dress in Anglo-Saxon England*, Woodbridge, England: Boydell Press.

Oxford *English Dictionary* (1989), 2nd edn. 20 vols, Oxford and New York: Clarendon Press; Oxford University Press.

Paine, S. (1990), *Embroidered Textiles: Traditional Patterns from Five Continents*, New York: Rivoli.

Parker, R. (1984), *The Subversive Stitch: Embroidery and the Making of the Feminine*, New York: Routledge.

Paulicelli, E. (2014), *Writing Fashion in Early Modern Italy: From Sprezzatura to Satire*, Farnham, Surrey: Ashgate.

Paulicelli, E., and H. Clark, eds (2009), *The Fabric of Cultures: Fashion, Identity and Globalization*, London and New York: Routledge.

Payne, B. (1965), *History of Costume*, New York: Harper and Row.

Payne, B., G. Winakor, and J. Farrell-Beck (1992), *The History of Costume*, New York: Harper Collins.

Peck, A. (2013), *Interwoven Globe: The World Textile Trade, 1500–1800*, New York: Metropolitan Museum of Art.

Pemberton, J. (1994), *On the Subject of "Java,"* Ithaca: Cornell University Press.

Penh, S. (2015), "Historical Events Impact Fashion," unpublished paper, University of Rhode Island, (December 9).

Péquart, M., and S. J. Péquart (1954), *Hoëdic, Deuxieme Station-nécropole du Mésolithique Côtier Armoricain*, Anvers: de Sikkel.

Péquart, M., and S. J. Péquart (1960), "Grotte du Mas d'Azil (Ariége), Une nouvelle galerie magdalénienne," *Annales de Paléontologie* 46: 127–94.

Péquart, M., S. J. Péquart, M. Boule, and H. Vallois (1937), *Téviec, Station-nécropole du Mésolithique du Morbihan*, Paris: Archives de L'Institut de Paléontologie Humaine XVIII.

Petersen, J. B., ed. (1996), *A Most Indispensable Art: Native Fiber Industries from Eastern North America*, Knoxville: University of Tennessee Press.

Pettersson, J. (2016), *Joona Pettersson*. Available online: http://www.joonapettersson.com/West-African-Street-Styles (accessed September 1, 2016).

Phillips, J. C. (2012), "On the Use and Re-use of Jewellery Elements," in R. Laffineur and M.-L. Nosch (eds.), *KOSMOS: Jewellery, Adornment and Textiles in the Aegean Bronze Age, Proceedings of the 13th International Aegean Conference, University of Copenhagen (21–26 April 2010)*, Aegaeum 32: Annales d'archéologie égéenne de l'Université de Liège et Centre for Textile Research, University of Copenhagen. Belgium: Kliemo: 483–91 & Plate CXXIII.

Piponnier, F., and P. Mane (1997), *Dress in the Middle Ages*, translated by C. Beamish, New Haven and London: Yale University Press.

Planché, J. R. (1879), *A Cyclopedia of Costume, or Dictionary of Dress*, London: Chatto and Windus.

Polhemus, T. (1994), *Street Style: From Sidewalk to Catwalk*, New York: Thames and Hudson.

Procopius of Caesarea, *The Secret History*, Internet Medieval Sourcebook: Fordham University. Available online: http://sourcebooks.fordham.edu/Halsall/basis/procop-anec.asp (accessed November 5, 2016).

Psellus, M. (n.d.), *Chronographia*, Internet Medieval Sourcebook: Fordham University. Available online: http://sourcebooks.fordham.edu/basis/psellus-chrono06.asp (accessed November 6, 2016).

Pulak, C. (2008), "The Ulunurun Shipwreck and Late Bronze Age Trade," in J. Aruz, K. Benzel and J. M. Evans (eds.), *Beyond Babylon: Art, Trade and Diplomacy in the Second Millennium B.C.*, 286–305, New York: The Metropolitan Museum of Art.

Purdy, D. L., ed. (2004), *The Rise of Fashion: A Reader*, Minneapolis: University of Minneapolis Press.

Rabine, L. W. (2002), *The Global Circulation of African Fashion*, Oxford and New York: Berg.

Racinet, A. (1876–1888), *Le costume historique. . . .,* Paris: Librairie de Firmin-Didot et cie, imprimeurs de l'institut.

Redaelli, A. (1994) "The Evolution of the Velvet Loom," in F. de' Marinis (ed.) *Velvet*, 196–99, New York: Idea Books.

Reich, C. A. (1970), *The Greening of America*, New York: Random House.

Reilly, A., and S. Cosbey, eds (2008), *The Men's Fashion Reader*, New York: Fairchild.

Reynolds, J. ([1776] 1831), "Discourse VII on the Distribution of the Prizes, December 10, 1776," in *Discourses Delivered to the Students of the Royal Academy*, London: M. Arnold.

Ribeiro, A. (1995), *The Art of Dress: Fashion in England and France, 1750 to 1820*, New Haven, CT: Yale University Press.

Ribeiro, A. (1999), *Ingres in Fashion: Representations of Dress and Appearance in Ingres's Images of Women*, New Haven, CT: Yale University Press.

Riello, G. (2006), *A Foot in the Past: Consumers, Producers, and Footwear in the Long Eighteenth Century*, Oxford: Oxford University Press.

Riello, G. (2013), *Cotton: The Fabric that Made the Modern World*, Cambridge, UK: Cambridge University Press.

Riello, G., and P. McNeil, eds (2010), *The Fashion History Reader: Global Perspectives*, New York: Routledge.

Roach, M. E., and K. E. Musa (1980), *New Perspectives on the History of Western Dress: A Handbook*, New York: NutriGuides.

Roach-Higgins, M. E., and J. B. Eicher (1992), "Dress and Identity," *Clothing and Textile Research Journal* 10 (4): 1–8.

Roche, D. (1994), *The Culture of Clothing: Dress and Fashion in the Ancien Régime*, Cambridge: Cambridge University Press.

Root, R. A., ed. (2005) *The Latin American Fashion Reader*, London and New York: Berg Publishers.

Root, R. A. (2013), "Mapping Latin American Fashion," in S. Black, A. de la Haye, J. Entwistle, A. Rocamora, R. Root, and H. Thomas (eds.), *The Handbook of Fashion Studies*, 391–407, London and New York: Bloomsbury Academic.

Rosenthal, M. F., and A. R. Jones (2008), *The Clothing of the Renaissance World: Europe, Asia, Africa, the Americas: Cesare Vecellio's Habiti Antichi et Moderni*, London and New York: Thames and Hudson.

Ross, R. (2008), *Clothing: A Global History: Or, The Imperialists' New Clothes*. Cambridge, UK: Polity Press.

Rovine, V. L. (2015), *African Fashion, Global Style: Histories, Innovations, Ideas You Can Wear*, Bloomington: Indiana University Press.

Rowe, A. P. (1984), *Costumes and Featherwork of the Lords of Chimor: Textiles from Peru's North Coast*, Washington DC: The Textile Museum.

Rowe, A. P. (1995–1996), "Inca Weaving and Costume," *The Textile Museum Journal* 34/35: 4–53.

Rowe, A. P. (2005), "Gods and Empire: Huari Ceremonial Textiles," *The Bulletin*, Washington, DC: Textile Museum.

Rowe, A. P., and L. A. Meisch (2011), *Costume and History in Highland Ecuador*, Austin: University of Texas Press.

Rowlandson, M. ([1682] 1981), "The Sovereignty and Goodness of God," in A. T. Vaughan and E. W. Clark (eds.), *Puritans Among the Indians*, Cambridge, MA: Belknap Press of Harvard University.

Ruhlen, R. N. (2003), "Korean Alterations: Nationalism, Social Consciousness, and 'Traditional' Clothing," in S. Niessen, A. M. Leshkowich and C. Jones (eds.), *Re-Orienting Fashion: The Globalization of Asian Dress*, 117–37, Oxford: Berg.

Russell, D. (1973), *Stage Costume Design: Theory, Technique, and Style*, New York: Appleton-Century-Crofts.

Rydell, R. (1984), *All the World's a Fair: Visions of Empire at American International Expositions, 1876–1916*, Chicago: University of Chicago Press.

Ryerson, R. A. ed. (1993), *Adams Family Correspondence*, The Adams Papers, series II, vol. 5. Cambridge, MA: Belknap Press.

Said, E. (1978), *Orientalism*, New York: Pantheon.

Saliklis, R. (1999), "The Dynamic Relationship Between Lithuanian National Costumes and Folk Dress," in L. Welters (ed.), *Folk Dress in Europe and Anatolia: Beliefs about Protection and Fertility*, 211–34, Oxford and New York: Berg.

Samwell, D. ([1788] 1967). "Some Account of a Voyage to South Sea's in 1776–1777–1778," in J. C. Beaglehole (ed.), *The Journals of Captain James Cook on His Voyages of Discovery: The Voyage of the* Resolution *and Discovery 1776–1780*, 987–1300, Cambridge: Cambridge University Press.

Sandhu, A. (2016), *Indian Fashion: Tradition, Innovation, Style*, London and New York: Bloomsbury.

Sapir, E. (1931), "Fashion," in E. R. A. Seligman (ed.), *Encyclopedia of the Social Sciences* 6, 139–44, New York: Macmillan Co.

Scarce, J. (1987), *Women's Costume of the Near and Middle East*, London: Unwin Hyman.

Scheinman, P. (1991), "A Line at a Time: Innovative Patterning in the Isthmus of (Isthmian) Mexico," in M. B. Schevill, J. C. Berlo and E. B. Dyer (eds.), *Textile Traditions of Mesoamerica and the Andes*, 63–87, New York: Garland.

Schevill, M. (1986), *Costume as Communication*, Bristol, RI: Haffenreffer Museum of Anthropology.

Schevill, M. (1991), "The Communicative Power of Cloth and Its Creation," in M. B. Schevill, J. C. Berlo and E. B. Dwyer (eds.), *Textile Traditions of Mesoamerica and the Andes*, 3–15, New York and London: Garland Publishing Company.

Schneider, J. (2006a), "Cloth and Clothing," in C. Tilley, W. Keane, S. Kuchler, M. Rowlands and P. Spyer (eds.), *Handbook of Material Culture*, 203–20, London: Sage.

Schneider, L. (2006b), "The Maasai's New Clothes: A Developmentalist Modernity and Its Exclusions," *Africa Today* 53 (1): 101–31.

Schulting, R. J. (1996), "Antlers, Bone Pins and Flint Blades: The Mesolithic Cemeteries of Téviec and Hoëdic, Brittany," *Antiquity* 70 (268): 335–50.

Seneca the Younger, (ca. 3 BCE–65 CE), *Declamations* Vol. I.

Sheng, A. (2010), "Textiles from the Silk Road: Intercultural Exchanges Among Nomads, Traders, and Agriculturalists," *Expedition* 52 (3): 33–43.

Sherrill, T. (2009), "Who Was Cesare Vecellio? Placing *Habiti Antichi* in Context," in R. Netherton and G. R. Owen-Crocker (eds.), *Medieval Clothing and Textiles* 5, 161–88, Woodbridge, Suffolk: The Boydell Press.

Shukla, P. (2015), *Costume: Performing Identities Through Dress*, Bloomington: Indiana University Press.

Silberstein, R. (2016), "Cloud Bands and Sleeve Bands: Commercial Embroidery and the Fashionable Accessory in Mid-to-Late Qing China," *Fashion Theory*, 1–34. Available online: http://dx.doi.org/10.1080/1362704X.2016.1150670 (accessed October 17, 2016).

Simmel, G. ([1904] 1954), "Fashion," *International Quarterly* 10 (1): 130–55, reprinted in *American Journal of Sociology* 62 (6): 541–58.

Slade, T. (2009), *Japanese Fashion: A Cultural History*, London: Berg.

Snodgrass, M. E. (2014) *World Clothing and Fashion: An Encyclopedia of History, Culture, and Social Influence*, Armonk, NY: M. E. Sharpe.

So, J. F. (2013), "Scented Trails: Amber as Aromatic in Medieval China," *Journal of the Royal Asiatic Society* 23 (1): 85–101.

Spencer, H. (1854), *Essays: Scientific, Political, and Speculative. Library Edition, containing Seven Essays not before republished, and various other Additions* (London: Williams and Norgate, 1891). Vol. 3. Available online: http://oll.libertyfund.org/titles/337 (accessed June 26, 2016).

Spencer H. ([1864] 2002), *Principles of Biology*, vol. 1, Honolulu, HI: University Press of the Pacific.

Sproles, G. B. (1974), "Fashion Theory: A Conceptual Framework," *Advances in Consumer Research* 1: 463–72, Association for Consumer Research. Available online: http://acrwebsite.org/volumes/5731/volumes/v01/NA-01 (accessed March 20, 2016).

Sproles, G. B. (1981), "Analyzing Fashion Life Cycles—Principles and Perspectives," *Journal of Marketing* 45 (4): 116–24.

"Staatsiejas van de Sultan Hamengku Buwono VI en VII van Yogyakarta" (2015), Nationaal Museum van Wereldculturen, object nr. TM-1595-2. Available online: http://collectie.wereldculturen.nl/Default.aspx?ccid=57842&lang= (accessed July 15, 2016).

Steele, V. (2001), *The Corset: A Cultural History*, New Haven, CT: Yale University Press.

Steele, V. (2005), "Preface," in V. Steele (ed.), *Encyclopedia of Clothing and Fashion*, Vol. 1, xv–xviii, New York: Charles Scribner's Sons.

Steiner, C. B. (1985), "Another Image of Africa: Toward an Ethnohistory of European Cloth Marketed in West Africa, 1873–1960," *Ethnohistory: The Bulletin of the Ohio Valley Historical Conference* 32 (2): 91–110.

Stephens, J. (2008), "Ancient Roman Hairdressing: (On) Hairpins and Needles," *Journal of Roman Archaeology* 21: 1110–32.

Strutt, J. (1842), *A Complete View of the Dress and Habits of the People of England*, with an introduction by J. R. Planché, London: H. G. Bohn.

Sturtevant, W. C. M. (1980), "Les Inuit du Québec-Labrador méridional/The Inuit of Southern Québec-Labrador," *Études Inuit / Inuit Studies* 4 (1/2): 47–49.

Styles, J. (2007), *The Dress of the People: Everyday Fashion in Eighteenth-Century England*, New Haven and London: Yale University Press.

Sylvanus, N. (2016), *Patterns in Circulation: Cloth, Gender and Materiality in West Africa*, Chicago: University of Chicago Press.

Taborin, Y. (1974), "La parure en coquillage de l'Epipaléolithique au Bronze ancien France," *Gallia Pre'histoire* 17 (1): 101–79 and 17 (2): 307–417.

Taylor, J. G. (2007), "Identity, Nation and Islam: A Dialogue About Men's and Women's Dress in Indonesia," in M. Roces and L. Edwards (eds.), *The Politics of Dress in Asia and the Americas*, 101–20, Sussex: Sussex Academic Press.

Taylor, L. (2002), *The Study of Dress History*, Manchester and New York: Manchester University Press.

Taylor, L. (2004), *Establishing Dress History*, Manchester and New York: Manchester University Press.

Taylor, L. (2013), "Fashion and Dress History: Theoretical and Methodological Approaches," in S. Black, A. de la Haye, J. Entwistle, A. Rocamora, R. Root and H. Thomas (eds.), *The Handbook of Fashion Studies*, 23–43, London and New York: Bloomsbury Academic.

Teilhet-Fisk, J. (1999), "The Miss Heilala Beauty Pagaent: Where Beauty Is More than Skin Deep," in M. L. Damhorst, K. A. Miller and S. O. Michelman (eds.), *The Meanings of Dress*, 67–77, New York: Fairchild.

Tezcan, H. (2000) "Fashion at the Ottoman Court," *Art Culture Antiques* 3: 2–49.

Tezcan, H. (2012), "The Evaluation of the Sultan's Costume Collection According to the Ottoman Fashion," *Endymatologika* 4: 25–29.

The Periplus of the Erythraean Sea: Travel and Trade in the Indian Ocean by a Merchant of the First Century, Ancient History Sourcebook: Fordham University. Available online: http://sourcebooks.fordham.edu/halsall/ancient/periplus.asp (accessed October 22, 2016).

The *Wild One* (1953), [film] Dir. László, Benedek, USA: Stanley Kramer Productions.

Thomas, P. A. (1979), "In the Maelstrom of Change: The Indian Trade and Cultural Process in the Middle Connecticut River Valley, 1635–1665," PhD diss., University of Massachusetts, Amherst.

Thomas, T. K. ed. (2016), *Designing Identity: The Power of Textiles in Late Antiquity*, Princeton: Princeton University Press.

Thomas, T. K. (2016), "Material Meaning in Late Antiquity," in T. K. Thomas (ed.), *Designing Identity: The Power of Textiles in Late Antiquity*, 20–53, Princeton: Princeton University Press.

Thomson, J. (1873–1874), *Illustrations of China and Its People, a Series of Two Hundred Photographs with Letterpress Description of the Places and People Represented*. 4 vols, London: Sampson Low, Marston Low, and Searle.

Tilke, M. (1923), *Orientalische Kostüme in Schnitt und Farbe* (*Oriental Costumes in Cut and Color*), Berlin: Verlag Ernst Wasmuth AG.

Tortora, P. G. (2010), "History and Development of Fashion," in J. B. Eicher and P. G. Tortora (eds.), *Global Perspectives*, Vol. 10, *Encyclopedia of World Dress and Fashion*, 159–70, Oxford and New York: Berg Publishers and Oxford University Press.

Tortora, P. G., and S. B. Marcketti (2015), *Survey of Historic Costume*, 6th ed., London and New York: Bloomsbury.

Trinkaus, E., A. P. Buzhilova, M. B. Mednikova and M. V. Dobrovolskaya (2014), *The People of Sunghir: Burials, Bodies, and Behavior in the Earlier Upper Paleolithic*, New York: Oxford University Press.

Tsui, C. (2016), "'Fashion' in the Chinese Context: An Academic Approach," in M. A. Jansen and J. Craik (eds.), *Modern Fashion Traditions: Negotiating Tradition and Modernity through Fashion*, 51–70, London and New York: Bloomsbury Academic.

University of Oxford (2009), "World's Oldest Manufactured Beads Are Older Than Previously Thought," *Science Daily*. Available online: http://www.sciencedaily.com/releases/2009/05/090505163021.htm (accessed August 8, 2016).

van Assche, A.M. (2010), "Overview of Japan," in J. E. Vollmer (ed.), *East Asia*, Vol. 6, *Encyclopedia of World Dress and Fashion*, 345–54, Oxford and New York: Berg Publishers and Oxford University Press.

van Buren, A. H. (2011), *Illuminating Fashion: Dress in the Art of Medieval France and the Netherlands, 1325–1515*, New York: The Morgan Library and Museum.

van Driel Murray, C. (1987), "Roman Footwear: A Mirror of Fashion and Society," in D. E. Friendship-Taylor, J. Swann and S. Thomas (eds.), *Recent Research in Archaeological Footwear*, 32–42, London: Association of Archaeological Illustrators and Surveyors.

Veblen, T. (1899), *The Theory of the Leisure Class: An Economic Study in the Evolution of Institutions*, New York: Macmillan.

Veldhuisen, H. C. (1993), *Batik Belanda, 1840–1940: Dutch Influences in Batik from Java, History and Stories*, translated by M. Ader, Jakarta: Gaya Favorit Press.

Vitalis, O. ([1075-1143?] 1854), *The Ecclesiastical History of England and Normandy*, Vol. III translated by T. Forester, London: Henry G. Bohn.

Vogelsang-Eastwood, G. (1993), *Pharonic Egyptian Clothing*, Leiden: E. J. Brill.

Vollmer, J. E. (1977), *In the Presence of the Dragon Throne: Ch'ing Dynasty Costume (1644–1911) in the Royal Ontario Museum*, Toronto, Canada: Royal Ontario Museum.

Voss, B. L. (2008), *The Archaeology of Ethnogenesis: Race and Sexuality in Colonial San Francisco*, Berkeley: University of California Press.

Ward, E. (1699), *A Trip to New-England with a Character of the Country and People, Both English and Indians*, Ann Arbor, MI: University Microfilms.

Warner, J. (1977), *China, The Land and Its People: Early Photographs by John Thomson*, Hong Kong: John Warner Publications.

Waugh, C. (1999), "'Well-Cut Through the Body': Fitted Clothing in Twelfth-Century Europe," *Dress* 26: 3–16.

Weiner, A. B., and J. Schneider (1989), *Cloth and the Human Experience*. Washington DC: Smithsonian Institution.

Weiss, H. (1864), *Kostümekunde*, Stuttgart: Ebner and Seubert.

Welters, L. (1988), *Women's Traditional Costume in Attica, Greece*, Nafplion: Peloponnesian Folklore Foundation.

Welters, L., and M. Ordoñez (2004), "Blue Roots and Fuzzy Dirt: Archaeological Textiles from Native American Burials," in P. B. Drooker (ed.), *Perishable Material Culture in the Northeast*, New York State Museum Bulletin 500, 185–96, Albany, NY: State Education Department.

Welters, L., and A. Lillethun, eds (2007), *The Fashion Reader*, Oxford and New York: Berg.

Welters, L., and A. Lillethun, eds (2011), *The Fashion Reader*, 2nd ed., Oxford and New York: Berg.

Welters, L., M. Ordoñez, K. Tarleton and J. Smith (1996), "European Textiles from Seventeenth-Century New England Indian Cemeteries," in L. D. De Cunzo and B. L. Herman (eds.), *Historical Archaeology and the Study of American Culture*, 193–232, Winterthur: The Henry Francis du Pont Winterthur Museum.

William Merritt Chase, Exhibition, Museum of Fine Arts, Boston, October 9, 2016 to January 16, 2017.

Williams, R. ([1643] 1936), *A Key into the Language of America*, Providence: The Rhode Island and Providence Plantations Tercentenary Committee.

Willmott, C. (2005), "From Stroud to Strouds: The Hidden History of a British Fur Trade Textile," *Textile History* 36 (2): 196–234.

Wilson, E. (1985), *Adorned in Dreams: Fashion and Modernity*, London: Virago.

Wilson, L. A. (2011), "'De novo modo': The Birth of Fashion in the Middle Ages," PhD diss., Fordham University, New York.

Winlock, H. E., and Arnold, D. (2010), *Tutankhamun's Funeral*, New York: Metropolitan Museum of Art.

Winner, V. H. (2001), "Abigail Adams and 'The Rage of Fashion'," *Dress* 28: 64–76.

Winthrop, J. (1908), *History of New England, 1630–1649*, vol. 1, edited by J. K. Hosmer, New York: Charles Scribner's Sons.

Wolf, E. R. (1982), *Europe and the People Without History*, Berkeley: University of California Press.

Wolf, E. R. ([1982], 1997), *Europe and the People Without History*, Berkeley: University of California Press.

Wood, W. ([1635] 1977), *New England's Prospect*, edited by A. T. Vaughan, Amherst: University of Massachusetts Press.

World Digital Library (2016), "Florentine Codex," Library of Congress, https://www.wdl.org/en/item/10096/ (accessed September 13, 2016).

Wroth, L. C. (1970), *The Voyages of Giovanni da Verrazzano, 1524–1528*, New Haven, CT: Yale University Press.

Zelinsky, W. (2004), "Globalization Reconsidered: The Historical Geography of Modern Western Male Attire," *Journal of Cultural Geography* 22 (1): 83–143.

Zorn, E. (2005), "Dressed to Kill: The Embroidered Fashion Industry of the Sakaka of Highland Bolivia," in R. A. Root (ed.), *The Latin American Fashion Reader*, 114–41, London and New York: Berg Publishers.

INDEX

References to figures are displayed in bold.